Desperation Entertaining!

Desperation Entertaining!

by Beverly Mills & Alicia Ross

Illustrations by Robin Zingone

Workman Publishing • New York

Desperation Dinners is a registered trademark of Beverly Mills
Gyllenhaal and Alicia Brady Ross.

Library of Congress Cataloging-in-Publication Data
Mills, Beverly.
    Desperation entertaining / by Beverly Mills and Alicia Ross; illustrated
    by Robin Zingone.
        p. cm.
    Includes index.
    ISBN 0-7611-1815-2 (alk. paper)—ISBN 0-7611-2796-8
      1. Entertaining. I. Ross, Alicia. II. Title.

TX731 .M48 2002
642'.4—dc21   2002016826

Cover design by Paul Hanson
Book design by Barbara Balch
Authors' photograph by Anthony Loew
Cover food styled by Ulli Stachl
Cover illustration by Lynn Rowe Reed
Book illustrations by Robin Zingone

Workman books are available at special discount when purchased in
bulk for premiums and sales promotions as well as for fund-raising
or educational use. Special editions or book excerpts can be created
to specification. For details, contact the Special Sales Director at the
address below.

Workman Publishing Company, Inc.
708 Broadway
New York, NY 10003-9555
www.workman.com

Manufactured in the U.S.A.

First printing April 2002

10 9 8 7 6 5

FOR ANDERS AND RON

With you the fun never stops.

THANK YOU JUST ISN'T ENOUGH!

It amazes us how many people have touched our lives during the writing of this book: recipes shared, stories told, helpful hints, broad suggestions, and enthusiasm beyond our wildest dreams. What a pleasure it has been to work with our editor, Suzanne Rafer, again. We are eternally grateful to have had your guidance and unwavering vision on this project. Carla Glasser, our agent, is the best cheerleader out there. Your "just checking in" phone calls and messages were always perfectly timed. It's so comforting to know you're always there when we need you.

This book simply couldn't have ever been finished if it weren't for Julie Realon. You are our friend and our one-woman optimism team. Your eleventh hour testing of recipes was above and beyond the call of duty.

Other invaluable friends, testers, and recipe sharers are not to be forgotten—Kats Barry, Martie Leming, Marietta Wynands, Denise Deen, Charlie and Mary Lou Halley, Cheryl Ross, Denise Thorpe, Liza Bennett, Linda Wilkerson, Laurie Kovolew, Sharon Thompson, Felicia Gressette, Sharon Gustafson, Sally Pike, Louise Agner, and Lynn Clark-Brady. Bless you all for opening your family cookbooks, your kitchens, and your hearts to the two of us.

Without our mothers, Dot Mills and Gayle Brady, we would have never written another book. Your love and support, loyalty and devotion humbles us beyond words. We love you.

Thanks must also go to the readers of our newspaper column and supporters of our first book, *Desperation Dinners!* Your constant encouragement kept us going. To all the newspapers who publish the column and to Mary Anne Grimes, Lisa Wilson, and the rest of the great folks at United Media, thank you for keeping the Desperation Dinners philosophy alive and well from week to week.

All of the terrific people at Workman Publishing are to be applauded. Thanks to Peter Workman for his leadership. Barbara Mateer, our copy editor extraordinaire, for her careful attention to detail. Kudos to Paul Hanson for a superb cover design, to Barbara Balch for her energetic and user-friendly inside design, and to Robin Zingone for her delightful illustrations. Nicole DuCharme, in production, and Beth Doty, in editorial, thank you for helping to move things along smoothly.

To Kate Tyler and Jim Eber, our "publicity people," you guys are terrific. Thank you for a wonderful tour and continuous confidence. To Jenny Mandel, thank you for pitching us to QVC and being there to cheer us on.

Thanks must go to Anthony Loew, our photographer; Ulli Stachl, our fantastic food stylist; and Mark Lindsey, for his magic with eyeliner. Who would have thought a photo shoot could have been so much fun!

We especially appreciate our children, Sam and Grey and Hannah and Rachel. We know how hard it is to hear Mom say one more time, "Don't touch that yet, I'm testing!" or to see us locked in our offices furiously trying to meet a deadline. Thank you for understanding and loving us anyway.

Last but not least, we are always grateful for Anders and Ron. You guys are the best. Your straightforward reasoning, unwavering support, and encouragement still blow us away. Thank you for being on this journey with us.

Contents

CHAPTER THREE:

ENTERTAINING ENTREES 80

Festive and substantial no-sweat main dishes. Look for Crispy Oven-Baked Chicken Fingers, Pepper-Sauced Pasta with Ham and Asparagus, Lazy Spinach Lasagna, and Baked Party Paella.

CHAPTER FOUR:

THE GOOD OL' CROCK-POT 128

Everything goes into the slow cooker effortlessly for dishes like New Old-Fashioned Pot Roast, Big Beefy Burritos, Our Favorite Spaghetti and Meatballs, or Chill-Out Chicken Chili.

CHAPTER FIVE:

THE CASUAL COOKOUT 150

Gather guests around the grill for Amazing Steaks, Stuffed Bacon-Cheddar Burgers, Vacation Fish Boats, and Portobello Mushroom "Steak" Sandwiches.

CHAPTER SIX:

STANDOUT SALADS 188

Delicious, main dish salads and side salads are a snap to throw together for company. Try Chunky Chicken Salad with Macadamia Nuts, Niçoise Salad with Dijon Vinaigrette, Louise's Big Bowl Slaw, or Rainbow Wild Rice Salad.

CHAPTER SEVEN:

SUPER SIMPLE SIDES 246

Reliable side dishes that get to the table without taxing the cook. Think of Perfect Baked Potatoes, Dressed-Up Asparagus, Can-Do Corn on the Cob, or Succotash with a Twist.

CHAPTER EIGHT:

EVERYBODY'S BRUNCH 268

Casseroles and quiches put together ahead of time are hot and tasty when guests arrive. Baked Omelet with Italian Salsa, Eggs Benedict Casserole, Overnight French Toast Casserole, and Three-Cheese Broccoli Quiche are all crowd pleasers.

CHAPTER NINE:
DECADENT DESSERTS 298

Fast and gratifying desserts like Easy Elegant Pears with Red Wine Glaze, Strawberry Shortcake Trifle, Apple Brown Betty, and Granny Zeta's Pecan Pies let you end the meal gracefully.

COME ON IN, WE'RE GLAD YOU'RE HERE!

From Alicia:

Shortly after my kids were born I realized entertaining regularly and my new reality were not going to coexist. For me, entertaining had always entailed ambitious tasks like spray painting pinecones for the dining room centerpiece and spending hours over a fancy sauce.

Sure the table would look great and the food would be terrific, but add kids to the game plan and at what point was I supposed to drive the car pool, straighten the living room, do the laundry, and pick up the baby-sitter? All the magazines on my coffee table assured me I could do it. But whose staff was going to offer assistance?

My dilemma led to a decision: If I couldn't be hostess of the year, then I'd stick to the impromptu and maybe no one would pass judgment. Call it entertaining by accident. If you happened to be hanging out with me at a daring moment, then maybe you'd get invited over. Not for anything fancy, more of a fly by the seat of your pants thing: Let's order pizzas, and we'll toss together a salad.

After several years of this, takeout started to get old and, frankly, a little embarrassing. I craved the successful feeling of sitting down to a homemade meal with couples I really wanted to spend time with. It would be nice if the appetizer was more than just celery stalks pulled out of the vegetable bin. But wasn't there a middle ground between the six-course dinner and carryout Chinese?

From Beverly:

Meanwhile across town I was busy concocting every excuse I could muster not to entertain at all. It was easy to exclude all of my gourmet friends—they wouldn't enjoy the meager meals I could manage in my constant state of desperation. The friends with the meticulously decorated dens were out, too. Our sofa is plain brown, and we still don't have end tables. And what about my lack of serving spoons and the glasses that never match?

However, my sociable, party-loving husband insisted on guests, and after months of whining, my protests started to sound lame. So I went from nothing to throwing the once-a-year extravaganza that took a month of snowballing worry and nearly two weeks recovery time. We invited far too many people, and since I had transformed myself into a one-woman catering company, I hardly got to talk to any of them.

Although I had conquered the need for perfect everyday meals, when it came to entertaining, I was still putting the pressure on myself. My mother's gracious gatherings had always featured bountiful meals topped off by at least two kinds of homemade dessert. When I turned on the TV, the daily cooking shows only made matters worse. Every single channel made perfection seem commonplace. Why was I making such a big deal out of a once-a-year event? What was wrong with me?

From both of us:

One day during a heart-to-heart chat, we each confessed our entertaining angst. After a good laugh over how similar our predicaments actually were, we realized that what we both wanted was to fill that huge gap in our lives that occurs when we neglect to gather with friends and family. We came to recognize that the rewards of offering hospitality—the warmth, laughter, and fellowship—are just what we need to put life back into perspective after a difficult

There's really nothing that substitutes for inviting people into your home.

week. Or more realistically these days, it's exactly what we crave after a grueling month. But, we just can't stand the idea of all that predinner worry and an all-day Saturday cooking marathon to make entertaining happen.

Sure, we could assemble everyone for dinner at a restaurant, and that's what lots of Desperate Cooks, us included, sometimes do. Yet it's around the family table where acquaintances are truly encouraged to become close friends. The trick was to find ways to open our doors and feed our friends and family without falling over from exhaustion after they all went home. We believe that entertaining should be a pleasure for everyone—including the host.

At its heart, this is a book simply about hospitality and about hospitality made simple. Simple hospitality is really Desperation Entertaining at its best. This philosophy lets you avoid the temptation to obsess over the centerpiece or the stains on the sofa. It steers clear of serving takeout when you really want more, but it also shows you where to draw the line. Simple hospitality focuses on the guests. It smiles and says, "Come on in. We're glad you're here."

We figure Desperate Cooks might find the energy to throw a giant wingding only once in a decade. But with the right approach and the right recipes, all included here, Desperate Cooks can invite a few folks over any time they like for a meal that nourishes friendship, fun, and family ties. The real question for all of us is, why in the world did we wait so long?

VISIT OUR WEB SITE

For the latest desperate tips and information, visit us at our Web site: www.desperationdinners.com

Desperation Entertaining!

How Desperate

DESPERATE DETAILS: GAME PLANS, EQUIPMENT, AND STOCKING THE PANTRY

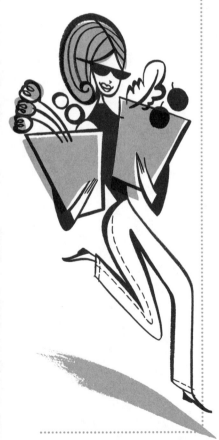

When it comes to entertaining, desperation has any number of sources. Perhaps you blurted out the impulsive words, "Why don't you all come over for dinner tonight," before you remembered that there was nothing at home to offer besides a bag of chips. Or maybe your spouse called to say that a prospective client is just a home-cooked meal away from signing on—so what's for dinner? This is when you need the recipes we call *Fast and Fabulous*. These entertainment-worthy recipes can be prepared quickly, sometimes in as few as 5 minutes and always in no more than 20.

At the other end of the spectrum lurks guilt. You've been to the Smiths' house for dinner four times and to the Johnsons' twice. Have you returned the invite yet? Go ahead and do it. You *need* to ask your friends to dinner. But, you say, you've barely got enough time to cook normal dinners—the project is due at work, you're out of town half the month, the twins are still in diapers. You've invited the Smiths and the Johnsons for dinner on the 24th? You think you've lost your mind.

Pause. Take a deep breath. You'll find the help you need in our *Phased and Flexible* recipes. These will enable you to pull together a meal by dividing the recipes into manageable steps so you can spread the preparation out over what time you have available.

Read on to learn entertaining strategies and what to keep on hand to help implement them. It's time to start bailing.

Are You?

Gotta Get a Plan!

First of all, come up with a game plan for feeding your guests. A game plan gives you a framework for preparing a meal without panicking. It helps you recognize which Fast and Fabulous recipes can be served together—without finding yourself trying to do five things simultaneously. It enables you to map out how to complete the stages of Phased and Flexible recipes. A game plan allows you to entertain without being tied to the stove while your guests wonder why you've neglected to show up at your own party. If you keep your pantry stocked for emergency entertaining (you'll find pantry suggestions beginning on page 18), you can even have a fallback game plan or two for spontaneous entertaining.

So how does a game plan work? To begin a plan you need to make three basic decisions: How many people will you invite? Where will you eat? What will you prepare?

Thinking through these simple questions can make all the difference. Eight people in the den eating spaghetti and meatballs off trays is not a good idea. A simple switch from long, stringy noodles to short penne pasta saves the day—and the potential for laundry hazards.

To flesh out a game plan you'll need to ask yourself two more questions: When will you shop? What time blocks can you carve out for cooking? Menu planning, shopping, and cooking—these are the essentials.

Whether you have a lot of time or a little, if your party boat is sinking, think of this book as a bucket.

As you pick a menu, be realistic. Consider your available time. You may feel comfortable whipping together a dip and the main course, but if your hectic schedule means you can't swing a homemade dessert, too, go to the experts. Stop by the bakery for a pie or cake, or pick up some exotic flavors of ice cream and your favorite toppers.

To help you create a menu, our recipes explain exactly how the preparation and cooking can be broken down into smaller steps. The idea is to give you flexibility. Some recipes can be started a week ahead and some a day ahead. Many can be cooked way in advance and frozen.

To start mapping out a plan, read through the recipes and make a complete shopping list to prevent emergency trips to the store. Also read the recipes with one eye on your daily schedule. Perhaps there are 20 minutes for chopping vegetables before you head off to work and there's another half hour in the evening before you turn in. Working on party prep during these small snatches of time allows you to produce a whole meal without headaches. While you're reading recipes, also keep in mind tasks that can overlap.

To get you started we've put together sample menus with game plans. These indicate how we'd be most likely to tackle the workload based on our typical schedules. Bear in mind that everything's designed to be flexible, and if your approach is different, that's okay. You'll find directions on page 16 for putting together game plans of your own. Each of our recipes contains the timing information you need to do that. In addition, all of the recipes that are broken into phases can be made start to finish if you prefer, usually by omitting the suggested refrigeration times and proceeding to the next step. And as you look at our projected times for completing recipes, you'll seldom see time allotted for serving. That's because most often we "serve" family style, and we encourage you to do the same.

Getting a game plan, whether it's yours or one of ours, means you can focus on entertaining your guests. Thanks to that game plan, the person at the table wearing the biggest smile might very well be you.

WHAT!
DINNER TONIGHT?
FAST AND FABULOUS

While we don't usually go around issuing invitations to come for dinner the very same night, there are at least 101 desperate reasons you may be feeding guests on the spur-of-the-moment—many of them your own doing! Call it emergency entertaining or crisis control, having company with no notice—or only a few hours' worth—can strike fear in the heart of any host, even if he or she's the reason company is on the way. There aren't as many options as when you plan ahead, but that's okay. At least options do exist.

When there isn't even time to swing by the grocery, you'll need to rely on your Desperation Entertaining Pantry (see page 18). For just this kind of no-notice rescue we always try to keep on hand the ingredients for the two Fast and Fabulous menus you'll see shortly with their game plans. The one for the grill features Chicken with Mustard Glazes and the one for the stove top includes Three-Bean and Meatball Chili.

Often an impromptu invitation will inspire one of the most welcome questions around: "What can I bring?" Seize the moment. Suggest, at the very least, that your guests bring the wine, the salad, or the bread (any of these can be picked up on the trip over).

Many times when you're entertaining you will get a *little* advance notice and a dash to the grocery is possible. Look to any of our other Fast and Fabulous, start-to-finish, recipes and relax. Dinner will be on the way in a flash if, for example, you turn to Stuffed Bacon-Cheddar Burgers or Amazing Steaks. You'll find menus and game plans built around each of these beginning on page 8.

In a true panic, takeout is sometimes the only sane option. (We've been there, too.) Put a homey touch on the menu by making your own salad dressing or whipping together a Desperation Dessert. Now, take a deep breath and answer the door—you're ready for the group to gather.

Close your eyes and repeat after us: "I will not panic. I am Fast and I am Fabulous."

Thanks to some pantry and freezer staples, this menu goes together with less than an hour's notice and no one dish will take more than 20 minutes to make. You don't even have to stop and shop. Whet your guests' appetites with smoked oysters and spiced-up olives while you boil a bit of pasta for our toss-together Pretty Pasta Salad with Peas and Carrots. (Those olives take only 3 minutes to prepare.) The chicken goes on the grill still-frozen and turns out burnished and juicy with mustard glazes for sophisticated flavor. After dinner comes our 10-minute Easy Elegant Pears with Red Wine Glaze, sure to leave your friends begging for more. All this without breaking a sweat? You bet!

FAST AND FABULOUS MENU 1

Ready-to-go nibble: Smoked oysters with crackers
Rosemary Olives, page 42
Chicken with Mustard Glazes, page 160
Pretty Pasta Salad with Peas and Carrots, page 236
Reheated frozen dinner rolls
Easy Elegant Pears with Red Wine Glaze, page 305
Your choice of beverages

Game Plan

WHEN	TO DO	TIME REQUIRED
50 minutes before dinnertime	Bring water to boil for the pasta. Meanwhile, prepare the olives. Set out the appetizers. Prepare and refrigerate the pasta salad. Preheat the oven for the rolls.	25 minutes
25 minutes before dinnertime	Prepare the glaze of your choice for the chicken. Place the rolls in the oven to warm, following the instructions on the package.	5 minutes
20 minutes before dinnertime	Preheat the grill and grill the chicken.	20 minutes
To end the meal	Prepare and serve the pears.	15 minutes

FAST AND FABULOUS MENU 2

Ready-to-go nibble: Vegetarian pâté
Ready-to-go nibble: Roasted cashews
Three-Bean and Meatball Chili, page 85
Packaged prewashed mixed salad greens and
Balsamic Vinaigrette, page 213
Plenty of assorted crackers
Tropical Bananas, page 307
Your choice of beverages

Game Plan

WHEN	TO DO	TIME REQUIRED
30 minutes before dinnertime	Set out the appetizers, including crackers for the pâté.	5 minutes
25 minutes before dinnertime	Prepare the chili. While the chili simmers, make the vinaigrette and get out the salad greens. Replenish the assortment of crackers.	20 minutes
To end the meal	Prepare and serve the bananas.	15 minutes

Is the weather making you yearn to huddle by the fire? Need a hearty meal on a moment's notice? Forget trekking for supplies, just saunter to your pantry and then kick back for a casual meal that starts off with a pâté, then features our Three-Bean and Meatball Chili. An assortment of crackers accompanies both. Preparations don't *really* have to start until less than half an hour before you ring the dinner bell. All you need to add is a green salad, and our Balsamic Vinaigrette will put the topspin on any combination of greens you may find in the veggie bin. Let your guests dress their own salads and there's no need to toss. To finish the meal, what could be more comforting than ice cream with a warm banana topping that makes you practically taste the tropics? Forget winter and focus on the fun.

It's hard to beat a burger on the grill unless it's a better burger on the grill. Our Stuffed Bacon-Cheddar Burger is just that, a dressed-up, company's coming combo guaranteed to make mouths water every time. Add a pan of Best Baked Beans—well, the name says it all. Less than an hour in the kitchen covers preparation for the whole menu, dip and dessert included. Frozen pound cake gives you a head start on lemon cake sandwiches, and all the work required for curry dip is a quick stir. Convince someone else to grill the burgers, and you're freed up to stand behind the video camera. Trust us, this easy way to entertaining deserves to be in pictures.

FAST AND FABULOUS MENU 3

Golden Curry Dip, page 44, with baby carrots
Stuffed Bacon-Cheddar Burgers, page 172
Best Baked Beans, page 253
Potato chips
Lemon Cake Sandwiches with Strawberry Purée, page 312
Your choice of beverages

Game Plan

WHEN	TO DO	TIME REQUIRED
10 to 2½ hours before dinnertime	Shop for the entire menu.	Varies
8 to 1½ hours before dinnertime	Prepare and refrigerate the dip. Prepare and refrigerate the hamburger patties. Prepare the beans for baking and then refrigerate them.	30 minutes
	Prepare and refrigerate, but do not garnish, the lemon cake sandwiches.	15 minutes
45 minutes before dinnertime	Preheat the oven for baking the beans.	Varies
30 minutes before dinnertime	Bake the beans. Set out the appetizer.	30 minutes total, mostly unattended baking time
15 minutes before dinnertime	Preheat the grill and grill the hamburgers. Set out the potato chips.	15 minutes
To end the meal	Garnish the lemon cake sandwiches and serve.	10 minutes

FAST AND FABULOUS MENU 4

Dilly of a Dip, page 44, with cucumbers and pretzels
Amazing Steaks, page 152
Red and Black Bean Salad, page 237
Sliced ripe, red tomatoes
Reheated frozen garlic bread
Your choice of ice cream with Old-Fashioned
Hot Fudge Sauce, page 300
Your choice of beverages

Game Plan

WHEN	TO DO	TIME REQUIRED
10 to 2½ hours before dinnertime	Shop for the entire menu.	Varies
8 to 1½ hours before dinnertime	Prepare and refrigerate the bean salad. Prepare and refrigerate the fudge sauce. Prepare and refrigerate the dip.	35 minutes
30 minutes before dinnertime	Preheat the oven for the garlic bread. Set out the appetizer. Prepare the steaks. Slice the tomatoes and cover them with plastic wrap.	12 minutes
15 minutes before dinnertime	Bake the garlic bread, following the instructions on the package. Preheat the grill and grill the steaks.	15 minutes
To end the meal	Reheat the fudge sauce and serve over the ice cream.	5 minutes

Our Amazing Steaks truly live up to their name. However, we have been known to make an entire meal of Red and Black Bean Salad, so it too is a welcome addition to a menu for any occasion. The fact that this side dish is ultraeasy (20 minutes start to finish) is better than dessert. Well almost. If dessert is the most decadent-tasting hot fudge sauce you can imagine that whips together in less than 10 minutes, what could be better than that?

THE DO-AHEAD SOLUTION:
PHASED AND FLEXIBLE

When we created our entertaining recipes, we knew we had to communicate exactly what to expect at each stage. We had to make the recipes fit into a Desperate Cook's real life.

After the guests arrive, we believe the cook should be having fun in the family room along with everybody else. Our goal is to get most of the work done before the doorbell ever rings, and so we've developed a way of approaching many of our entertaining recipes that allows you to reach the finish line without running out of steam. These recipes are the ones we call Phased and Flexible.

Who says a recipe absolutely has to be prepared from start to finish all at once? What about the Desperate Cook who has precious little uninterrupted time to spend in the kitchen? To make the most of the blocks of time that are available, our Phased and Flexible recipes are divided into segments that give you the option of working in what we call phases. We discovered this to be particularly appealing because all too many times we have chosen a recipe based on the preparation time it professes, then found out halfway through that we would need two assistants to pull it off on schedule. Nothing pushes us over the edge in the kitchen faster, so in our recipes we have taken nothing for granted. We account for peeling and chopping onions, melting butter, and browning chicken. The only time not factored in is that needed for preheating the oven or bringing a pot of water to a boil, since these vary from kitchen to kitchen.

At the end of each phase in a recipe you can proceed to the next if you have the time, or you can store the partially finished dish until your schedule allows for another opportunity to cook. Most phases that involve hands-on preparation take 15 to 20 minutes. Some of them take even less time than that. If you are free for a little while before the Saturday morning soccer game, for example, you can chop up all of the vegetables for Shrimp Creole à la Beverly and cook it later. You'll find menus and game plans featuring this recipe and ones for lasagna and for spaghetti and meatballs in the pages that follow, along with a menu and game plan for brunch.

PHASED AND FLEXIBLE BRUNCH

Ready-to-go nibble: Cheese straws
Curried Walnuts, page 40
Mother's Brunch Casserole, page 286
Fastest Fruit Salad, page 270
Mini croissants from the bakery
Fruity Tea Punch, page 29, and coffee

Game Plan

WHEN	TO DO	TIME REQUIRED
4 to 2 days before brunch time	Shop for the entire menu.	Varies
3 to 2 days before brunch time	Prepare and refrigerate the fruit salad.	7 minutes
1 day before brunch time	Prepare the tea punch. While the tea is steeping, prepare the walnuts.	40 minutes
The night before brunch time	Prepare and refrigerate the brunch casserole.	18 minutes
1¼ hours before brunch time	Preheat the oven.	Varies
1 hour before brunch time	Bake the casserole. Wrap the croissants in aluminum foil. Make coffee.	50 minutes mostly unattended baking time
30 minutes before brunch time	Set out the cheese straws and walnuts.	5 minutes
15 minutes before brunch time	Add the croissants to the oven to warm.	15 minutes unattended baking time
5 minutes before brunch time	Set out the fruit salad and punch.	5 minutes

Whether it's for sleepover guests or a morning gathering of old college roommates, overnight casseroles have been our brunch mainstay for decades. We'll admit that we're not the types to rise at daybreak, so brunch recipes that you prepare a day or more before by definition are just the ticket. And as you'll see, the preparation for this menu can be spread out over five days. Any of our overnight recipes can be substituted for Mother's Brunch Casserole and easily adjusted to fit this game plan. If you can stumble out of bed with enough wits to make coffee and preheat the oven, this is the menu for you.

When the household is running smoothly and our schedules aren't overloaded, that's the time we like to use to get prepared for special company. If you've got a freezer stocked with shrimp Creole sauce and one or two pecan pies (the recipe makes two), entertaining becomes a possibility even when regular life veers out of control. With this bounty stashed away up to a month ahead and the dip made the day before, the remaining few chores for this dinner are manageable indeed. Bring on the boss!

PHASED AND FLEXIBLE MENU 1

Hot Spinach Dip, page 49, with pita points
Shrimp Creole à la Beverly, page 121, served over rice
Marietta's Mandarin Salad, page 219
Corn muffins from the bakery
Granny Zeta's Pecan Pie, page 328
Your choice of beverages

THE BASIC EQUIPMENT

Here is some of the equipment you must have to pull off cooking for a crowd. All of these items can be purchased anywhere from discount stores to shops selling fancy kitchenware.

- **Large pot:** A pot that holds at least 4½ quarts and has a lid. A nonstick interior is great but not mandatory.
- **12-inch nonstick, extra-deep skillet:** A skillet with an extra-high side (2 inches or more) and a large cooking surface makes for easier sautéing and stirring. Look for a skillet with a lid.
- **Oblong, glass casserole dishes:** Use these for everything from sheet cakes to egg casseroles to enchiladas. We recommend the 13 × 9-inch size. Having two can expand your menu options. Serve from them right at the table.
- **Large roasting pan:** A pan that measures 15 × 10 inches is perfect for roasted vegetables and Baked Party Paella (see page 116).
- **Serving trays:** Whether supercheap bamboo or designer ones that double as kitchen art, you'll want a few of these handy helpers. They're ideal for serving drinks, passing appetizers, and/or providing "table space" for the casual buffet.

Game Plan

WHEN	TO DO	TIME REQUIRED
Up to 1 month before dinnertime	Shop for the shrimp Creole and pecan pies.	Varies
	Prepare the shrimp Creole through Phase 3 and then freeze it.	1 hour
	Prepare the pecan pies and then freeze them.	20 minutes, plus 1 hour unattended baking time and cooling time
1 day before dinnertime	Shop for the beverages, spinach dip and pita points, salad, corn muffins, and topping for the pie.	Varies
	Prepare the rice and refrigerate it according to the instructions on page 120.	30 minutes
	While the rice is steaming, prepare the dip through Step 2 and refrigerate it.	
The morning before dinnertime	Prepare the salad through Step 4 and refrigerate it.	20 minutes
	Remove a pie from the freezer to thaw on a counter top.	
1 hour before dinnertime	Add the mandarin oranges, bacon, and almonds to the salad.	5 minutes
30 minutes before dinnertime	Preheat the oven.	10 minutes
	Heat the spinach dip and set it out.	
	Wrap the corn muffins in aluminum foil for heating.	
20 minutes before dinnertime	Cook the shrimp in the Creole sauce and reheat the rice.	15 minutes
	Heat the corn muffins.	
To end the meal	Serve a pie with whipped topping.	5 minutes

13

Just about everybody likes lasagna, so it's a dish we naturally turn to when we're entertaining. Especially when we're entertaining vegetarians. With Mushroom Lasagna Alfredo, everyone at your table will be equally enthusiastic. All of the assembly and preparation can be done the day before, and the baking time is a smooth fit with the cocktail hour. Mediterranean Blue Cheese Salad and Flexible Fruit Fondue can be stashed in the refrigerator up to two hours ahead, leaving you plenty of time to shower and relax. (Or in our case, hide the laundry baskets.)

PHASED AND FLEXIBLE MENU 2

Roasted Garlic Artichoke Dip, page 69, with crackers
Mushroom Lasagna Alfredo, page 101
Mediterranean Blue Cheese Salad, page 216
Crusty Italian rolls
Flexible Fruit Fondue, page 309
Your choice of beverages

Game Plan

WHEN	TO DO	TIME REQUIRED
Up to 3 weeks before dinnertime	Prepare roasted garlic.	30 minutes
Up to 2 weeks before dinnertime	Prepare the red wine vinaigrette for the salad.	5 minutes
2 days before dinnertime	Shop for the rest of the menu.	Varies
1 day before dinnertime	Prepare the lasagna through Phase 1. Prepare the dip through Phase 1.	45 minutes total
2 hours before dinnertime	Prepare the salad. Assemble the fruit and cake platter for the fondue.	30 minutes total
1½ hours before dinnertime	Preheat the oven.	Varies
1¼ hours before dinnertime	Bake the lasagna. Wrap the rolls in aluminum foil for heating.	50 minutes unattended baking time
1 hour before dinnertime	Bake the dip.	30 minutes
30 minutes before dinnertime	Set out the appetizer.	5 minutes
About 10 minutes before dinnertime	Remove the lasagna from the oven and let rest. Heat the rolls.	10 minutes total
To end the meal	Heat the chocolate fondue sauce and serve with the fruit and cake platter.	5 minutes

PHASED AND FLEXIBLE MENU 3

Easiest Marinated Mushrooms, page 66
Our Favorite Spaghetti and Meatballs, page 142
Spinach Salad with Sweet Poppy Seed Dressing, page 229
Crunchy Italian bread sticks
Rocky Road Brownie Sundaes, page 318,
with chocolate ice cream sauce
Your choice of beverages

Game Plan

WHEN	TO DO	TIME REQUIRED
3 days before dinnertime	Shop for the mushrooms, spaghetti and meatballs, salad dressing, and brownies.	Varies
2 days before dinnertime	Prepare and refrigerate the mushrooms. Prepare and refrigerate the salad dressing.	20 minutes total
	Prepare the brownies.	5 minutes, plus 30 minutes unattended baking time
1 day before dinnertime	Shop for the spinach salad and bread sticks.	Varies
	Prepare the pasta and refrigerate it according to the instructions on page 88.	Varies
30 minutes before dinnertime	Preheat the oven. Prepare the salad. Set out the appetizer.	10 minutes
10 minutes before dinnertime	Wrap the bread sticks in aluminum foil and heat.	10 minutes
5 minutes before dinnertime	Reheat the pasta.	5 minutes
To end the meal	Assemble and serve the brownie sundaes.	5 minutes

Weekends won't let you slow down? First it's the trip to the hardware store, then one to the swim meet, and on to stock up on supplies for next week. Glance over this game plan, and you'll understand why the Crock-Pot was invented. Walk in the door half an hour before your guests (or even with them in tow), and you can still be named host of the year if you serve Our Favorite Spaghetti and Meatballs followed by Rocky Road Brownie Sundaes. Who knows, dinner parties could become the highlight of your weekends.

TIME SAVER

Our Favorite Spaghetti and Meatballs isn't the only Crock-Pot recipe in the book. You'll find a whole chapterful starting on page 128. Many of the dishes can be prepared an entire day or two ahead, and others can be frozen for up to a month.

HOW TO MAKE YOUR OWN GAME PLANS

You've followed several of our game plans for entertaining and now you're ready to branch out and create your own plan. The steps that follow are designed to help you do just that. We've found that the easiest way to stay on top of the details is to jot them down in order on 3-by-5 cards. After you've plotted out a couple of game plans, it's likely you'll start thinking the steps through without writing them down. That's great—but why not record them anyway? Even though we've been drawing up game plans for years, when we're really desperate, having them in writing makes entertaining mindlessly easy. For us, that's the goal.

Think Flowchart

1. Select a menu, then write down everything you want to serve and whether you'll buy it ready-made or prepare it.
2. Flag the recipes in the book so you can flip to them easily.
3. Check the preparation time for each recipe and add it to your game plan. Review each recipe's do-ahead instructions.
4. Make a note of the dishes you can prepare completely ahead of time or begin assembling a day or more in advance. For example, you can boil the eggs and make the dressing for our spinach salad four days before the date of your dinner.
5. Pick a day to prepare things that can be frozen.
6. Now take a careful look at the preparation times for each of the remaining recipes. If several need last-minute attention that can raise a red flag. You may want to rethink your choice of recipes.
7. Do you want to serve Hot Chicken Salad and peach cobbler? Since these both go in the oven, check to be sure they bake at the same temperature.
8. Once you've decided on a menu, make a detailed shopping list. Be sure to include nonfood items, such as paper napkins, disposable plates, or candles.
9. Reserve time for shopping.

SANITY SAVER

Put the game plan in action by posting it in a convenient place for easy reference—we like to put it on the refrigerator or inside a cabinet door. (If you get nervous or distracted, just take another look at the plan.) Then, when the evening is over, save your game plan. You'll find it a handy reference to help when you put together the next one.

Set the Clock

1. Refine the game plan by filling in the timing. Most likely some of the recipes on your menu can be prepared in stages throughout the day you'll serve them or can be completed earlier that day. Suppose you want to serve a dinner of paella, spinach salad, and key lime pie starting at 7 o'clock. Make a note to move the pie, which you baked several weeks earlier, from the freezer to the refrigerator to thaw before you go to bed the night before your dinner.

2. Plan to finish the first phase of the paella when you get up in the morning, since it can be refrigerated for up to 8 hours.

3. The spinach salad can be assembled and refrigerated for up to 4 hours before serving, so note on the game plan that any time between 3:00 and 7:00 you can fix the salad.

4. The paella takes about 15 minutes to get ready for the oven and bakes for 75 minutes, but it can rest once it's baked. If you finish putting it together between 5:00 and 5:30, it will be done when you want to serve it.

5. Last but not least, you'll need to dress the salad. If you plan on taking a couple of minutes to do this at 6:45, you'll have time to wash your hands before setting dinner on the table.

6. Once you've mapped out the time frame of each recipe, you'll notice that the order in which to prepare them falls into place.

7. Look back over your menu. Add any steps not accounted for in the recipe times, tasks like preheating the oven or warming the bread. Don't forget to add thawing and reheating times for frozen dishes.

8. Double check that none of your work times overlap and that no activities are duplicated. Make adjustments where necessary.

9. Before making the schedule final, factor in your personal needs on the day you entertain. For example, you'll want to allow yourself time to change clothes before your guests arrive.

10. Think the plan through step by step one last time. Did you forget anything?

11. Now that you've drawn up your game plan, implementing it will be a cinch.

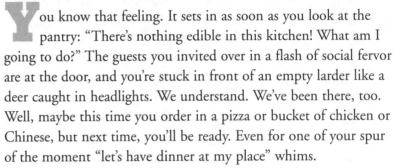

THE DESPERATION ENTERTAINING PANTRY

You know that feeling. It sets in as soon as you look at the pantry: "There's nothing edible in this kitchen! What am I going to do?" The guests you invited over in a flash of social fervor are at the door, and you're stuck in front of an empty larder like a deer caught in headlights. We understand. We've been there, too. Well, maybe this time you order in a pizza or bucket of chicken or Chinese, but next time, you'll be ready. Even for one of your spur of the moment "let's have dinner at my place" whims.

The secret is to prepare ahead, but hoarding loads of food for a possible entertaining crisis just isn't smart budgeting. So here's the compromise: Know that in most Desperation Entertaining situations you'll have a chance to shop at least once before the guests arrive. You can confidently turn to any of our Phased and Flexible recipes and work out a plan for your menu. Or if you're really stressed and need the details spelled out, turn to one of our game plans and menus and simply follow along (see pages 6 through 15). There we even offer instructions on when to head to the grocery.

When guests are literally waiting on the threshold, resort to one of our two menus that go from the pantry to the table in less than an hour. In addition to the usual staples (flour, sugar, milk, butter, onions . . .), stock your kitchen with the ingredients that follow and you'll never get that sinking feeling of being unprepared again. Here's how:

• First, change the way you think about the word *pantry*. It's not just the cupboard. It's your whole kitchen—your refrigerator, your freezer, *and* the cupboard—the whole enchilada.

• Then take our list of what to keep on hand with you to the store and stock up on these items. Most of them will work their way into your desperate midweek meals before you know it, so even when a month has passed and you haven't needed them for entertaining (and, why haven't you?), they're not going to waste. Just be sure not to let your stock diminish completely before the item goes back on the shopping list.

• Finally, relax. You're prepared.

SANITY SAVER

Most of the ingredients in the Desperation Entertaining Pantry will live practically forever on your shelves. For refrigerated and frozen items, always check the "use by" dates on the packages and look for those that will give you the longest storage time possible.

Once open, mayonnaise, salsa, and pickle relish and bottled ginger, horseradish, and garlic should be refrigerated. Loose olives should also be kept in the refrigerator. It's best to freeze nuts to prevent them from turning rancid.

WHAT TO KEEP IN A DESPERATE PANTRY

DRIED HERBS, SPICES, AND SEASONINGS

Celery seed
Poppy seeds
Dried basil
Dried oregano
Dried red pepper flakes
Dried rosemary
Dried thyme
Ground allspice
Ground cinnamon
Cinnamon sticks
Ground coriander
Ground cumin
Apple pie spice
Cayenne pepper
Paprika
Dry mustard
Chili powder
Curry powder
Garlic powder
Onion powder
Italian-style seasoning
Seafood seasoning, such as
    Old Bay
Cajun seafood seasoning,
    such as Chef Paul
    Prudhomme's Seafood Magic
Italian salad dressing mix,
    such as Good Seasons

PRESERVES AND CONDIMENTS

Orange marmalade
Chinese plum sauce
Assorted mustards, including
    Dijon, brown and yellow
    prepared, and Chinese
Tabasco sauce
Reduced-sodium soy sauce
Worcestershire sauce
Mayonnaise
Prepared salsa
Sweet pickle relish
Bottled fresh ginger
Bottled prepared horseradish
Bottled minced garlic
Kalamata olives, preferably pitted
Sliced black olives in cans

VINEGARS AND OILS

Apple cider vinegar
Balsamic vinegar
Distilled white vinegar
Red wine vinegar
Rice wine vinegar
Extra-virgin olive oil
Asian (dark) sesame oil

CANNED GOODS

Artichoke hearts packed in water
Marinated artichoke hearts
Beans: kidney, black, navy,
    great Northern
Chickpeas
Chopped green chiles
Tomato sauce
Tomato paste
Chili-style seasoned tomatoes,
    such as Del Monte
Diced tomatoes seasoned with
    garlic and onions
Italian-style stewed tomatoes
Mexican-style stewed tomatoes,
    such as Del Monte
Mandarin orange segments
Pear halves packed in juice
Pineapple tidbits packed
    in juice

The ingredient lists in our recipes call for what we have found to be the most common package or can sizes. If what you find has a similar weight—say a can of red kidney beans that weighs 15¼ ounces rather than 15½—feel free to make the substitution. A little more or a little less won't make a difference. And while these are all nationally available items, if there are any that your supermarket doesn't carry, ask the manager for them and he or she may order them for the store.

PASTA, CRACKERS, AND CHIPS

Pasta shells
Penne
Rotini
Spaghetti
Assorted crackers
Bread sticks
Cheese straws
Assorted chips

DAIRY PRODUCTS

Cream cheese
A variety of already-shredded
    cheeses, including Mexican
    blend and Cheddar
Already-grated Parmesan cheese
Heavy (whipping) cream
Sour cream
Premium ice cream: vanilla and
    chocolate

FRESH FRUITS
AND VEGETABLES

See page 54 for a list of fresh
vegetables that are good for
dipping. In addition, you'll
want to keep on hand:
Already-peeled baby carrots
A selection of prewashed
    salad greens
Garlic
Apples, in season
Bananas
Limes
Lemons
Orange juice
Strawberries, in season

FROZEN FOODS

Artichoke hearts
Corn kernels
Green peas
Precooked meatballs
Individually quick-frozen skinless,
    boneless chicken breasts
Rolls and garlic bread
All-butter pound cake, such as
    Sara Lee

SPIRITS

Dry red wine
Dry white wine
Madeira
Marsala
Rum
Triple sec or another liqueur

OTHER INGREDIENTS

Brown sugar
Honey
Light corn syrup
Pure vanilla extract
Raisins
Already-cooked bacon
Fancy nuts—roasted cashews,
    smoked almonds, sugared
    peanuts, pistachios
Smoked oysters, mussels, and
    clams, in cans
Pâtés, including vegetarian ones,
    in cans

DESPERATION SYMBOLS

Throughout the book you'll find recipes that are accompanied by symbols. Some of these alert you to set aside a little bit of time not accounted for in the recipe (in Phased and Flexible recipes they'll appear at the beginning of the phase to which they apply). Others tip you off to a particular advantage of that recipe. Here's what to look for:

These symbols indicate that you need to allow time for the oven to preheat or for water to come to a boil (for pasta, for example) before you can begin to cook. How much time this will take depends upon your equipment; just be sure to turn on the oven or put the pot on the stove before beginning the stage of the recipe where the symbol appears.

When you want a recipe that is especially appealing to kids, look for this symbol.

When you see this symbol, you'll know that freezing instructions are included for the recipe it accompanies; this will allow you to make the dish well in advance.

CHAPTER ONE

Beguiling

It's tempting to let party drinks slip to the position of last detail. There's so much that has to be done in the kitchen. But beverages are the first offering of hospitality, and they do deserve at least a bit of thought. However, there's no need to think all *that* hard. Nor do you need to work particularly hard, either. Fortunately, when it comes to drinks, today's hosts get a lot of help. Stores are filled with interesting choices—everything from wine coolers and microbrewed beers to flavored seltzers, gourmet ginger ales, and margarita mixes. With such a plethora available, our advice is simple: Experiment and then serve what you like.

For the times when we feel the need for a homemade touch, we've assembled our favorite beverage recipes, which we think you'll enjoy as much as we do. You'll find Beverly's Bloody Mary mix, Alicia's easiest way ever to brew iced tea, plus her fruit tea punch, a sock-it-to-you sangria, an attention-getting frozen wine punch, and some ultrasmooth fruit smoothies. Last but not least, do try our superquick hot chocolate that's as good as a warm hug on a cold day.

Grab a glass or a mug, and let's start by considering alcoholic beverages: For several of our friends, tending the bar is one of the biggest barriers to entertaining. "But we don't have a liquor cabinet," lamented one who wanted to invite her neighbors for dinner. "We have water glasses and wineglasses, but I'm not even sure what a highball glass looks like." Our feeling is this:

Beverages

If a liquor cabinet is not your style, there's nothing inhospitable about an offer of beer, wine, coffee, or tea.

Serving mixed drinks can indeed get complicated, involving everything from the right glasses to garnishes and mixers. Trying to anticipate everyone's tastes will require deep pockets and a bar recipe book, too. If you don't know your guests intimately, they certainly won't expect you to know their favorite drinks. On the other hand, if close friends have a penchant for a particular scotch or bourbon, you can simply pick up a bottle and let them mix their own concoctions.

It's not that we're against serving mixed drinks, we've just learned over the years that it's best to stick with what you know. A friend of ours makes a fabulous frozen margarita, so whipping up blenders full of this specialty became part of her evening's entertainment. Perhaps you've made a personal quest for the perfect martini, and you already have the required gadgets. Go for it. If single malt scotch is your passion, your guests might enjoy a guided tasting tour.

When it comes to alcohol, there's only one essential responsibility the host does have, and that's to offer acceptable alcohol-free alternatives. We'll give you some suggestions for these, but let's look at wine and beer first.

After "How are you?" and "Let me take your coat," one of the first things a thoughtful host asks is "Would you like something to drink?"

SERVING WINE?

From Alicia:

Was I hearing correctly? The experts were suggesting what? "Basically, we're saying, drink what you like."

Huh? That's it? Here Beverly and I have spent countless times worrying whether the wine we were serving was the right one for the meal. Yet two highly acclaimed wine professionals were advising an assembly of food writers to throw out all of the traditional rules and drink what they like.

After I stopped resenting all my wasted worries, I was actually relieved. No more stressing over whether white or red was better suited to the entrée and then doubling my anxiety by wondering which color wine my guests preferred. Some folks drink only very dry, almost chocolaty reds. Some don't drink red wines because of the headaches they can cause. Others like the lighter tastes of whites better. How could I please everybody?

What I usually ended up doing was serving both a red and white wine that my husband and I enjoyed, secretly hoping I wasn't making a huge gourmet faux pas. Or at least hoping no one would notice. You just never know when the gourmet police will arrive. . . . But now my method had been validated. Here were two wine professionals saying, "Drink what you like."

The old rules do still apply somewhat. The reasoning behind white with white meat and red with red is that white meats, seafood included, are lighter in flavor than their red counterparts. White wines are usually lighter as well, so it's logical not to serve a heavy red wine with a light, delicate fish, for instance.

But then there's always the tricky entrée, such as Beverly's shrimp Creole on page 121. There's shrimp in it, sure, but the dish is anything but light and delicate. It's bold and spicy and cries out for an assertive wine. So the wines we choose for serving with this amazing New Orleans specialty are a hearty Côtes-du-Rhône for the red wine drinkers and a dry chardonnay for those who prefer white.

Wine has become so readily available that (depending upon where you live) even large grocery stores have extensive wine departments and wine stewards on hand to answer questions. That means it's much easier to make an informed decision about which wine to serve. When all else fails, and you just can't decide, ask for help. Take the recipe for what you plan to serve along if you want. If your larger grocery stores don't have wine masters, then go to a wine shop. Describe your dinner dilemma and trust the answer the staff gives you. After all, he or she will want you to come back again, so the suggestion is bound to please.

Wine prices range vastly; know what your budget is before you get to the store. If you're asking for help, explain what that budget is. Don't be shy to say, "I'd like to stay under $10 a bottle please," or whatever your limit might be. (We've found that wines from Chile and Argentina are economical and delicious.)

Table wines, including those made from blends of several grape varieties, are easy, trusty ways to get more for your money. Then of course there's always the special. Take advantage of the weekly one wherever you buy wine. Making a wine punch, such as our sangria on page 35, is also an excellent way to extend a tight wine budget. Adding fruit juices and other ingredients stretches the wine, and the infusion of flavors masks the fact that the vintage may not be the very finest.

As far as how much wine to buy, count on about four to five glasses (depending on the size of your wineglasses) per bottle. The easiest thing to do is buy two bottles of white and two of red—that's about two glasses each for a party of eight. Know that any leftovers can be saved for cooking or later consumption. We find the vacuum-style wine saver indispensable for saving unfinished bottles (see the box at right). Above all, don't stress over serving wine. It's not a big deal. Even the professionals say so.

MONEY SAVER

What do you do when there's wine left over after a dinner party? We love our handy, dandy wine saver. It's nothing more complicated than a rubber stopper with a suction pump device that removes the air, resealing the wine bottle. Reasonably priced, the VacuVin is manufactured in Holland and was the first vacuum-seal wine saver to hit the market. Other brands are also available at most wine or kitchen stores. Extra stoppers are sold separately. Investing in one of these useful gadgets makes it more economical to buy that additional bottle of wine since you know you'll be able to cook with it or drink it later if it's not finished off.

BEER BUYING RULES

From Beverly:

I t didn't matter who we invited over, it happened every time. My husband would buy the beer, the guests would come, they'd go home, and we'd be left with a panoply of bottles stacked in the refrigerator. "Oh, we'll drink it," my husband would say, and two months later I'd find myself stashing those same bottles down in the basement to clear room for food. I couldn't bear to throw them away.

Two problems were at work here. Obviously my spouse was overestimating how much beer our friends would drink. But he was also trying way too hard to please everybody, buying every brand of beer he could imagine anybody requesting. Anybody but us.

"Why don't you just buy beer *we* like," I finally reasoned. "That way you can buy as much as you think we'll need, and it won't go to waste." He had to admit I was right. That's how we came upon our beer buying rules. They're simple, and they work every time. No more lone soldiers in the fridge.

- Buy lots of the beer you normally drink.
- Buy a reasonable amount of the other kind. That means if you drink light beer, buy some full-bodied beer or vice versa.
- You may also want to buy at least one six-pack of nonalcoholic beer (see page 33).
- If you do end up with a few leftovers not to your taste, offer to send the unopened bottles home with your guests.

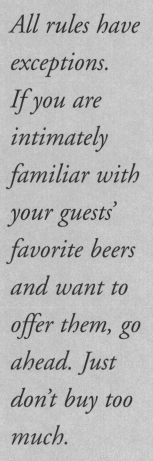

All rules have exceptions. If you are intimately familiar with your guests' favorite beers and want to offer them, go ahead. Just don't buy too much.

fast and fabulous

Frozen Fruit Smoothies

2 very ripe bananas, frozen
1 cup blend of 100 percent fruit juices, such as
  orange-pineapple
1 container (8 ounces) fruit-flavored yogurt, such as
  blueberry
1 cup (8 ounces) frozen strawberries (see Note)

START TO FINISH: 3 TO 4 MINUTES

1. Cut the bananas into chunks, about 4 pieces each. Place them in the container of a blender. Add the fruit juice blend, yogurt, and strawberries.

2. Blend the yogurt mixture on medium-low or pulse until well blended. Stir midway through to mix well. The smoothies are done when all the fruit is puréed. Serve at once.

■ *Makes 4 one-cup servings*

Note: Be sure to buy the strawberries that come frozen in a plastic bag so they'll separate and blend easily. The bags usually weigh 16 ounces. One batch of smoothies uses half a bag.

With just the right balance between tart and sweet, these smoothies will be a welcome refresher for kids of all ages. One of their bonuses is that they provide a purpose for that overripe banana that always seems to lurk at the bottom of the fruit bowl. Just peel it, toss it in a heavy-weight zipper-top plastic bag, and stash it in the freezer for up to a month. Before long, you'll have all the bananas you need for an endless smoothie supply.

This recipe makes a blenderful, which serves about four. However, since the smoothies whir together in less than 5 minutes, it's no trouble to whip them up even while guests are standing around in the kitchen.

This is tea brewing at its Desperate best. Instead of steeping huge quantities on the stove top like our mothers did, we turn to the microwave to speed us through the process. But your guests will never know. They'll just enjoy the sweet, delicious results.

Extra-Easy Peppermint Iced Tea

3 family-size regular or decaffeinated tea bags
1 cup sugar
⅛ teaspoon peppermint extract
Ice cubes, for serving
Lemon slices and mint leaves (optional), for garnish

START TO FINISH: 10 MINUTES PREPARATION, PLUS 30 MINUTES STEEPING TIME

1. Fill a 4-cup glass measure with cold water. Remove the paper tabs on the tea bags, if necessary (see Note), and place the tea bags in the water. Microwave, uncovered, on high for 8 minutes. Carefully remove the glass measure from the microwave and place a plate over the top to cover. Let steep for 30 minutes.

2. Meanwhile, mix the sugar and peppermint extract with about 1 cup of cold water in a gallon-size beverage container. Stir until the sugar is dissolved. Remove the tea bags from the tea (do not squeeze the bags!), pour the tea into the sugar water, and stir briskly.

3. Add cold water to fill the pitcher to 1 gallon. Cover and refrigerate for up to 24 hours. To serve, fill 8 iced tea glasses with ice and add the peppermint tea. Garnish each glass with a lemon slice and/or mint leaves, if desired.

■ *Makes 1 gallon*

Note: Some manufacturers are producing tea bag "rounds" without strings and tabs attached. If you can find these, it makes it easier to toss them in the water and not worry about the tabs. If your tea bags have paper tabs, pull them off before you add the tea bags to the pot. Don't worry about the strings. You might open the bags if you try to remove them.

Fruity Tea Punch

3 family-size regular or decaffeinated tea bags
1 cup sugar
1 can (6 ounces) frozen lemonade concentrate
2½ cups unsweetened pineapple juice
Ice cubes, for serving
Lemon and/or pineapple slices (optional), for garnish

START TO FINISH: 10 MINUTES PREPARATION, PLUS 30 MINUTES STEEPING TIME

1. Fill a 4-cup glass measure with cold water. Remove the paper tabs on the tea bags, if necessary (see Note opposite), and place the tea bags in the water. Microwave, uncovered, on high for 8 minutes. Carefully remove the glass measure from the microwave and place a plate over the top to cover. Let steep for 30 minutes.

2. Meanwhile, mix the sugar with about 1 cup of cold water in a gallon-size beverage container. Add the lemonade concentrate and pineapple juice, stirring well to dissolve the sugar and lemonade. Set aside until the tea has finished steeping.

3. Remove the tea bags from the tea (do not squeeze the bags!), pour the tea into the lemonade mixture, and stir briskly.

4. Add cold water to fill the pitcher to 1 gallon. Cover and refrigerate for up to 24 hours. To serve, fill 8 iced tea glasses with ice and add the punch. Garnish each glass with a lemon slice and/or pineapple slice, if desired.

■ *Makes 1 gallon*

A concoction perfect for brunch—even children who say they don't like tea will enjoy Fruity Tea Punch. Be sure to purchase unsweetened pineapple juice. The sweetened kind will overpower the other ingredients.

SANITY SAVER

When extending your invitations, tell your guests everything they need to know. That means what time the gathering starts and also when it ends. Tell your guests whether the majority of time will be spent indoors or out (weather permitting), the dress code, and whether or not children are included. It's also nice to mention who else is coming.

ABOUT SERVING HOT BEVERAGES

From Beverly:

I keep threatening to buy a thirty-cup coffeemaker, but in my wiser moments, I remind myself that I probably wouldn't use it enough to justify the expense. In the meantime, I've discovered the perfect compromise—two of them actually.

When the group isn't too large, I make a pot of coffee several hours ahead and store it in a thermal carafe. This is like an old-time thermos jug only with a side handle and spout. These 1-liter carafes are inexpensive and available at most any store that sells pots and pans. Two of these are also a good solution when half the group drinks decaf and the other half wants regular coffee.

For sizable gatherings, my second solution is the "press and pour" pot. This, too, is a thermal container that keeps beverages hot for hours, but it is a larger (not quite 2-liters), taller jug that has a press-down pump in the top. When you push on the top, coffee comes squirting out of the spout. These pots are handy for setting up a beverage bar that allows guests to serve themselves. I was so pleased with how my first one worked, I promptly splurged and bought a second one. Again, this is a perfect caf/decaf solution and also works well for serving hot chocolate or hot water for tea alongside the coffee. So far, my inexpensive ones from the discount store work great.

Coffee, tea?
With caffeine
or without?
With the
right pots,
you're ready.

Rich Hot Chocolate

½ gallon milk (low-fat is fine)
3 squares (3 ounces) semisweet chocolate
1 pint half-and-half
Dash of salt
2 teaspoons pure vanilla extract
8 cinnamon sticks (each 3 inches long), for serving
Marshmallows, or whipped cream from an aerosol can,
  for serving (optional)

START TO FINISH: 10 MINUTES

1. Put the milk in a 4½-quart Dutch oven or soup pot and begin heating over medium-high heat.

2. Meanwhile, coarsely chop the chocolate and place it in a 4-cup microwave-safe container. Add the half-and-half and salt to the chopped chocolate. Cover with a paper towel and microwave, on high, until the chocolate is almost melted, about 4 minutes. Remove from the microwave and whisk briskly just until the chocolate is completely melted.

3. Add the chocolate mixture to the milk in the pot on the stove. Add the vanilla extract. Whisk until the chocolate is completely mixed in and the mixture is steaming hot, about 2 minutes more. If not serving the cocoa immediately, reduce the heat to low and let simmer, stirring from time to time, for up to 30 minutes, taking care not to let the mixture boil. Serve in mugs and garnish each with a cinnamon stick and marshmallows or a squirt of whipped cream, if desired.

■ *Serves 8*

Want to be known as the best parents to visit in a snowstorm? Whip up a pot of this infinitely-better-than-instant cocoa during the next blizzard and serve it with a plate of cookies or doughnuts for a winter celebration your kids will long remember. That's what we did during the famous Raleigh blizzard of 2000—the year 22 inches of snow socked in our fair Southern city and shut it down tight for two weeks. Even if your audience is strictly grown-up chocoholics, watch for smiles with every sip.

DO-AHEAD

The cocoa can be refrigerated, covered, for up to 2 days. Reheat the cocoa over medium-high heat, stirring frequently, until it begins to get hot, about 10 minutes. Reduce the heat to medium and continue to stir frequently until steaming hot, being careful not to let the cocoa boil, about 5 minutes more.

Phased and Flexible

Virgin Mary Punch (Extra "Punch" Optional)

From Beverly:

When I was just a little girl, my parents would rave about Cousin Jim Clark's Bloody Marys. From time to time, I was allowed a taste before the "serious stuff" got added. So from a tender age I learned to love the taste of spicy tomato juice mixed with Cousin Jim's secret ingredient—a touch of horseradish. It's probably Cousin Jim's fault, but I simply adore Bloody Marys. I order them—often without vodka—everywhere I travel. None can compare to the Jim Clark version. It took me years to develop, but my own rendition tastes even better than what I remember from my child-hood. With or without the vodka, this punch is sure to be a hit with tomato juice lovers. Keep extra ingredients on hand in case your guests demand second helpings.

1 bottle (46 ounces) low-sodium vegetable juice, such as V8
1 bottle (8 ounces) clam juice
1 lime
3 tablespoons Worcestershire sauce
2 tablespoons prepared horseradish
1 teaspoon celery salt
⅛ teaspoon finely ground black pepper
1 cup vodka, or to taste (optional)
Ice cubes, for serving
8 celery sticks or lime wedges (optional), for garnish

PHASE 1: 5 MINUTES

1. Pour the vegetable juice and clam juice into a very large pitcher or container. Cut the lime in half and squeeze the juice into the pitcher. Add the Worcestershire sauce, horseradish, celery salt, and pepper. Stir until well blended. *The punch can be refrigerated for up to 2 days.*

PHASE 2: 5 MINUTES

2. Stir the vodka, if using, into the pitcher just before serving or pour the desired amount into individual glasses. Serve the punch in tall glasses over ice cubes, garnished with celery sticks or lime wedges, if desired.

■ *Serves 8*

DESIGNATED DRIVERS MUST DRINK, TOO

Whether it's because Cousin Clara just isn't ready to announce her pregnancy to everyone or your friend Joe has a heavy workload tomorrow, you'll want to offer something nonalcoholic that's more pleasing than tap water for them to sip. You'll also want to serve these benign beverages right alongside the others so guests won't feel awkward about choosing them.

We've covered some recipes for wonderful drinks that won't leave your friends feeling deprived, including Extra-Easy Peppermint Iced Tea (see page 28), Fruity Tea Punch (see page 29), and Virgin Mary Punch (opposite). For other options, look no further than the supermarket. Here's a list of easy-to-stock bar alternatives:

• **Individual bottles of water:** Whether sparkling or still, plain or with a twist of lime built right in, there's something about having your own bottle of water that's definitely special.

• **Gourmet sodas:** There's nothing wrong with the standard fare, but your guests will appreciate a fancy twist on the same old, same old soda.

• **Sparkling grape juice:** When everyone's lifting the glass to toast, glasses of this bubbly make everybody happy. Nonalcoholic sparkling cider is sometimes available, too. Look for both in the regular juice aisle of the supermarket.

• **Nonalcoholic beer:** Brands abound, and our friends say the only thing they miss when they drink nonalcoholic beer is the hangover.

• **Fruit juices and juice blends:** Fresh-squeezed OJ and grapefruit juice spell pure luxury, but your best friends are worth it. Or look to the refrigerator case near the dairy department for cartons of blends featuring everything from banana-pineapple to strawberry-tangerine. It's not quite fresh squeezed, but it's close. If these juices are a bit too intense for your guests' tastes, suggest that they mix them with an equal amount of seltzer, ginger ale, or a lemon-lime flavored soda.

Alcohol is not for everyone. The list of reasons people choose not to imbibe is long—and often private.

THE PERFECT PITCHER

From Beverly:

One aspect of making beverages for a crowd caught me off guard the first time around. You need a lot of liquid. And a gallon-size pitcher, an essential piece of party equipment I simply didn't own. So, I poured my iced tea into a clean leftover plastic milk jug and set out to buy the perfect pitcher. But as I was rushing from store to store on the afternoon before my guests were to arrive, I discovered that giant-size pitchers are not that easy to find. Okay, there are lots of cheap, plain, plastic ones out there, but if you want something that looks snazzy, it's another matter. I've still never seen a 128-ounce glass pitcher. Most manufacturers must figure a piece of glass that big risks too much shatter potential.

After extensive shopping, here's what I discovered: The perfect pitcher doesn't have to be plain, but when you're talking plastic, it does have to be in season. In the early spring when retailers' thoughts turn to pool and patio, you'll find a host of acrylic and plastic serving pieces with designs that are far from ho-hum. Manufacturers must reason that folks drink more by the pool, because in this category, the gallon-size pitcher is plentiful.

For fancier fare and indoor occasions, we've settled on using a half-gallon glass pitcher and simply refilling it. You can keep a cheap plastic spare in the refrigerator or buy two nice pitchers and switch them. Either way, be sure to choose a container that's not too tall to fit on the average refrigerator shelf (I learned this the hard way). As for price and design in the glass realm, you'll find everything from functional (read cheap) to cut glass. Watch for sales and discount outlets and retailers that specialize in overstocked or discontinued merchandise for the best buys.

When I make a beverage, I like to mix it in a big vat that has room for vigorous stirring with no chance of any liquids escaping over the side. A stock pot or a really large mixing bowl does the trick. When you are done, use a soup ladle or a 2-cup glass measure to fill your pitcher quickly with no spillage.

Once you've stirred up a gallon of brew, where do you put it all? In a gallon-size pitcher, of course.

Super Sangria

2 bottles (750 milliliters each) dry red wine
1 cup rum or brandy
1 cup orange-flavored liqueur, such as triple sec
1 can (6 ounces) frozen lemonade concentrate
⅔ cup orange juice
1 lemon
4 cups chilled ginger ale
Ice cubes, for serving
2 oranges sliced (optional), for garnish

PHASE 1: 8 MINUTES, PLUS 2 HOURS CHILLING TIME

1. Put all of the ingredients except the ginger ale, ice cubes, and garnish in a 1-gallon container that has a lid. Stir well and refrigerate, covered, until chilled through, about 2 hours. *The sangria can be refrigerated, covered at this point for up to 24 hours.*

PHASE 2: 5 MINUTES

2. Just before serving, stir in the ginger ale. Serve in wineglasses filled with ice and garnish each glass with an orange slice, if desired.

■ *Serves 8 to 10*

From Alicia:

I've been making this delicious wine punch for years. Because of all the "extras" in the sangria, you can use an inexpensive red table wine if you choose.

SANITY SAVER

On your last trip to the supermarket before your guests arrive, if you have room for it in your freezer, pick up an extra bag of ice. You can never have enough.

ABOUT ICE

Y ou know what beverages you plan to serve, but if your freezer space is limited, stocking up on ice before your bash can be a challenge. Here are some suggestions:

• Are there nooks and crannies in your freezer? Put cubes from your ice maker into zipper-top plastic bags and stash them away. Start several days ahead.

• Canvass the neighbors to see who has extra freezer space. A gallon bag or two of ice cubes may not be an imposition. After all, freezers work better when full.

• If there's a guest who must pass a grocery or convenience store on the way to the party, ask him or her to pick up a couple of bags of ice for you. Good friends will be glad to help. You can return the favor later.

• When all else fails, head out to buy ice a few hours before the gathering. Buy an extra bag (to allow for any melting), and store it all in a cooler until your guests arrive.

ABOUT THE ICE BUCKET

I ce buckets are handy additions to the entertaining equipment closet. They're insulated, which means ice can sit out during the cocktail hour allowing easy access. We've found guests are more apt to help themselves to refills (thus cutting down on chores for the host) if everything is readily available. Get the largest ice bucket you can find since refilling it is an unwelcome interruption.

For serving the ice, most of the plastic tongs that come with ice buckets just don't work. Substitute metal tongs with a real ability to grip or place a slotted serving spoon nearby.

We got our ice buckets by putting them on our wish lists. If you don't have an ice bucket yet and your birthday is months away, one serviceable substitute is a small foam cooler or a lunch-size ice chest. Or, if you don't mind a bit of melting, just put the ice in a large pretty serving bowl.

SANITY SAVER

I f you've come to the very last minute and need to chill a bottle of wine or a six-pack of beer quickly, place the bottle or bottles in a tall container (such as a bucket) and fill it with ice. Then add enough cold water to rise three quarters of the way up the bottle(s).

White Wine Granita with Peaches

1 bottle (750 milliliters) chardonnay
⅔ cup sugar
2 cinnamon sticks (each 3 inches long)
4 to 6 large fresh peaches (for about 2 cups slices)

PHASE 1: 20 MINUTES, PLUS 6 HOURS TO FREEZE

1. Heat the wine, sugar, and cinnamon sticks with 1 cup of water in a 2-quart or larger saucepan over medium heat, stirring occasionally, until the sugar dissolves, about 2 minutes. Remove from the heat and let cool for 10 minutes.

2. Pour the wine mixture into a shallow 2-quart glass, ceramic, or stainless steel dish so that it will form about a 1-inch layer (see Note). Cover with plastic wrap and place in the freezer until frozen crystals form throughout, at least 6 hours but no longer than 24.

PHASE 2: 10 MINUTES

3. Rinse the peaches, cut them in half, and remove and discard the pits. Peel and slice the peaches, then place an equal amount of slices in each of 8 wine glasses. Reserve 8 slices for garnish, if desired.

4. Remove the granita from the freezer and scrape it into chunks with a serving spoon. Spoon it into the glasses over the fruit. Top each serving with a peach slice, if desired, and serve. *The individual servings of granita may be kept in the freezer for up to 1 hour.*

■ *Serves 8*

Note: A 10 × 8-inch baking dish holds 2 quarts. You may find it easier to fit the granita into your freezer if you divide it between two containers.

B efore dinner, after dinner, or not for dinner at all, this refreshing beverage is easy to make ahead and will really impress your guests. If it's not quite peach season and you just can't wait, serve it with whatever berries are in season, instead.

CHAPTER TWO

Welcoming

When guests arrive at your door, a little something before dinner never fails to please.

Don't let yourself fall into the hors d'oeuvre trap, spending hours artistically layering tiny bits of food only to spend hours more arranging them on trays. Unless this sounds like fun, it's just not worth it. To delight guests, there's only one thing you really need: dip.

Everybody—from the tiniest two-year-old to the hunkiest he-man—loves dips and spreads. There's just something about dunking chips, crackers, and veggies into a bowl of saucy, surprising flavors that seems to satisfy the practically universal human need to nibble.

There's another essential advantage. Dips and spreads are easy. They're fast. They're whipped together long before the doorbell rings. This chapter contains nearly two dozen varieties, and it's safe to say that every single one is our favorite. We're two women who'd just as soon the dinner menu be chips and dip most any night of the week; we found it hard to narrow the playing field. It would be like leaving out a child, so we just included them all—everything from Beverly's mom's crab dip to a skinny version of guacamole to our updated twist on the ever-popular artichoke dip.

The food processor plays an important part in getting many of the dips and spreads you'll find here to have just the right consistency. All it takes is a quick spin and then an easy transfer to a pretty serving bowl or a storage container, if you're preparing the recipe in advance.

Light Bites

In our estimation, a light bites lineup for most gatherings would contain a choice of two dips (or a dip and a spread) and perhaps one other nibble. Of course, there are a few finger foods that have made it into our repertoire as well. They don't require artistic arrangement yet are guaranteed to draw raves. Cajun Barbecued Shrimp, Curried Walnuts, and Pinwheels Primavera come immediately to mind. Our goal is to focus on fast, rich flavors, not prissy perfection.

Whether you're looking for a start to a full evening's menu or just offering guests a chance to gather for cocktails and conversation before the show, you need an arsenal of recipes you can count on. Here it is.

fast and fabulous

Curried Walnuts

2 cups walnuts
1 tablespoon plus 1 teaspoon sugar
¾ teaspoon curry powder
½ teaspoon salt
1 tablespoon vegetable oil
1 tablespoon butter

START TO FINISH: 10 MINUTES, PLUS 10 MINUTES COOLING TIME

1. Spread the walnuts in a single layer on a microwave-safe dish. Microwave, uncovered, on high until fragrant and lightly toasted, 6 to 8 minutes, stopping once halfway through to stir. Using oven mitts, remove from the microwave.

2. While the nuts are toasting, stir 1 tablespoon of sugar together with the curry powder and salt in a medium-size bowl.

3. When the nuts have finished toasting, combine the vegetable oil and butter and the remaining 1 teaspoon of sugar in a small saucepan. Heat over medium heat, whisking constantly, until the butter melts. Add the toasted walnuts to the glaze and stir. Cook until the walnuts are shiny and coated with most of the glaze, about 1 minute.

4. Transfer the nuts to the bowl with the spice mix and toss to coat. Let the nuts cool on waxed paper or parchment paper for about 10 minutes.

■ *Makes 2 cups*

These have been one of our favorite munchies for years. Curried walnuts are perfect before dinner or to round out a larger appetizer spread. We've translated the traditional oven recipe into this superfast, very desperate, microwave version that will amaze you. A coarse salt, such as kosher or sea salt, is especially nice on these nuts. While they keep well, if your crew knows they're around, they won't last long.

DO-AHEAD

The walnuts can be stored, covered, in an airtight container for up to 2 weeks.

Winter Spiced Pecans

2 cups pecans
1 tablespoon plus 1 teaspoon sugar
¾ teaspoon apple pie spice (see Note)
½ teaspoon salt
1 tablespoon pure vanilla extract
1 tablespoon pure rum extract or rum
1 tablespoon butter

START TO FINISH: 10 MINUTES, PLUS 10 MINUTES COOLING TIME

1. Spread the pecans in a single layer on a microwave-safe dish. Microwave, uncovered, on high until fragrant and lightly toasted, 6 to 8 minutes, stopping once halfway through to stir. Using oven mitts, remove from the microwave.

2. While the nuts are toasting, stir together 1 tablespoon of sugar with the apple pie spice and salt in a small mixing bowl.

3. When the nuts have finished toasting, combine the vanilla and rum extracts, the remaining 1 teaspoon of sugar, and the butter in a small saucepan. Heat over medium heat, whisking constantly until the butter melts. Add the toasted pecans to the glaze and stir. Cook until the pecans are shiny and coated with most of the glaze, about 1 minute.

4. Transfer the nuts to the bowl with the spice mix and toss to coat. Let the nuts cool on waxed paper or parchment paper for about 10 minutes.

■ *Makes 2 cups*

Note: What else can you do with apple pie spice? Make apple pies, of course, and hot spiced cider. Boiled with water the spice makes a great room-scenter.

Wow! will most likely be the number one response for these beauties. And you won't believe how easy they are to make, thanks to the microwave roasting technique. So, it's easy to serve them for everything from a quick and casual afternoon snack to the most formal of evening functions.

The secret is the use of wintery apple pie spice in the coating. Using a coarse salt—kosher or sea—will add an extra crunch. Get ready to crave these pecans.

DO-AHEAD

The pecans can be stored, covered, in an airtight container for up to 2 weeks.

An appetizer buffet is never complete without our friend Denise Thorpe's spiced olives. The original recipe came from a cookbook by the Junior League of Denver called *Colorado Collage*, but we've turned Denise's adaptation into one for the Desperate Cook by using the microwave instead of the oven and adding other favorite time-savers. Denise uses fresh rosemary, and if you happen to have a sprig, just place it in the dish instead of dried. If your olives have pits, provide a small bowl nearby for easy discards. The flavor of the olives improves after a day or two, so this is one task you can zip off in a flash long before the guests arrive.

DO-AHEAD

The olives can be prepared through Step 1 and refrigerated, covered, for up to 2 days. The microwaved olives can be refrigerated, covered, in a storage container for up to 1 week. To reheat before serving, microwave, uncovered, on high, for 2 minutes.

Rosemary Olives

2 teaspoons extra-virgin olive oil
1 cup dry white wine
1 tablespoon bottled minced garlic
1 teaspoon dried rosemary, or 1 sprig fresh rosemary
2 cups kalamata olives, pitted or unpitted (see Note)

START TO FINISH: **3 MINUTES, PLUS 5 MINUTES UNATTENDED MICROWAVE TIME**

1. Whisk together the olive oil, wine, garlic, and rosemary in a small microwave-safe baking dish. Drain the olives, add them to the dish, and stir.

2. Cover the dish with microwave-safe plastic wrap and cut a small vent in the center. Microwave, on high, until the wine mixture is boiling and the olives are aromatic, about 5 minutes. Use a slotted spoon to transfer the olives to a serving dish. Discard the rosemary sprig, if using. Serve the olives warm or at room temperature.

■ *Makes 2 cups*

Note: Many supermarkets now offer lots of kinds of olives in bulk in the cheese or deli department. A mix of various olives also works beautifully in this recipe.

LIGHT BITES ONLY

Let's say you'd like to have friends over but want to avoid the whole dinner dilemma. One good solution is to invite them for mid- to late-afternoon drinks and nibbles. Another idea is to gather them together before heading out to a restaurant, show, or other event, such as a child's music recital. Just make it clear when you extend the invitation what's involved, and don't apologize. "We'd love to have you over for drinks and dips from four to six on Saturday," is enough to get the idea across.

How many folks to include depends on the size of your house, deck, or yard; how much time you have to spend on the food; and how much you can budget for drinks. If you really need to include the whole neighborhood, light bites only is definitely a good way to go. Here's how:

• Buy some ice and bury some bottles of beer, white wine, sparkling water, and/or "gourmet" soda in it.

• Get bags of chips, boxes of assorted crackers, and some of those baby carrots that are already peeled. Spend 3 minutes whipping up our Rosemary Olives (opposite) and, while they're in the microwave and cooling down, invest another 8 minutes on Smoked Salmon Spread (see page 51). If you've got 6 more minutes, you can add Hot Spinach Dip (see page 49) to the line-up.

• Put the food into bowls. That chip-and-dip server that came as a wedding gift frankly looks a little too formal for most desperate gatherings. We put dips in pottery soup bowls and set each bowl on a dinner plate that holds the crackers and carrots. Chips go in wicker baskets or another larger bowl lined with colorful paper napkins. Lately we've noticed an explosion in attractive plastic party ware at discount stores, and the prices are extremely reasonable. Think about investing in a cheap, pretty bowl or two. Or maybe go for the plastic chip-and-dip set.

Now, less than an hour has elapsed (minus the shopping time), and your party food is ready. With a few successful gatherings under your belt, you'll soon be confident enough to graduate to dinner.

Entertain with light bites only. It's so easy even a child can do it.

Put this dip into the too-simple-to-be-so-good category. The distinctive flavor of dill goes especially well with pretzels or sliced cucumbers. Or you can take a hint from Beverly's brother-in-law Roger Rosenthal and dollop it atop smoked salmon on party pumpernickel slices.

DO-AHEAD

The dill dip can be refrigerated, covered, for up to 4 days.

Dilly of a Dip

½ cup mayonnaise
½ cup sour cream
2 tablespoons Dijon mustard
1½ teaspoons dried dill, or 1 sprig fresh dill

START TO FINISH: 5 MINUTES

Stir all of the ingredients together in a small serving bowl or 2-cup storage container that has a lid. If using fresh dill, mince finely first, avoiding tough stems; you'll need about 3 tablespoons.

■ *Makes about 1 cup*

Save this secret for your friends on diets: Our remarkable curried veggie dip has less than a gram of fat per tablespoon. Nonfat yogurt gets the thanks for the skinny side of things, and good-quality curry powder is the key to the flavor. The dip goes well with all kinds of fresh vegetables. For suggestions, check out the box on page 54.

DO-AHEAD

The curry dip can be refrigerated, covered, for up to 3 days. Store the scallion garnish separately in a small plastic bag.

Golden Curry Dip

1 scallion (for 2 tablespoons minced, white and green parts)
1 small container (8 ounces) plain nonfat yogurt
2 tablespoons low-fat mayonnaise
2 tablespoons chili sauce or ketchup
1 tablespoon curry powder

START TO FINISH: 7 MINUTES

1. Rinse and mince the scallion. Place 1 tablespoon of the minced scallion in a small, pretty bowl or a 2-cup or larger storage container that has a lid. (Be aware that curry powder will stain some plastics.) Set the remaining minced scallion aside.

2. Add the yogurt, mayonnaise, chili sauce, and curry powder to the bowl or container. Stir well to combine. Garnish with the reserved minced scallion just before serving.

■ *Makes about 1¼ cups*

Hercules's Cucumber Dip

1 large (about ¾ pound) cucumber (see Notes)
½ cup sour cream (see Notes)
¼ cup hummus
Salt and black pepper

START TO FINISH: 7 MINUTES

Peel the cucumber (see Notes) and cut it into bite-size pieces. Place the cucumber in a medium-size serving bowl or storage container that has a lid. Stir in the sour cream and the hummus until well combined. Season with salt and pepper to taste.

■ *Makes about 1¼ cups*

Notes: You can use low-fat sour cream here, if you like.

Hothouse (seedless English) and Kirby cucumbers do not need to be peeled.

The supermarket deli has become quite international in its offerings, and we now rely on hummus when we're in a hurry. This Middle Eastern dish is traditionally a smooth spread of chickpeas and sesame paste that's flavored with olive oil, garlic, and lemon juice, but we've paired it with cucumber and sour cream to expand its horizons. See pages 46 and 54 for a variety of suggestions on crackers and other things to serve the dip with.

DO-AHEAD

The cucumber dip can be refrigerated, covered, for up to 2 days.

THE HUM ON HUMMUS

Commercially prepared hummus is usually sold refrigerated in plastic containers, much like pesto. Sometimes it's sold by the pound in the deli case. Brands vary in the amount of garlic and lemon juice they contain, so taste the hummus before starting the recipe. If it tastes flat, add lemon juice or minced garlic. Experiment to find the brand that best suits your taste.

Since hummus keeps for more than a week in the refrigerator and you need only a quarter cup for Hercules's Cucumber Dip, you'll have enough left over to use as a quick snack with pretzels or baby carrots. Hummus also adds an easy zing when dolloped on grilled chicken breasts or used instead of mayonnaise on sandwiches. Any way you spread it, hummus is never ho-hum.

ABOUT CRACKERS

Crackers, flat bread, pita points, cocktail bread, or chips? What's a desperate cook to choose? Truth is, it doesn't really matter—most of the time. There are only a few dips that die without the perfect scoop, but in all other cases, we tend to buy whatever cracker and chip assortment happens to catch our eye.

When the dipper does make a noticeable difference, we've said so. One example is our BLT Dip on page 67. We like to serve it with melba toast, which makes the whole concoction reminiscent of a BLT sandwich. We discovered by accident that the flavor of dill goes amazingly well with pretzels, so we've paired those with our Dilly of a Dip on page 44. Blue corn chips are our suggestion with the Roasted Garlic Salsa (see page 50), mainly because they are unusual and the color makes a more impressive presentation.

The thing to remember when picking your dipper is the flavor of the dip. Strong crackers will fight, not complement, a strong dip, so don't pick garlic crackers if the dip is already loaded with garlic, for example.

Keeping your crackers crisp is essential. Nothing is more annoying than dipping a soggy cracker into a delicious dip. Because we live in a very humid climate, we leave opening the crackers to the very last minute before the guests arrive. Leftover crackers, if they've not been left out too long, are best stored in a tin.

Other than these very few guidelines, don't worry about which cracker, chip, or bread you choose. Here are a few of our favorites:

- Corn chips—blue, white, and regular
- Mediterranean flat bread, sliced into points
    (or pie-shaped slices)—whole wheat and white
- Pita bread, sliced into points—whole wheat and white
- Sour dough, rye, and pumpernickel cocktail bread slices
- Plain and hearty wheat crackers
- Buttery crackers
- Melba toast
- Pretzels

There are scads of ready-to-go dippers out there. If you want to get fancy, mix a couple of different ones in a basket.

Black Bean "Hummus"

3 cloves fresh garlic
About ½ cup densely packed fresh cilantro
1 can (15 ounces) black beans
3 tablespoons smooth peanut butter, preferably with
*   little or no added sugar*
1 tablespoon peanut oil
2 limes
Tortilla chips, bagel chips, or pita triangles, for serving

START TO FINISH: 12 MINUTES

1. Peel the garlic. Rinse the cilantro well and shake the leaves to remove any excess water. Remove and discard the tough lower stems but do not worry about the smaller, upper stems. You should have about ½ cup of leaves. Rinse and drain the black beans.

2. Drop the garlic cloves 1 at a time through the feed tube of a food processor with the motor running and finely chop. Drop in the cilantro and chop well. Stop the machine and use a rubber spatula to scrape down the side of the processor bowl, then add the beans, peanut butter, and peanut oil. Halve the limes and squeeze the juice from 3 halves into the processor bowl.

3. Process until the beans are puréed and the dip is mixed well, about 1 minute. Stop once midway to scrape down the side of the processor bowl. Taste the hummus. Add juice from the remaining lime half, if desired. (If the hummus is tart enough, reserve the remaining lime half for another use.) Serve with the chips or pita triangles.

■ *Makes about 1½ cups*

Here's a twist on traditional hummus that substitutes black beans for chickpeas and relies on peanut butter instead of sesame paste. The delightful dip never fails to elicit several requests for the recipe whenever we serve it. The secret to this innovative spread is using a natural-style peanut butter with little or no added sugar, such as Simply Jif or Smucker's Natural. Serve the dip with tortilla chips, bagel chips, or pita triangles.

DO-AHEAD

The black bean dip can be refrigerated, covered, for up to 3 days.

Don't tell anyone about the secret ingredient and your guests will never suspect. Granted, frozen green peas and avocados sound like strange bedfellows, but the peas prevent the guacamole from turning dark, so you can make it a day ahead. Also, the peas cut half the fat out of our favorite traditional guacamole recipe.

Choose an avocado that feels soft when pressed with your thumb. California avocados, also known as Hass, are the smaller pear-shaped variety that is almost black in color with bumpy skin. We prefer them for their fuller flavor. If you don't have a food processor, you can make the dip in a blender. The texture will be slightly smoother. Serve the guacamole with tortilla chips.

Guiltless Guacamole

1½ cups frozen green peas
3 cloves fresh garlic
½ medium-size red onion (for about ½ cup chopped)
About ½ cup densely packed fresh cilantro
1 very ripe, medium-size California avocado
½ cup spicy hot prepared salsa
1 lime
Salt (optional)

START TO FINISH: 15 MINUTES

1. Pour the peas into a colander and run slightly warm water over them for 2 minutes to thaw. Set aside to drain well.

2. Peel the garlic. Peel the onion and cut it into 4 pieces. Rinse the cilantro well and shake the leaves to remove any excess water. Remove and discard the tough lower stems but do not worry about the smaller, upper stems. You should have about ½ cup of leaves.

3. Drop the garlic cloves 1 at a time through the feed tube of a food processor with the machine running and finely chop. Drop in the onion pieces and chop well. Drop in the cilantro and chop well. Stop the machine before each addition and after all the cilantro is chopped and use a rubber spatula to scrape down the side of the processor bowl.

4. Cut the avocado in half around the seed. Twist the halves in opposite directions to separate them. Remove and discard the seed. Use a spoon to scoop out the avocado flesh and add it to the processor along with the thawed peas and the salsa. Halve the lime and squeeze the juice into the processor bowl. Process until very smooth, stopping once to scrape down the side of the bowl. Season with salt, if desired (this won't be necessary if serving the guacamole with salted chips). Transfer to a serving bowl and serve.

■ *Makes about 2 cups*

DO-AHEAD

The guacamole can be refrigerated, covered, for up to 3 days.

Hot Spinach Dip

1 package (9 ounces) frozen creamed spinach
*1 small package (3 ounces) cream cheese, at room
   temperature*
½ cup already-shredded Swiss cheese (see Note)
¼ cup mayonnaise
½ teaspoon onion powder
½ teaspoon garlic powder
¼ teaspoon black pepper

There's nothing to cut or chop for this simple, yet savory dip. Its taste belies the fact that all you have to do is just measure, stir, and microwave, thanks to our secret ingredient—a pouch of frozen creamed spinach. Feel free to substitute Neufchatel for the cream cheese and use low-fat mayonnaise. For ideas about things to use for dipping see pages 46 and 54.

**START TO FINISH: 6 MINUTES, PLUS 5 MINUTES MOSTLY
UNATTENDED MICROWAVE TIME**

1. Thaw the spinach by cutting a small slit in the plastic bag, placing it on a microwave-safe plate, and microwaving it on high until thawed, about 2 minutes.

2. Combine the thawed spinach with all of the remaining ingredients in a small, microwave-safe serving bowl. Stir well until the cream cheese is thoroughly incorporated. Some small clumps of cream cheese may remain.

3. Microwave the spinach dip, uncovered, on high, until bubbly, about 5 minutes, stopping once halfway through to stir. Serve the dip at once.

◼ *Makes about 2 cups*

Note: If you can't find any already-shredded Swiss cheese, it just takes a couple of minutes to shred your own. You'll need about 2 ounces.

DO-AHEAD

The dip can be prepared through Step 2 and refrigerated, covered, for up to 24 hours.

From Alicia:

Pairing roasted garlic with my favorite homemade salsa was quite accidental. In a wild roasting spree, I baked every last clove of garlic in the pantry. Then, that night we were craving the So-Simple Salsa, from our first book, *Desperation Dinners!* But not one unroasted garlic clove was to be found. Well, I figured, I've got ten heads of roasted garlic in the refrigerator, why not give them a try?

This salsa has all the depth and zip of our original but with the added mellow goodness of the roasted garlic. You can substitute one to two cloves of fresh garlic for the roasted, if you choose.

Roasted Garlic Salsa and Blue Chips

4 cloves already-roasted garlic (see page 262)
About ¼ cup densely packed fresh cilantro
1 can (14½ ounces) Mexican-style
    stewed tomatoes (see Note)
½ lime
1 bag blue corn chips

START TO FINISH: 5 MINUTES

1. Peel the garlic. Rinse the cilantro well and shake the leaves to remove any excess water. Remove the tough stems and discard but do not worry about the smaller, upper stems. You should have about ¼ cup of leaves.

2. Drop the garlic cloves 1 at a time through the feed tube of a food processor or through the top of a blender, with the machine running, and chop well. Drop in the cilantro and chop well. Stop the machine, add the tomatoes and squeeze the juice from the lime half directly into the processor bowl. Pulse to slightly chop the tomatoes. Pour the salsa into a serving bowl and serve with blue corn chips.

■ *Makes about 2 cups*

Note: If you can't find Mexican-style stewed tomatoes, you can make the salsa with canned diced tomatoes seasoned with jalapeños, for a hotter salsa, or with green chiles, for a milder salsa. You'll need to add ½ teaspoon of sugar when using tomatoes that haven't been stewed.

DO-AHEAD

The salsa can be refrigerated, covered, for up to 3 days.

Smoked Salmon Spread

1 package (4 ounces) smoked salmon
1 package (8 ounces) cream cheese
⅓ cup sour cream
1 tablespoon A.1. steak sauce

START TO FINISH: 8 MINUTES

Cut the salmon into small pieces and the cream cheese into 1-inch cubes. Place the salmon pieces in a food processor and pulse until finely chopped. Add the cream cheese cubes and the sour cream and steak sauce and process until well blended and creamy.

■ *Makes about 2 cups*

ABOUT MEXICAN TOMATOES

Canned "Mexican recipe" stewed tomatoes are a vital part of our pantry, and over the years we have come to trust the Del Monte brand. These tomatoes are cooked with jalapeño peppers, onions, garlic, green peppers, and celery, so the flavor is complex without the raw taste of plain canned tomatoes.

Del Monte also has a line they call "Zesty"—diced tomatoes seasoned either with jalapeños (medium hot) or with mild green chiles. These tomatoes contain onions and other spices and can be substituted for the Mexican stewed variety in all of our recipes.

Although Del Monte's tomatoes are nationally distributed, not all grocery stores carry them. Several other brands are available, including many store brands, and while these may be substituted, we can't swear you'll get the same results. Our best hint is this: When asked, most grocery store managers will order and begin to stock specific items their regular customers want to buy.

From Alicia:

After I was a guest on Brian Poor's talk radio show *The Poor Man's Kitchen* on KOMO Newstalk 1000 in Seattle, we got down to real business, sharing recipes. Poor, who was also the executive chef at Six Degrees restaurant, shared the basics of this delicious spread. We've adapted his restaurant-size recipe for the home kitchen, and it's perfect for entertaining.

Sealed packages of smoked salmon, stored unopened in your refrigerator, will stay fresh for weeks, making it easy to keep on hand for spur-of-the-moment guests. The very pink, smoked Nova salmon—or any other kind of smoked salmon— will work well in this recipe. So do Neufchatel cheese and low-fat sour cream in place of the cream cheese and full-fat sour cream. What to serve the spread with? You'll find some suggestions on pages 46 and 54.

DO-AHEAD

The Smoked Salmon Spread can be refrigerated, covered, for up to 2 days. Let return to room temperature before serving.

From Beverly:

My mom's signature crab dip never turns out exactly the same way twice since she is not prone to measure when she makes it. She just takes crab meat fresh from the bay in front of her Topsail Island home and stirs in whatever happens to look about right. When I asked for the recipe, it took several months to convince her it could be written down. In the end, I found myself driving to Topsail and standing watch in the kitchen with measuring spoons. Boy, was it worth it. This recipe offers the perfect balance for the delicate crab meat, and even though some of the ingredients come in small amounts, don't leave anything out. It is such a splurge anyway that I tend to make it with real cream cheese, sour cream, and mayonnaise, but if you're used to the reduced-fat alternatives, they can be substituted in equal amounts. You'll find serving suggestions on pages 46 and 54.

DO-AHEAD

The crab dip can be refrigerated, covered, for up to 24 hours.

Dot's Crab Dip

1 small package (3 ounces) cream cheese, at room temperature
¼ cup sour cream
3 tablespoons mayonnaise
1 small onion (for ½ teaspoon juice)
1½ teaspoons lemon juice
¾ teaspoon seafood seasoning, such as Old Bay
½ teaspoon Worcestershire sauce
8 ounces crab meat (see Note)
Lemon slice or paprika, for garnish

START TO FINISH: 15 MINUTES

1. In a medium-size serving bowl, stir together the cream cheese, sour cream, and mayonnaise. Peel the onion and place a grater in a pie pan or on a piece of waxed paper. Grate the onion using the smallest holes of the grater; juice will simply puddle at the bottom. You will be able to scoop up ½ teaspoon of juice easily. Add the onion juice to the cream cheese mixture and reserve what remains of the onion for another use. Stir in the lemon juice, seafood seasoning, and Worcestershire sauce.

2. Pick over the crab meat, flake it with your fingers, and remove any pieces of shell and discard. Add the crab to the cream cheese mixture and stir well to mix. Garnish with a lemon slice or a light sprinkling of paprika.

■ *Makes about 1¾ cups*

Note: The outcome of your dip will depend heavily on the quality and freshness of the crab. Though claw meat is sweeter, it commands only half the price of fancy lump or backfin meat and will work just fine. If you aren't lucky enough to have the ocean at your doorstep, containers of pasteurized crab meat should be available in the supermarket's fresh seafood section late spring through mid-September.

THE QUICK OIL AND VINEGAR TRICK

Want a two-second way to impress your guests? This works every time: Pour enough extra-virgin olive oil in a shallow dish, saucer, or salad plate to make a pool in the bottom. Drizzle in a little balsamic vinegar, say a teaspoonful, and serve it alongside a loaf of hearty bakery bread for dipping.

When our favorite Italian restaurants started serving this oil-and-vinegar combo with bread instead of butter, we realized we were impressed, so our guests were bound to be as well. The fact that it's so easy is an extra bonus.

You do need a good-quality, robust olive oil, thus the extra-virgin specification. We started out with a plain-old bottle of oil, but once we realized this would be an entertaining mainstay, we splurged on a slightly better quality bottle. Ditto with the vinegar. Most balsamic vinegar is aged, but some is aged longer. The longer the aging process, the sweeter and more flavorful the vinegar—and the more expensive it will be. But since you only use a few drops at each serving, your investment in a bottle of imported vinegar will last a while. As for the bread, you want a slightly chewy texture and an assertive crust. Sourdough varieties and peasant, farm, or hearth breads all work well. Assuming the bread is fresh, you don't even need to heat it. Slice it and let guests tear off dipping-size pieces.

If you have individual bread plates, you can serve each guest his or her own oil and vinegar, but two or three dinner guests can easily share, depending on the seating arrangements.

This dish has been so popular with our guests that we are asked to bring it along instead of wine to friends' dinners.

Introducing our favorite desperate standby to bring along to last minute potlucks.

DESPERATE VEGETABLES FOR DIPPING

When it comes to choosing vegetables that are perfect for dipping, we think the no-need-to-peel and the already-peeled are most appealing.

When you're in a hurry, don't you just hate to peel stuff? Truth is, we're not fond of peeling, period. Fortunately for all of us, the supermarkets are catching on to the no-peel craze. You'll find an array of fresh vegetables that are ready to eat with minimal work. Here are some of our favorites:

- **Broccoli florets:** They may be a bit more expensive per pound than the whole stalks, but remember, you're not paying for all that stalk that you'd just throw away.
- **Carrots:** Baby carrots come already peeled. No work needed.
- **Carrot sticks:** A longer version of the baby carrots. They come in plastic bags.
- **Celery sticks:** Ditto on the plastic bags. All the work's done. Hooray!
- **Cherry tomatoes:** Any stems you find must go in the garbage. Otherwise, a quick rinse does it. We like the variety called grape tomatoes for their smaller, one-bite size advantage.
- **Cucumbers:** If you don't want to peel and seed, choose the seedless variety with a thin skin, which goes by various names, depending on the store. The names we have seen most often are hothouse, English, and European. Kirby cucumbers, also called pickling cukes, are a smaller variety and work well, too. Give them a quick slicing and you're done.
- **Fresh mushrooms:** Do give them a rinse and check for woody stems. If you find any, break 'em off.
- **Yellow squash and zucchini:** Choose small, slender ones and slice them into circles about a quarter inch thick.

Topsail Shrimp Dip

½ small onion (for about ¼ cup chopped)
1 large rib celery
12 ounces already-cooked and -peeled medium-size
*   shrimp, thawed if frozen*
1 package (8 ounces) cream cheese, at room temperature
*   (see Note)*
3 tablespoons ketchup
1 tablespoon prepared horseradish
1½ teaspoons seafood seasoning, such as Old Bay

START TO FINISH: 10 MINUTES

1. Peel the onion and cut it into 2 pieces. Rinse the celery and cut it into 1-inch pieces. Drop the onion pieces through the feed tube of a food processor with the machine running and finely chop. Drop in the celery pieces and finely chop. Stop once to scrape down the side of the processor bowl with a rubber spatula.

2. Stop the machine, add the shrimp to the processor bowl, and process about 5 seconds, then pulse the motor just enough to finish coarsely chopping the shrimp.

3. Add the cream cheese, ketchup, horseradish, and seafood seasoning and process to blend well, about 30 seconds. Stop the machine once to scrape down the side of the processor bowl.

■ *Makes about 3 cups*

Note: You can use Neufchatel cheese here, if you like.

You never know when Beverly's mom, Dot Mills, will pull out one of her famous seafood dips. It might be shrimp or crab, but it's no wonder that neighbors are apt to stop by for a visit along about 5 o'clock most any summer Saturday. We like to serve our adaptation of the shrimp dip with mild crackers or vegetables. Leftovers are terrific spread on Sunday morning bagels.

DO-AHEAD

The shrimp dip can be refrigerated, covered, for up to 2 days. Let return to room temperature before serving.

Here's a French-inspired spread that draws on flavors from a classic *niçoise* salad. With the help of a food processor, the ingredients are transformed into a creamy tuna spread. It's perfect on crackers, bagel chips, or cocktail bread slices.

Riviera Tuna Spread

1 clove fresh garlic
About ¼ cup densely packed fresh parsley
½ small red onion (for about 2 tablespoons chopped)
¼ cup already-pitted imported black olives,
    such as kalamata
¼ cup mayonnaise (see Note)
4 teaspoons Dijon mustard
1 lemon
1 tablespoon extra-virgin olive oil
1 large can (12 ounces) white tuna packed in water

START TO FINISH: 15 MINUTES

1. Peel the garlic. Rinse the parsley well and shake the leaves to remove any excess water. Remove and discard the tough stems but do not worry about the smaller, upper stems. You should have about ¼ cup of leaves. Peel the onion.

2. Drop the garlic clove through the feed tube of a food processor with the machine running and finely chop. Drop in the parsley and process until finely chopped. Drop in the onion and olives and process until the onion and olives are finely chopped.

3. Add the mayonnaise and mustard. Cut the lemon in half and squeeze the juice through a small strainer (to catch the seeds) directly into the processor bowl. Process until just combined. While the machine is running, drizzle the olive oil through the feed tube very slowly until all has been added.

4. Drain the tuna well, pressing to remove excess liquid. Place the tuna in the processor bowl. Process until the spread is well mixed. Transfer to a storage container and cover or place in a decorative serving bowl and cover with plastic wrap. Refrigerate until ready to use.

■ *Makes about 3 cups*

Note: You can use low-fat mayonnaise here, if you like.

DO-AHEAD

The tuna spread can be refrigerated, covered, for up to 24 hours.

Smoked Oyster Spread

1 can (3.75 ounces) smoked oysters
1 package (8 ounces) cream cheese, at room temperature
*   (see Note)*
¼ cup already-grated Parmesan cheese
1 teaspoon Worcestershire sauce
Paprika, for garnish

START TO FINISH: 10 MINUTES

1. Drain the oysters well and pat with paper towels to remove as much oil as possible. Place the oysters in a food processor and process just until minced, about 10 seconds.

2. Add the cream cheese, Parmesan cheese, and Worcestershire sauce. Process until well blended, about 30 seconds. Serve in a pretty bowl garnished with a light sprinkling of paprika.

■ *Makes about 1¼ cups*

Note: You can use Neufchatel cheese in place of the cream cheese here, if you like.

Tins of smoked oysters are a great secret weapon to keep in the pantry. They're a bit messy to open and drain, but they pack so much flavor that the effort is well worthwhile. (A handheld can opener does the job better than an electric model.) This easy spread is elegant, with a subtle seafood taste. See if your guests can guess the main ingredient. Serve the spread with assorted hearty wheat crackers.

DO-AHEAD

The smoked oyster spread can be refrigerated, covered, for up to 3 days. Bring to room temperature and garnish with paprika before serving.

GARNISH IN AN INSTANT

From Beverly:

When it comes to garnishes, there are entire books devoted to explaining how to carve vegetables into swans and watermelons into baskets. The recommended tool kit costs extra.

Once I spent a significant slice of a weekend trying to get tomato peelings to come off in one continuous strand. The resulting red ribbons were then twisted to form tomato roses. They were elegant, but by the end, my nerves were shot.

Nowadays, given all of life's normal demands, I'm lucky just to get the food ready before my guests arrive. But I still want it to look nice. Here are some favorite tricks for fast and easy garnishes. You'll find other suggestions on pages 197 and 308.

- **Edible leaves:** Bright green sprigs of parsley, mint, cilantro, basil, chives, and other herbs enhance just about everything they touch. These decorator's dreams are widely available at supermarkets, but if you have a sunny patch of earth or even a clay pot and a bright windowsill, it's easy and cheap to grow your own. When it comes time to garnish, the trick is not to get too complicated. Placing a strand of chives artfully across the top of your food makes just as pretty a picture as tying chive bundles.

- **Big shapely leaves:** This category includes curly lettuce, red cabbage, and the outer leaves of all varieties of green cabbages. These leaves can be arranged to cover an entire serving plate and also serve as a nest for the food.

- **Stems and twigs:** Sometimes at a regular grocery you can find fruit with the stems and leaves still attached. Sources tell us this is a very sophisticated garnish these days, and the smaller the fruit the better. You can put these fruits in the middle of a platter or alongside it. Either way they'll be attractive.

- **Tomatoes:** Cherry tomatoes or full-size ones cut into wedges or chunks provide a splash of color either around or on top of chicken salad, potato salad, pasta salad—most any salad. Works with platters, too, for that matter.

- **Nuts and seeds:** A few toasted nuts scattered over the tops of steamed or roasted vegetables add an elegant touch. And don't forget sesame seeds; a few will add flavor as well as a nice finishing touch.

Just arrange parsley into a ring around the edge of a platter, and you can't miss.

Herbed Cheese Spread

2 cloves fresh garlic
1 package (8 ounces) Neufchatel cheese,
  at room temperature
½ cup low-fat cottage cheese
¼ teaspoon dried thyme
¼ teaspoon dried basil
¼ teaspoon black pepper
¼ teaspoon Worcestershire sauce

START TO FINISH: 9 MINUTES

1. Peel the garlic and cut the Neufchatel cheese into 4 pieces. Drop the garlic cloves 1 at a time through the feed tube of a food processor with the machine running and finely chop. Drop in the cheese pieces and continue processing until the cheese is smooth.

2. Add the cottage cheese, thyme, basil, pepper, and Worcestershire sauce and process until smooth, stopping once or twice midway through to scrape down the side of the bowl. Refrigerate the cheese spread until ready to use.

■ *Makes about 1¼ cups*

The flavors of garlic and herbs are so fantastic your guests will never realize that this is a reduced-fat version of a traditional Boursin-type spread. It's actually better made a day ahead to let the herb flavors permeate the cheese. Good served with wheat crackers, the spread also makes a fine topping for baked potatoes.

DO-AHEAD

The spread can be refrigerated, covered, for up to 3 days.

My Best Blue Cheese Spread

From Beverly:

I like the flavor of blue cheese a lot—provided that it's not overpowering. Most blue cheese dips and spreads I'd tasted were too strong for me, so a while back I set out to create one that would suit my taste perfectly. What I didn't know at the time was how many other people were yearning for a mild blue cheese flavor, but with just the right tang. I always get raves when I serve my version.

¼ cup plus 2 tablespoons already-chopped pecans
2 packages (8 ounces each) cream cheese,
*   at room temperature*
4 ounces blue cheese, such as Maytag or Saga
⅓ cup already-grated Parmesan cheese
1 teaspoon Worcestershire sauce
3 drops Tabasco sauce

START TO FINISH: 10 MINUTES

1. Spread the pecans in a single layer on a microwave-safe dish and microwave, uncovered, on high until fragrant and lightly toasted, about 2 minutes, stopping once halfway through to stir. If you plan on freezing the spread, toast only ¼ cup of pecans here. Using oven mitts, remove the nuts from the microwave.

2. Meanwhile, cut each cream cheese block into 4 pieces and place these in a food processor. Add all the remaining ingredients except the pecans. Process until smooth and well blended, stopping once or twice midway to scrape down the side of the bowl.

3. When the pecans have cooled slightly, add ¼ cup of the pecans to the processor and process until well mixed. Stop the machine and scrape down the side of the bowl, if necessary.

4. Transfer the cheese spread to a serving bowl and sprinkle the remaining toasted pecan pieces evenly over the top. Refrigerate, covered, until ready to serve.

■ *Makes about 3 cups*

DO-AHEAD

The blue cheese spread can be refrigerated, covered, for up to 4 days. Store the pecans for the garnish separately in an airtight container. Sprinkle them over the top of the spread a few hours before you plan to serve it.
• Or you can freeze the spread for up to 1 month in a covered plastic container. To thaw, place the container in the refrigerator at least 24 hours ahead. To garnish the thawed spread, you'll need to microwave 2 tablespoons of pecans on high until fragrant and lightly toasted, about 30 seconds.

Old English Cheese Spread

½ cup walnuts

1 clove fresh garlic

½ small onion

¼ medium-size green or red bell pepper

1 package (8 ounces) cream cheese (see Notes)

1 jar (5 ounces) sharp Cheddar cheese spread, such as Kraft Old English

1 jar (5 ounces) blue cheese spread, such as Kraft Roka

1 teaspoon Worcestershire sauce

⅛ teaspoon Tabasco sauce, or more to taste

For some reason, this spread particularly appeals to men. Women like it too, but our men friends can't get enough. If you don't find Roka blue cheese spread, use two jars of the sharp Cheddar cheese spread; of the two, it's the one that's most available. The spread goes together easily in 15 minutes or less. Serve it with butter crackers and celery sticks for dipping.

START TO FINISH: **15 MINUTES**

1. Place the walnuts in a food processor and chop medium-fine (see Notes). Put the chopped nuts in a small dish and set aside.

2. Peel the garlic and onion. Cut the onion into fourths. Rinse, core, seed, and dice the bell pepper. Drop the garlic clove through the feed tube of the processor with the machine running and finely chop. Drop in the onion pieces and finely chop. Stop the machine and add the cream cheese, cheese spreads, Worcestershire sauce, and Tabasco sauce to the processor bowl. Process to mix, then stop the machine and use a rubber spatula to scrape down the side of the processor bowl.

3. Add the diced bell pepper and chopped walnuts to the processor and pulse 3 or 4 times just to mix in.

■ *Makes about 2½ cups*

Notes: You can use Neufchatel cheese in place of the cream cheese, if you like. Whichever you use, have it at room temperature.

If you don't have a food processor, just chop the nuts, garlic, and onion by hand. If the cream cheese and cheese spreads are all at room temperature, you can stir the ingredients together easily with a spoon or use an electric mixer to combine them.

DO-AHEAD

The Old English Cheese Spread can be refrigerated, covered, for up to 1 week. Let return to room temperature before serving.

From Alicia:

As much as Beverly and I insist on making things easy, I sometimes forget to translate time-saving tips to my oldest favorite recipes.

Most of our conversations revolve around food, and one morning I boasted, "I used to make the best pimento cheese."

"So why don't you anymore?" Beverly asked.

Without thinking, I answered honestly. "I hate getting the food processor out to shred all that cheese. And cleaning the processor is the pits."

Being the level-headed journalist she is, Beverly asked, "Is there a reason you can't use already-shredded cheese?"

The answer was "No."

We decided to see how fast we could mix up that tasty, old-fashioned cheese spread. This recipe is the delicious result.

Roasted Red Pepper Cheese Spread

1 package (2 cups) already finely shredded Cheddar cheese (see Notes)
1 already-prepared roasted red pepper, drained (for about ½ cup chopped; see Notes)
1 cup cottage cheese (see Notes)
¼ cup mayonnaise (see Notes)
⅛ teaspoon (4 drops) Tabasco sauce (optional)
Cocktail bread slices or crackers, for serving

START TO FINISH: 15 MINUTES

Place the Cheddar cheese in a serving bowl. Finely chop the pepper and add it to the bowl. Stir to distribute the pepper evenly. Stir in the cottage cheese, mayonnaise, and Tabasco sauce, if using. Serve on cocktail bread slices or crackers.

■ *Makes about 2½ cups*

Notes: The spread is equally good made with 2 percent milkfat Cheddar and cottage cheese and light mayonnaise.

Roasted red peppers are available in jars. You'll have some left over; refrigerate them for use later.

DO-AHEAD

The cheese spread can be refrigerated, covered, for up to 5 days. If it seperates just give it a quick stir before serving.

Chickpea Spread with Roasted Garlic

1 head already-roasted garlic (for about ¼ cup cloves;
*   see page 262)*
About ¼ cup densely packed fresh parsley
2 cans (15 ounces each) chickpeas (garbanzo beans)
1 lemon
¼ cup tahini (sesame paste)
2 tablespoons olive oil
½ teaspoon ground cumin
¼ teaspoon cayenne pepper
¼ teaspoon ground coriander
¼ teaspoon salt, or more to taste
⅛ teaspoon black pepper, or more to taste
Pita bread cut into triangles, for serving

START TO FINISH: 20 MINUTES

1. Peel the garlic cloves. Rinse the parsley well and shake the leaves to remove any excess water. Remove and discard the tough stems but do not worry about the smaller, upper stems. You should have about ¼ cup of leaves. Drain the chickpeas well.

2. Drop the garlic cloves through the feed tube of a food processor with the machine running and chop well. Add the drained chickpeas and process until smooth. Cut the lemon in half and squeeze the juice through a small strainer (to catch the seeds) directly into the processor bowl.

3. Stop the machine and add the tahini, olive oil, cumin, cayenne, coriander, salt, and black pepper to the processor bowl. Process until smooth and creamy in texture. Stop the machine and scrape down side of the bowl once or twice. Taste for seasoning, adding salt and pepper as necessary. Serve with pita triangles.

■ *Makes about 2½ cups*

From Alicia:

I first came across this delicious variation on hummus in Key West, Florida. We were eating at Mangoes on Duval Street.

I never introduce myself as a food journalist in restaurants—the waitstaff thinks food critic and gets jittery. But I *really* wanted to know how they made this spread. So, I introduced myself to our waiter, and with all the southern charm I could conjure, I asked if the chef would share his recipe. I was prepared for a quick "No." Instead, the waiter returned with the recipe and a note from the chef apologizing for the large quantities!

I've "desperized" the ingredients (look for tahini in the specialty section of larger groceries or health food stores). Thanks go to executive chef Paul Orchard.

DO-AHEAD

The chickpea spread can be refrigerated, covered, for up to 3 days.

READY-TO-GO NIBBLES

Our favorite nibbles are those that don't require much effort beyond opening the container and setting out the crackers.

Sometimes you just need a little extra something for your guests to nibble on. And sometimes you don't have any extra time. That's when you grab for the bag, pry open the tin, and thank the heavens above that the expiration date on cream cheese seems never to come. That's when you're happy to have a stash of crackers on hand.

We're also partial to tidbits that won't spoil, so you can keep them on hand for emergencies. You somehow burned the Pesto Pizza with Tomatoes? If you've got these other options, it's not such a catastrophe. Here are some of our trusted bail-out bites:

• **Assorted olives:** Buy them in jars, then mix and match. Or, some groceries and delicatessens have olive bars where you can just scoop out the varieties you want.

• **Fancy nuts:** Ever watched guests grab for the cashews? Smoked almonds and sugared or honey-roasted peanuts are equally popular. Trail mix works, too. Several companies offer nut mixes of only the gourmet stuff minus the ordinary peanuts. Pistachios in the shell? Yes! It's amazing, but people *will* stand around at parties and shell their own. Maybe they like the fact that it gives them something to do. Just be sure to provide small bowls for the shells.

• **Vegetable chips:** A bowl of plain potato chips is fine for a cook-out, but we'd hesitate to dish them up any other time. Vegetable chips are a different matter entirely. These crispy curls of sweet potato and other unexpected vegetables, such as taro, parsnip, and yuca, are colorful and offer intense flavor, plus they're downright fascinating. Poured in a glass bowl, they look like flower petals. "They're not chips, they're art," one guest commented.

• **Japanese cracker mixes:** A close cousin to vegetable chips, again these are colorful and novel, plus they come in a variety of flavors, such as hot and spicy.

• **Smoked fish:** Smoked Nova Scotia salmon is readily available in supermarket delis, though sometimes it's kept alongside the hot dogs. No time to make dip? Cut the slices into bite-size pieces (we're talking three quick whacks with the knife) and serve them with toothpicks or crackers. Tins of smoked oysters, mussels, or clams do have to be drained, but the sophisticated result is worthwhile. Again, spear them with toothpicks.

• **Cream cheese:** We've never served it plain, but there are zillions of things that come in bottles that you can simply pour on top of a block of cream cheese for an instant cracker spread. Combinations of sweet and spicy or sweet and sour flavors seem to be the key to success. Our favorites include Indian chutney; the Jamaican sauce sold under the brand name Pickapeppa (or substitute A.1. sauce); hot pepper jelly; and bottled cocktail sauce mixed with a can of shrimp (drained first)—or use thawed frozen cocktail shrimp. Pour a saucy topper over the cream cheese and let it pool down the sides onto a plate. Present this masterpiece with assorted crackers and don't forget a small cocktail knife for serving. You can use light cream cheese as well.

• **Marinated artichokes:** Drain away the marinade, cut the artichokes in half lengthwise, and spear them with toothpicks.

• **Pâtés:** Tins of assorted pâtés can be found in the supermarket with the imported foods or specialty foods. The brand names tend to vary from grocery to grocery, so you may have to experiment to find your favorite. We've tried a vegetarian variety that's super. Just open the tin, and depending on the consistency, transfer the pâté to a plate, crock, or small dish and serve with crackers and a knife for spreading or slicing.

• **Cheese straws:** Alone on a tray these delicate cheese crackers make an impressive statement. They're available in specialty stores and some supermarkets.

Phased and Flexible

Easiest Marinated Mushrooms

Can a recipe that goes together in just 10 minutes pack this much taste? The answer is a resounding "Yes." But don't wait until the last minute to start. The mushrooms need to marinate for at least 8 hours but no longer than 48. However, if you drain the mushrooms after two days, they can hold in the refrigerator for two days more. The flavor will improve each day. Serve the mushrooms with small wooden toothpicks for spearing, and they become finger food.

24 ounces fresh button mushrooms
½ cup extra-virgin olive oil
¼ cup balsamic vinegar
1 package (0.7 ounces) Italian salad dressing mix,
*   such as Good Seasons*

PHASE 1: 10 MINUTES

1. Rinse the mushrooms and drain well. Cut off any tough portions of the stems and cut the mushrooms in half to make bite-size pieces. If any mushrooms are very large, cut them in quarters. Place the mushrooms in a 2-quart storage bowl or zipper-top plastic bag.

2. Place the olive oil, vinegar, and salad dressing mix in a small bowl with 3 tablespoons of water and whisk to combine. Pour the marinade over the mushrooms. Cover the bowl or zip seal the bag.

PHASE 2: 8 HOURS MOSTLY UNATTENDED MARINATING TIME

3. Refrigerate the mushrooms in the marinade for 8 hours or up to 2 days. If possible, stir the mushrooms or turn the bag once or twice while the mushrooms are marinating.

4. To serve, drain the mushrooms and place in a small serving bowl. *The marinated mushrooms can be refrigerated, drained and covered, for up to 2 days.*

■ *Makes about 5 cups*

BLT Dip

12 slices already-cooked bacon (see box on page 218)
1¼ cups sour cream
½ cup mayonnaise
½ teaspoon garlic powder
½ teaspoon onion powder
Pinch of cayenne pepper
1 large, ripe tomato, or 3 ripe plum tomatoes
    (for 1 cup chopped)
¼ head iceberg lettuce (for 2 lightly packed cups
    chopped)

**PHASE 1: 7 MINUTES, PLUS AT LEAST 4 HOURS
REFRIGERATION TIME**

1. Place the already-cooked bacon on a microwave-safe plate, cover with a paper towel, and microwave on high for 2 to 3 minutes to crisp. Remove from the microwave and blot off any excess grease with paper towels. Set the bacon aside to cool.

2. Meanwhile, mix together the sour cream, mayonnaise, garlic powder, onion powder, and cayenne in a medium-size serving bowl. Coarsely crumble in the crisped bacon. Stir well, cover, and refrigerate for at least 4 hours. *The dip can be refrigerated at this point for up to 24 hours.*

PHASE 2: 5 MINUTES

3. Rinse, seed, and finely chop but do not peel the tomato, sprinkling the pieces over the refrigerated dip as you chop. Chop the lettuce into bite-size pieces. Sprinkle the lettuce over the tomato. Just before serving, stir the lettuce and tomato into the dip. *The dip can be refrigerated for up to 1 hour before serving.*

■ *Makes about 4 cups*

From Alicia:

When I first sampled a version of this bacon, lettuce, and tomato dip, I wasn't sure if it was the setting—a huge summer house party on the North Carolina coast—or the food that had me so intrigued. But when I got back home, it was the easy-as-pie dip that I couldn't stop thinking about, with its flavors of my all-time favorite summer sandwich. I added in a few of my own ingredients including pre-cooked bacon and threw in a pinch of cayenne for a little zip. Thanks go to my friend Linda Wilkerson for first introducing the idea to me. For an authentic crunch, serve the dip on melba toast or enjoy it on everything from corn chips to wheat crackers. And if you prefer, substitute the low-fat varieties of sour cream and mayonnaise.

This is a Southwestern version of our favorite baked artichoke dip. The addition of low-fat cottage cheese and mayonnaise and 2 percent milkfat Cheddar cuts the fat grams in half (this is one recipe that can be made with reduced-fat Cheddar without suffering). Without the Tabasco sauce the dip is mild enough for children, but if you like a kick, be sure to add it. Bake the dip in an attractive—but ovenproof—ceramic dish since it goes straight from the oven to the table. For a dramatic garnish, place blue corn chip triangles in the dip around the edges of the dish when you serve it.

South of the Border Artichoke Dip

*1 can (about 14 ounces) artichoke hearts packed
    in water
1 can (4 ounces) chopped green chiles
1 cup already finely shredded low-fat sharp
    Cheddar cheese
½ cup low-fat cottage cheese
½ cup low-fat mayonnaise
1 teaspoon bottled minced garlic
½ teaspoon chili powder
½ teaspoon ground cumin
½ teaspoon Tabasco sauce, or more to taste (optional)
Cooking oil spray
Blue corn tortilla chips or bagel chips, for serving*

PHASE 1: 7 MINUTES

1. Drain the artichoke hearts, pressing out any excess moisture. Coarsely chop the artichokes and place them in a small mixing bowl. Drain the chiles and add them to the bowl.

2. Stir in the Cheddar and cottage cheeses, mayonnaise, garlic, chili powder, cumin, and Tabasco sauce, if using, until well blended. Spray a 1- to 2-quart refrigerator-to-oven-safe baking dish with cooking oil spray. Place the dip in the dish. *The dip can be refrigerated, covered, at this point for up to 24 hours.*

PHASE 2: 30 MINUTES UNATTENDED BAKING TIME

3. Preheat the oven to 350°F.

4. Uncover the baking dish, if necessary, and bake the dip until hot and bubbly, about 30 minutes. Serve warm with tortilla chips or bagel chips.

■ *Makes about 2½ cups*

Roasted Garlic & Artichoke Dip

1 can (about 14 ounces) artichoke hearts packed
  in water
4 cloves already-roasted garlic (see page 262)
1 cup mayonnaise (see Note)
1 cup already-grated Parmesan cheese
Cooking oil spray
Hearty wheat crackers, cocktail bread, or tortilla chips,
  for serving

PHASE 1: 13 MINUTES

1. Drain the artichoke hearts pressing out any excess moisture.
Coarsely chop the artichokes and place them in a small mixing bowl.
Mince the roasted garlic and add it to the chopped artichokes. Add
the mayonnaise and Parmesan cheese and stir to mix well.

2. Spray a 1- to 2-quart refrigerator-to-oven-safe ceramic baking dish
with cooking oil spray. Place the dip in the dish. *The dip can be
refrigerated, covered, at this point for up to 24 hours.*

PHASE 2: 30 MINUTES UNATTENDED BAKING TIME

3. Preheat the oven to 350°F.

4. Uncover the baking dish, if necessary, and bake the dip until the
edges are lightly browned and bubbly, about 30 minutes. Serve
warm with crackers, bread slices, or chips.

■ *Makes about 2½ cups*

Note: You can use low-fat mayonnaise here, if you like.

From Alicia:

My first recipe for
classic artichoke dip
came from my good friend
Laurie Kovolew. Laurie
would often double the
recipe of this family favorite
and bring half to us.
Whatever night that hap-
pened to be, I'd bake it and
call it dinner! My children
have been eating the creamy
artichoke spread since they
got their first teeth.

To make a good thing
even better, when I roast
garlic, I add a few cloves to
this simple dish. If you don't
have roasted garlic or don't
want to take the time to roast
some, then use one or two
cloves of fresh instead.

TIME SAVER

*If you're making dips
at the last minute,
mix them right in their
serving bowls and wipe
away any splatters from
around the sides with
a clean cloth.*

Traditional *baba ghanoush* is made with eggplant, but our zucchini version is prettier, lighter, easier to make, and just as exotically wonderful. At a recent dinner party we practically had to beg our guests to come away from the dip bowl to gather for the main course. You'll find suggestions for crackers to serve it with on page 46.

Za-Za Ghanoush

3 medium-size zucchini (about 1½ pounds total)
3 large cloves fresh garlic
About ½ cup densely packed fresh parsley
¼ cup tahini (sesame paste)
1 tablespoon olive oil
¼ teaspoon salt, or more to taste
1½ lemons

PHASE 1: 10 MINUTES, PLUS 10 MINUTES COOLING TIME

1. Rinse the zucchini and trim the ends. Cut each zucchini into pieces about 1 inch wide. Place the zucchini pieces on a microwave-safe dish or pie pan. Cover with microwave-safe plastic wrap and cut a small vent in the center. Microwave, on high, until tender throughout when tested with a sharp knife, about 7 minutes. Remove from the microwave, uncover, and refrigerate until cool enough to handle, about 10 minutes. *The zucchini can be refrigerated in a covered storage container at this point for up to 24 hours.*

PHASE 2: 8 MINUTES

2. Peel the garlic. Rinse the parsley well and shake the leaves to remove any excess water. Remove and discard the tough lower stems but do not worry about the smaller, upper stems. You should have about ½ cup of leaves. Drop the garlic cloves through the feed tube of a food processor with the machine running and finely chop. Drop in the parsley and process until finely minced. Stop the machine and use a rubber spatula to scrape down the side of the processor bowl.

3. Drain off any liquid from the zucchini pieces and drop the zucchini through the processor feed tube with the motor running. Process until finely chopped. Stop the processor.

4. Add the tahini, olive oil, and salt to the processor bowl. Squeeze the lemon juice through a small strainer (to catch the seeds) directly into

SANITY SAVER

When you're facing a stretch when a whole meal is more than you can handle but you still want to get together with friends, remember the words drop by. *It's all in how you extend the invitation. If you ask folks to drop by—nothing fancy—just for a drink, especially on the spur-of-the-moment, their expectations won't be that grand. That means your workload doesn't have to be, either.*

the processor bowl. Scrape down the side of the bowl, then process until all of the ingredients are well combined and the mixture reaches a dip consistency, about 45 seconds. Taste for seasoning, adding more salt if necessary. Transfer to a storage container or to a decorative serving bowl and cover with plastic wrap. Refrigerate until chilled through. *The dip can be refrigerated, covered, for up to 2 days. Stir the dip again before serving, if necessary, to recombine.*

■ *Makes about 2¾ cups*

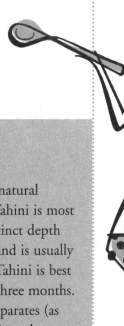

ABOUT TAHINI

Having trouble understanding tahini? Think all-natural peanut butter, only made from sesame seeds. Tahini is most often used in Middle Eastern cooking and lends a distinct depth and flavor. It is available in many large supermarkets and is usually found in the international or specialty foods section. Tahini is best stored in the refrigerator, where it will keep for about three months.

The only difficulty in using tahini is that the oil separates (as in natural peanut butter) and needs to be stirred back into the sesame paste that settles to the bottom of the container. If possible, let the tahini come to room temperature before stirring it vigorously with a fork. Expect to spend a few minutes stirring.

Mexican Cheese and Jalapeño Spread

Thanks to the already-shredded Mexican cheese blends found in the dairy case, this zippy little spread is easy to throw together. The only real work is seeding and mincing the jalapeño peppers. If you don't normally work with gloves when handling hot peppers, be sure to wash your hands thoroughly after mincing the jalapeños. Feel free to use low-fat sour cream and mayonnaise here.

5 fresh jalapeño peppers (for about ½ cup minced)
3 scallions (for about ¼ cup minced, white and
  green parts)
1 package (8 ounces) already-shredded Mexican or
  taco cheese blend
½ cup sour cream
¼ cup mayonnaise
⅛ teaspoon white pepper
⅛ teaspoon salt
Tabasco sauce, to taste (optional)
Blue and white corn chips, for serving

PHASE 1: 19 MINUTES, PLUS 2 HOURS CHILLING TIME

1. Rinse, core, and seed, then mince the jalapeños (see Handling Hot Peppers on page 156). Place them in a medium-size serving bowl. Rinse the scallions and mince, using enough green tops to make ¼ cup. Add the minced scallions and the cheese, sour cream, mayonnaise, white pepper, and salt to the jalapeños and stir until well blended.

2. Cover and refrigerate for at least 2 hours. When ready to serve, stir well and taste to determine if Tabasco sauce is desired, adding it to taste. If you've chilled the spread for less than 24 hours, it can be served cold or hot. If you've chilled it for a longer time, it is best hot. *The spread can be refrigerated, covered, for up to 48 hours.*

PHASE 2: 5 MINUTES

3. If serving the spread hot, place it in a microwave-safe serving dish and microwave on high until heated through, 4 to 5 minutes, stopping once halfway through to stir. Serve with chips.

■ *Makes about 2 cups*

MONEY SAVER

Cheese trays are lovely, but huge hunks of Brie, chèvre, and imported Swiss can cost a small fortune. Cheese spreads, on the other hand, are a cinch to make and are always a hit at parties. They cost a fraction of what the cheese tray costs, too.

Cajun Barbecued Shrimp

1 tablespoon butter

2 tablespoons olive oil

3 teaspoons bottled minced garlic

1 can (14½ ounces) chicken broth

1 cup chili sauce

2 teaspoons Cajun seafood seasoning, such as
    Chef Prudhomme's Seafood Magic

2 teaspoons Worcestershire sauce

1 teaspoon dried thyme

2 pounds already-peeled medium-size raw shrimp
    (20 to 25 per pound), thawed if frozen

Tabasco sauce

There never seems to be enough of these shrimp when we make them. They are just that habit forming. The recipe will serve four to five shrimp per person, but if you would like to increase the number of shrimp, there's enough sauce for up to half a pound more. Add Tabasco sauce to suit your taste, making the dish as hot and spicy as you like. Set out cocktail forks or toothpicks alongside and the shrimp become finger food.

PHASE 1: 15 MINUTES

1. Melt the butter in the olive oil in a large nonstick skillet over medium heat. Add the garlic and cook for 30 seconds. Add the chicken broth, chili sauce, seafood seasoning, Worcestershire sauce, and thyme. Stir well and let cook until heated through and beginning to bubble, about 5 minutes. *The sauce can be refrigerated, covered, at this point for up to 2 days.*

PHASE 2: ABOUT 10 MINUTES

2. Return the sauce to the nonstick skillet, if necessary. Heat over medium heat until warmed through and beginning to bubble, about 5 minutes. Add the shrimp. Add Tabasco sauce to taste and cook until the shrimp are just done (pink), 5 to 7 minutes, stirring them frequently.

3. Transfer the shrimp and sauce to a serving dish and serve immediately. *The shrimp will also hold in a chafing dish for up to 30 minutes for a buffet.*

■ *Serves 8 to 10*

From Alicia:

In my household, Easter lunch is second only to Thanksgiving in its magnitude. There's always enough food for the proverbial army—there are plenty of hungry family members and others to enjoy it. We don't just do the traditional ham, we roast a turkey breast as well. Fresh asparagus, green beans, creamed potatoes, and corn soufflé are just a few of the side dishes that grace the table.

There's only one problem. Everyone starts to get desperate for a nibble after arriving home from church, and yet lunch won't be ready for another hour. That's when this extra-simple appetizer comes in handy. Just a few bites of these jewels will tide everyone over until the feast begins—no matter what the occasion. Pinwheels Primavera are easy to put together in the morning and are waiting when the hungry hoards arrive. You and your guests will be grateful.

Pinwheels Primavera

1 container (8 ounces) vegetable-flavored cream cheese
 spread
2 large (10-inch) flour tortillas
2 cans (2½ ounces each) sliced black olives
1½ cups already-shredded carrots (see Note)

PHASE 1: 15 MINUTES

1. Spread ½ cup of cream cheese (half of the container) over each tortilla. Drain the olives. Scatter half of the olives and half of the carrots over each tortilla. Roll up each tortilla tightly like a jelly roll. Cut off ½ inch from each tortilla roll edge and discard. If not serving immediately, cover the tortilla rolls with plastic wrap and refrigerate. *The tortilla rolls can be refrigerated, covered, at this point for up to 24 hours.*

PHASE 2: 5 MINUTES

2. Place the tortillas seam side down on a cutting board and cut each into nine 1-inch slices. Arrange on a platter. *The sliced tortilla rolls can be refrigerated, covered, for up to 30 minutes.*

■ *Makes 18 pinwheels*

Note: Can't find the already-shredded carrots? Just peel and shred 2 medium-size carrots instead.

Crostini di Firenze

1 baguette (at least 12 inches long)
1 large clove fresh garlic
3 tablespoons extra-virgin olive oil
1 tablespoon balsamic vinegar
⅛ teaspoon salt
Pinch of black pepper
¼ pound ripe strawberries (for about ⅓ cup chopped)
1 large ripe tomato (¾ to 1 pound)
5 or 6 large, fresh mint leaves (for about 2 teaspoons chopped)

PHASE 1: 10 MINUTES

1. Turn on the broiler.

2. Cut off one end of the baguette, then cut 20 slices, each about ½ inch wide (reserve the remaining bread for another use). Place the bread slices on a baking sheet and toast in the hot broiler about 3 inches from the heat source until golden brown, about 1 minute. Remove, turn the slices over, and toast until golden brown on the second side, about 45 seconds. Remove the toasted bread from the baking sheet and let cool to room temperature.

3. Peel the garlic and put the clove through a garlic press or finely mince. Place the garlic in a small bowl. Add the olive oil, vinegar, salt, and pepper. Whisk well to blend and set aside at room temperature until ready to serve. *The vinaigrette and toast slices can be stored at this point for up to 8 hours. Cover the vinaigrette. Place the toast slices in an airtight container.*

PHASE 2: 10 MINUTES

4. Rinse the strawberries and drain thoroughly. Remove the leaf caps of the strawberries and cut the berries in half. Place the strawberry halves on a cutting board and coarsely chop to roughly ¼-inch pieces. Put the strawberries in a small mixing bowl.

From Beverly:

Tomatoes and strawberries mixed together? As an appetizer? It was hard for us to believe, but the two joined on a piece of crusty bread is a blissful marriage made in, well, Tuscany. On a summer trip through this sun-drenched region of Italy, my husband and I sampled *crostini* at every stop. Most of the time this truly addictive appetizer featured ripe tomato chunks bathed in a light vinaigrette. But in a tony trattoria in Florence, we experienced *crostini* made with the unexpected zing of tomatoes paired with juicy strawberries. The only time during the trip we swooned more dramatically was at the first glimpse of Michelangelo's statue of David. Upon returning to Raleigh, we just had to duplicate this slice of heaven. Try our version of it when tomatoes and strawberries are at the height of summer freshness. Choose a European-style baguette that's no more than 3 inches in diameter.

5. Core and seed the tomato. Chop it into small dice. Add these to the strawberries. Rinse and dry the mint leaves and finely chop; you should have about 2 teaspoons. Add the mint to the strawberries and tomato. *The strawberry-and-tomato mixture can be refrigerated, covered, at this point for up to 2 hours.*

PHASE 3: 5 MINUTES, PLUS ABOUT 10 MINUTES STANDING TIME

6. Whisk the vinaigrette to remix, pour over the fruit mixture, and stir well to blend. Arrange the toasts on a serving platter and spoon about 2 heaping teaspoons of the topping over each slice. Let the *crostini* stand at room temperature for about 10 minutes before serving to allow the vinaigrette to penetrate the bread. Standing longer than 20 minutes makes *crostini* soggy.

■ *Makes 20 crostini*

HOMEMADE PIZZA IN A FLASH

Can homemade pizza be desperate? Absolutely. Thanks to partially baked pizza crusts available in supermarkets, even pizza made at home can be fast enough for the frantic cook, and not just as dinner. Our simple pies, cut into tiny wedges, make a fun appetizer either alone or alongside some nuts or a dip.

It takes only 6 minutes to throw together pizza nibbles. Try Pesto Pizza with Tomatoes (opposite), Roasted Garlic and Mozzarella Pizza (see page 78), or the slightly more sophisticated combination in Artichoke and Feta Pizza (see page 79).

Preheating the oven actually takes longer than the baking does, that's just how quick and easy these pizzas are. The trick is getting your hands on one of the work-free crusts. The most widely distributed brand is Boboli, but there are many others available now, too. You can top the crusts and bake them right away or wait until closer to party time and pull out a steaming hot pizza ready to slice and serve. Cut it into eight slices or into multiple pieces if you have a larger crowd.

Pesto Pizza with Tomatoes

1 large (12 inch) partially baked pizza crust,
  such as Boboli
¼ cup commercially prepared pesto
⅓ cup already-shredded mozzarella cheese
¼ cup already-grated Parmesan cheese
2 large or 3 medium-size, ripe plum tomatoes

PHASE 1: 6 MINUTES

1. Place the pizza crust on an ungreased baking sheet. Use the back of a spoon to spread the pesto over the crust, leaving the edge bare.

2. Sprinkle the mozzarella and Parmesan cheeses over the pesto.

3. Rinse the tomatoes and cut off the stem ends. Cut the tomatoes into ¼-inch slices and arrange these evenly over the crust. *The pizza can be covered with plastic wrap at this point and kept at room temperature for up to 1 hour or can be refrigerated for up to 4 hours.*

PHASE 2: 8 TO 10 MINUTES UNATTENDED BAKING TIME

4. Preheat the oven to 450°F.

5. Bake the pizza until the crust begins to brown and crisp slightly, 8 to 10 minutes. Cut the pizza into 8 wedges and serve at once.

■ *Serves 8*

This is no ordinary pizza. Skipping the traditional tomato sauce and adding already-prepared pesto from the supermarket adds a gourmet flare. You can find several brands of pesto both on the grocery shelf and in the refrigerated case near the fresh pastas.

Assembly takes only a short 6 minutes. Then pop the pizza in the oven while you are pulling out the candles, plates, and napkins. When your guests arrive not only will your whole kitchen smell divine but hot nibbles will be ready to serve.

SPACE SAVER

A cooler on wheels is the perfect ice chest to chill beverages, saving precious space in the refrigerator.

Plain cheese pizza may appeal to the kids, but this mellow, rich pizza is great for both the adults and children in your crowd. Because the garlic is so mild, kids won't mind that the tomato sauce is missing, either.

If you've got a stash of already-roasted garlic on hand, making this pizza is especially easy. Placing the roasted garlic under the cheese not only protects it from burning while baking but keeps the surprise ingredient hidden until the first bite.

Roasted Garlic and Mozzarella Pizza

1 large (12 inch) partially baked pizza crust, such as Boboli
1 tablespoon olive oil
1 head already-roasted garlic (for about ¼ cup cloves; see page 262)
1 cup already-shredded mozzarella cheese
2 large or 3 medium-size, ripe plum tomatoes

PHASE 1: 6 MINUTES

1. Place the pizza crust on an ungreased baking sheet. Use the back of a large spoon to spread the olive oil over the crust, leaving the edge bare.

2. Coarsely chop the garlic and sprinkle over the crust. Top with the mozzarella cheese.

3. Rinse the tomatoes and cut off the stem ends. Cut the tomatoes into ¼-inch slices and arrange these evenly over the crust. *The pizza can be covered with plastic wrap at this point and kept at room temperature for up to 1 hour or can be refrigerated for up to 4 hours.*

PHASE 2: 8 TO 10 MINUTES UNATTENDED BAKING TIME

4. Preheat the oven to 450°F.

5. Bake the pizza until the crust begins to brown and crisp slightly, 8 to 10 minutes. Cut the pizza into 8 wedges and serve at once.

■ *Serves 8*

Artichoke and Feta Pizza

1 large (12 inch) partially baked pizza crust,
   such as Boboli
1 jar (6 ounces) marinated artichoke hearts
1 package (4 ounces; about ½ cup) already-crumbled
   feta cheese
2 large or 3 medium-size, ripe plum tomatoes

PHASE 1: 6 MINUTES

1. Place the pizza crust on an ungreased baking sheet.

2. Drain and coarsely chop the artichoke hearts and sprinkle them evenly over the crust, leaving the edge bare. Top with the feta cheese.

3. Rinse the tomatoes and cut off the stem ends. Cut the tomatoes into ¼-inch slices and arrange these evenly over the crust. *The pizza can be covered with plastic wrap at this point and kept at room temperature for up to 1 hour or can be refrigerated for up to 4 hours.*

PHASE 2: 8 TO 10 MINUTES UNATTENDED BAKING TIME

4. Preheat the oven to 450°F.

5. Bake the pizza until the crust begins to brown and crisp slightly, 8 to 10 minutes. Cut the pizza into 8 wedges and serve at once.

■ *Serves 8*

The bold flavors of this amazing appetizer pie come from marinated artichokes. These come in jars and can be found alongside the plain cans of artichoke hearts and stems. Packed in a blend of oil, vinegar, and spices, marinated artichokes burst with flavor. Feta cheese and fresh, ripe plum tomatoes round out the terrific combination.

SANITY SAVER

Plastic tablecloths are worth their weight in gold for outdoor gatherings. Thin plastic, disposable covers are available in every color imaginable at party stores. Reuseable plastic cloths are also inexpensive and are readily available. Just be sure to dry the cloth completely before storing, or the next time you pull it out, you'll realize mold and mildew have come a-visiting.

CHAPTER THREE

Entertaining

What we want is some middle ground between potluck and a meal that ends up shish kebabing the host.

Your favorite neighbors are moving. The Big Game is finally on. A dear friend is hitting that birthday milestone. Whatever the occasion, a dinner is in order. When everyone gathers around the table the conversation is bound to be special, and the food must fit the festive mood.

Whether you drag out the good china or eat off bamboo trays at halftime, when company's coming, you probably have higher expectations for your dinner menus than your guests do. But if you get all stressed out over preparing a meal that's too complex, you miss the whole point of socializing in the first place. What if, just for fun, you refocused your attention on spending a relaxed evening with your favorite people and viewed the food as merely an accompaniment to good conversation and the joy of shared company? Not ready to go quite that far? Neither are we.

We've spent years searching for the perfect compromise between too much work and catch-as-catch-can. One solution that works for us is to concentrate our efforts on a single dish that, while spectacular, doesn't make us feel like we're arm wrestling an octopus. Quite often, that means a hearty, one-pot soup with some exotic twist. Or it could be a dressed-up pasta sauce with an intriguing secret ingredient. We take dishes that are familiar and not difficult to cook and give them a slightly new angle. For example, we've given traditional lasagna a twist with a mixed-mushroom version featuring a creamy Alfredo sauce.

Entrées

The real key to success, however, is to forget the need to serve way too many time-consuming side dishes. Since the entrées in this chapter are substantial and usually have starch and vegetables built in, all that's really needed to round out the meal is good-quality bread and a salad. But if you opt to add another simple side, check out our favorites in the "Super Simple Sides" chapter, starting on page 246.

As for that bread, those of you who make a hobby out of getting up-close and personal with yeast will want to labor over your loaves. Everybody else should buy company bread from a dependable bakery. And what about the salad? When you're desperate, forget the idea of spending hours tearing and chopping. Prewashed, bagged greens coupled with our streamlined recipes in the "Standout Salads" chapter, starting on page 188, make light work of filling a spectacular salad bowl.

As soon as your guests get a whiff of our Baked Party Paella, Pepper-Sauced Pasta with Ham and Asparagus, or Lazy Spinach Lasagna, they'll wonder where you've hidden the caterer. When you gaze at your guests through eyes that aren't glazed over with fatigue, you'll be glad you turned to our entertaining entrées.

fast and fabulous

Tex-Mex Chicken Soup

Our soup here features a mildly spicy brew chock-full of chicken and corn, but the real treat is this: Guests get to customize their own bowls with goodies like shredded cheese, black olives, sour cream, and tortilla chips. Put out a bottle of Tabasco sauce for guests who like to really breathe fire. The soup demands so little effort, it might be just the excuse you need to host a spur of the moment gathering. Dig out the cowboy boots, line up some Lyle Lovett tunes, and you're all set.

2 teaspoons olive oil
2 medium-size onions (for about 1½ cups chopped)
1⅓ pounds skinless, boneless chicken breasts
2 teaspoons bottled minced garlic
3 cans (14½ ounces each) fat-free chicken broth
2 cans (14½ ounces each) Mexican-style stewed
  tomatoes (see page 51) or diced tomatoes seasoned with
  jalapeño or chile peppers
1½ cups frozen corn kernels
½ teaspoon ground cumin
½ lime
2 cans (2½ ounces each) sliced black olives, for serving
Tortilla chips, for serving
Already-shredded cheese, such as Cheddar or
  a Mexican blend, for serving
Sour cream, for serving
Tabasco sauce, for serving (optional)

START TO FINISH: 20 MINUTES

1. Heat the olive oil over medium heat in a 4½-quart Dutch oven or soup pot. Peel the onions and coarsely chop, adding them to the pot as you chop. Cut the chicken into bite-size chunks, adding them to the pot as you cut. After the first breast is in the pot, raise the heat to medium-high. Continue until all the chicken is added. Add the garlic. Cook the chicken, stirring from time to time, until it is no longer pink outside, about 3 to 4 minutes.

DO-AHEAD

The soup can be prepared through Step 2 and then after cooling, refrigerated, covered, for up to 24 hours. To reheat, place the soup in a pot over medium-high heat, bring to a low boil, and let cook until heated through, about 10 minutes.

2. Add the chicken broth, tomatoes, and corn. Raise the heat to high, cover, and bring to a boil. Uncover, reduce the heat to low, and add the cumin. Squeeze the lime juice into the soup. Continue to simmer to let the flavors develop, about 5 minutes more.

3. While the soup simmers, drain the olives and break the tortilla chips into smaller pieces (a few firm whacks on the counter does the trick). Place the olives, chips, cheese, and sour cream in small serving bowls. Ladle the soup into bowls, and invite guests to garnish their soup as desired, passing Tabasco sauce on the side.

■ *Serves 8*

Crispy Oven-Baked Chicken Fingers

Cooking oil spray
1 cup milk
1 cup already-grated Parmesan cheese
1 cup fine bread crumbs
1 teaspoon onion powder
1 teaspoon garlic powder
8 skinless, boneless chicken breast halves
    (about 2⅔ pounds total; see Note)
Assorted dips (see suggestions at right)

START TO FINISH: 12 TO 14 MINUTES, PLUS 16 TO 18 MINUTES UNATTENDED BAKING TIME

1. Preheat the oven to 425°F. Spray a large baking sheet and wire rack with cooking oil spray.

2. Pour the milk into a shallow dish such as a pie pan.

3. In a large zipper-top plastic bag, combine the Parmesan cheese, bread crumbs, and onion and garlic powders. Zip the bag closed and shake to mix.

Children are dippers. Give them a food they can dab into a sauce and they're content. Carrot sticks, french fries, broccoli florets, mozzarella sticks, and the all-time favorite—chicken fingers—are perfect for little ones to dip.

It's not an accident that just about every children's menu in just about every restaurant offers chicken fingers. That's because kids love them. They're fun for adults, too, especially with a variety of dipping sauces. We suggest ranch dressing, Honey-Mustard Vinaigrette (see page 203), a commercial barbecue sauce, and our Warm Ginger-Peanut Sauce (see page 178).

4. Slice each breast into 6 to 8 thin strips. Drag the chicken strips through the milk, pop 8 to 10 into the bag with the bread crumb mixture, zip it closed, and shake to coat. Place the coated strips on the prepared rack. Repeat until all of the chicken is coated well. Sprinkle any remaining bread crumbs over the coated chicken. Bake without turning, until the chicken is just cooked through (it will no longer be pink inside) and the crumbs start to brown, 16 to 18 minutes.

5. Place the dips in small bowls and serve alongside the chicken fingers.

■ *Serves 8*

Note: Chicken tenderloins (sometimes called tenders) are available in many stores. Although they can be a little pricey, they make even quicker work of this perennial favorite since you won't have to slice them into strips. Buy about ⅓ pound per person.

DO-AHEAD

When cool, the baked chicken fingers can be refrigerated, covered, for up to 1 day. To reheat, place in a single layer and wrap in aluminum foil. Bake at 350°F for 10 minutes or until heated through.

MAKING MORE SPACE AT THE TABLE

You've finally done it. You've invited three couples over for dinner and one look at your dining room table tells you it's not going to work—it seats only six.

Never fear. We've got the perfect solution.

Place a card table at one end of your dining table. This efficiently adds the extra two seats you need. It doesn't matter if your main table is round or oval. Do you think anyone will care that the table at which they're eating is an odd shape?

We've pushed two tables together so often that we purposefully buy a matching tablecloth for the card table or an extra-large one that will cover both.

Still have cramped quarters? Turn the tables so they spill out into a hall or even into the kitchen. For those times when it's important that everyone be together, it's unlikely that any of your guests will pay attention to the layout.

Three-Bean and Meatball Chili

1 bag (18 ounces) precooked frozen meatballs
2 teaspoons olive oil
2 large onions (for about 2 cups chopped)
1 tablespoon bottled minced garlic
3 cans (14½ ounces each) chili-style seasoned tomatoes
1 large can (15 ounces) tomato sauce
1 can (15½ ounces) red kidney beans
1 can (15½ ounces) black beans
1 can (15½ ounces) navy beans
1 teaspoon chili powder

START TO FINISH: 20 MINUTES

1. Place the meatballs on a microwave-safe plate and microwave, uncovered, on high for 4 minutes to begin defrosting.

2. Meanwhile, heat the olive oil in a 4½-quart Dutch oven or soup pot over medium heat. Peel and coarsely chop the onions, adding them to the pot as you chop. Add the garlic and cook until the onions are soft, about 4 minutes.

3. Add the tomatoes with their juice and the tomato sauce to the pot with the onions. Stir to mix. Put the kidney, black, and navy beans in a colander, rinse, and drain well. Add the beans to the tomato mixture. Add the chili powder and stir well.

4. Remove the meatballs from the microwave and cut them in half. Add the meatball halves to the pot with the tomato and bean mixture. Raise the heat to medium-high. Stir well to mix. Bring the chili to a boil, stirring occasionally. Reduce the heat to low and simmer 5 minutes to blend the flavors. Serve at once or continue to simmer until ready to serve, stirring from time to time.

■ *Serves 8*

From Alicia:

What an interesting spin this recipe takes on one of my all-time favorite casual dinners—chili! Its history is a desperate tale indeed. Craving the comfort of my favorite chili, I realized I had no meat except a lonely package of frozen meatballs. So, I thought, meatballs are just seasoned ground beef, right? Why can't they go in chili? That night dinner was quick and delicious and my family raved.

The next time we discussed chili on the company menu, my husband asked for the "meatball kind." What started as a desperate act of getting a dinner on the table had turned out to be a meal good enough for guests.

Looking for some desperate toppings to go with the chili? Serve it with already-shredded Cheddar or Monterey Jack cheese or a cheese blend, chopped scallions, and/or sour cream.

DO-AHEAD

When cool, the chili can be refrigerated, covered, for up to 24 hours. To reheat, place it in a pot over medium heat and stir frequently until heated through, about 20 minutes.

PASTA PERFECT FOR A CROWD

Here are our essential tricks for cooking huge vats of pasta—or at least enough for a gathering of eight. We've borrowed these pointers from a friend who cooks pasta for hundreds at a local high school's fund-raisers.

• **What type of pot?** You need a pot large enough for the water to surround the pasta so that it cooks evenly. If you don't have a large pot (6-quart capacity) or a pasta pot (see page 93), then divide the pasta between two pots each of which have a capacity of at least 4½ quarts.

• **How much water?** You need enough water to boil the pasta, but you don't have to drown it. For 1 pound of pasta just fill your pot(s) two thirds full.

• **How much pasta?** Many American pasta manufacturers routinely suggest cooking 2 ounces dry pasta per person, and even though it may not look like enough when you're putting it into the pot, we find that amount to be exactly right. You might want to cook extra for second helpings. (Our friends with Italian backgrounds scoff at cooking any less than 4 ounces per person.) Since cooking pasta is so easy and can be done ahead, there's no need to fret about a few extra ounces. If you want more than a pound of pasta, cook it in batches with 4 quarts of water for every pound.

• **How long does it take to cook?** Use the cooking times printed on pasta packages as a guide. There's no one rule because the thickness of pasta varies so much from brand to brand and shape to shape. There's also the matter of personal preference. Many people like pasta al dente (firm), while those of us who grew up on SpaghettiOs might want to cook ours a bit longer for a softer consistency. As a guideline, it will generally take from 9 to 12 minutes for the water to come to a boil, plus from 4 to 12 minutes cooking time, depending on the type of pasta being cooked.

• **How do you cook pasta ahead?** Here's our favorite trick that's essential to cooking pasta in advance: After the pasta is done, drain it in a colander (or use the handy colander insert from your pasta pot) and then immediately dunk the colander of pasta into a sink full of

You don't need to baby-sit a pot of pasta when you should be enjoying your guests.

ice water (for a complete how-to, see page 88). This stops the pasta from cooking, rinses off the starch, and allows you to store and reheat the noodles without ending up with a gummy mess. After the water bath, put your perfectly cooked pasta in a zipper-top plastic bag and store it in the refrigerator for up to 24 hours. Adding oil to the pasta is not necessary.

• **How do you reheat it?** A few minutes before serving, simply place the pasta back in the colander, put the colander in the sink, and run very hot water over the pasta for a minute or two, tossing it to make sure all of the pasta gets hot. Drain it well and then top with your favorite heated pasta sauce.

This convenient method means you don't steam up the kitchen during your gathering, and you'll have the confidence of knowing there's a stash of perfect pasta just waiting to go.

PERFECT BASIC PASTA

You can make quick work of preparing pasta for company once you realize unsauced cooked pasta can be reheated. Use this method for preparing pasta to serve with any of the pasta sauce recipes in this book. The recipe makes exactly eight portions with no leftovers based on 2 ounces of dried pasta per person. For more information on serving pasta to a group, see page 86.

1 teaspoon salt (optional)
1 package (1 pound) pasta of your choice
About 2 cups or 1 tray ice cubes

START TO FINISH: 9 TO 12 MINUTES FOR THE WATER TO BOIL, PLUS 4 TO 12 MINUTES COOKING TIME

1. Fill a 6-quart or larger pot (preferably with a colander insert; see page 93) with 4 quarts of water. Place the pot over high heat and bring the water to a boil; this will take 9 to 12 minutes.

2. When the water boils, add the salt, if using, followed by the pasta. Note the cooking time indicated on the pasta package and check the pasta for doneness a couple minutes before the time is up. Continue checking it frequently until the pasta is cooked to the degree of softness you prefer.

3. Meanwhile, fill a sink with cold water and add the ice cubes. When the pasta is done, drain it immediately in a colander. Submerge the colander full of hot pasta in the ice water in the sink. After about 30 seconds, toss the pasta gently, making sure all of it is chilled; this stops the cooking. Remove the pasta from the ice water and drain completely.

4. The cooled pasta can be stored in zipper-top plastic bags in the refrigerator for up to 24 hours. To reheat, put the pasta back in the colander and run very hot water over it. Toss to make sure all of the pasta gets hot. Drain well and serve with the heated pasta sauce of your choice.

■ *Serves 8*

With this method you'll never worry about whether your pasta will be perfect. Rest assured, it will be.

Too-Good-to-Be-True Pepper Sauce with Pasta

1 tablespoon olive oil
1 large onion (for about 1 cup chopped)
1 tablespoon bottled minced garlic
⅛ teaspoon black pepper
2 bags (1 pound each) frozen bell pepper strips (see Note)
¾ cup half-and-half
1 package (1 pound) pasta of your choice, cooked
    (see opposite for cooking instructions), for serving

As beautiful to look at as it is wonderful to eat, this versatile sauce takes less than 10 minutes to make and can be frozen for a month. As well as using it as the base for Pepper-Sauced Pasta with Ham and Asparagus (see page 91), you can serve it as is over noodles.

START TO FINISH: 10 MINUTES

1. Heat the olive oil in an extra-deep, 12-inch nonstick skillet over medium-high heat. Peel and coarsely chop the onion, adding it to the skillet as you chop. Reduce the heat to medium when all of the onion has been added. Add the garlic and black pepper. Cook until the onion is soft, about 3 minutes.

2. While the onion cooks, put the bell pepper strips in a colander and rinse with cool water until thawed, about 1½ minutes. Drain well, pressing the bell peppers with the back of a spoon to remove as much water as possible.

3. Remove the onion from the heat and put it in the container of an electric blender. Add the thawed bell pepper strips and the half-and-half. Blend on high until the vegetables are well blended but the sauce is still slightly chunky, 30 to 45 seconds. Scrape down the sides of the blender midway through, if necessary.

4. Place the sauce in a microwave-safe container and microwave 3 minutes, uncovered, on high, stopping once halfway through to stir. Serve at once over hot, drained pasta.

■ *Serves 8*

Note: Some brands of frozen bell pepper strips contain onions. This type is fine to use in this recipe.

DO-AHEAD

The sauce can be refrigerated in the blender container for up to 24 hours before serving. Whir it again in the blender to remix before using.

• The sauce can be frozen for up to 1 month in an airtight, microwave-safe container. If the sauce has been frozen, thaw it in the microwave oven on the defrost setting, following the manufacturer's directions.

• To reheat the sauce, place in a pot over medium-low heat and stir frequently until heated through, about 15 minutes.

From Beverly:

From Beverly:

My friend Martie Leming has worked for fifteen years to perfect this recipe. It's economical, easy, and fast, so she made a giant batch once to feed twenty-eight school kids on a field trip to Blue Jay Point County Park in Raleigh, North Carolina. Hence the name. The addition of vegetables along with a hint of cinnamon gives the sauce its distinctive character. We like to serve it over thin spaghetti.

Blue Jay Point Pasta

1 teaspoon olive oil

1 medium-size onion (for about ¾ cup chopped)

1 cup already-sliced fresh button mushrooms

1 pound extra-lean ground beef

½ medium-size green bell pepper (for about ¾ cup
    bite-size pieces)

1 medium-size (about ½ pound) zucchini

½ cup already-shredded carrots (see Note)

2 teaspoons dried Italian-style seasoning

2 teaspoons garlic powder

1 teaspoon sugar

⅛ teaspoon ground cinnamon

1 can (14½ ounces) Italian-style stewed tomatoes

1 can (8 ounces) tomato sauce

1 can (6 ounces) tomato paste

1½ teaspoons cornstarch

Salt and black pepper (optional)

1 package (1 pound) thin spaghetti or other pasta of your
    choice, cooked (see page 88 for cooking instructions),
    for serving

START TO FINISH: 20 MINUTES

1. Heat the olive oil in an extra-deep, 12-inch nonstick skillet over medium heat. Peel and coarsely chop the onion, adding it to the skillet as you chop. Add the mushrooms and beef and raise the heat to medium-high, stirring occasionally to break up the meat.

2. Rinse the bell pepper and zucchini. Core and seed the bell pepper. Chop it and the zucchini into bite-size pieces, adding them to the skillet as you chop. Add the carrots, Italian-style seasoning, garlic powder, sugar, cinnamon, stewed tomatoes, tomato sauce and paste, and 2 cups of water. Stir until the tomato paste is well incorporated.

3. Mix the cornstarch with 1 tablespoon of cold water in a small jar that has a lid. Shake well until the lumps disappear and then

DO-AHEAD

The sauce can be refrigerated, covered, for up to 24 hours or frozen for up to 1 month in a microwave-safe container. If the sauce has been frozen, thaw it in the microwave oven on the defrost setting, following the manufacturer's directions.
• To reheat, place the sauce in a skillet over medium heat and stir frequently until heated through, about 20 minutes.

drizzle the cornstarch mixture over the sauce. Stir well, then let cook 2 minutes. Season the sauce with salt and black pepper, if desired. Serve at once over hot, drained pasta.

■ *Serves 8*

Note: Can't find the already-shredded carrots? Just peel and shred a small carrot instead.

Pepper-Sauced Pasta with Ham and Asparagus

Too-Good-to-Be-True Pepper Sauce (see page 89)
2 pounds fresh asparagus
1 pound Virginia baked or other good-quality ham,
    presliced ⅛ inch thick
1 package (1 pound) penne or other short pasta
    of your choice, cooked (see page 88 for cooking
    instructions), for serving

START TO FINISH: 20 MINUTES

1. Bring 1 quart of water to a boil in a pot large enough to hold the asparagus.

2. Meanwhile, make the Too-Good-to-Be-True Pepper Sauce.

3. Snap the tough ends off the asparagus where they naturally break and discard. Rinse and drain the asparagus spears. Cut the ham slices into ⅛-inch strips. Cut the strips in half.

4. Boil the asparagus just until crisp-tender and bright green in color, 2 to 2½ minutes, and drain.

5. Put the drained, hot penne on a large serving platter. Pour the warm pepper sauce over the pasta and toss to coat with sauce. Scatter the warm asparagus spears and the ham strips over the pasta. Serve at once.

■ *Serves 8*

If you need a perfect springtime meal for entertaining, this is it. Bright green, crisp-tender asparagus and rosy pink ham make mouths water before you even sit down to eat.

DO-AHEAD

The recipe can be prepared through Step 4 up to 24 hours ahead. Refrigerate the sauce, cooked asparagus, and sliced ham separately. When ready to serve, whir the sauce in the blender to remix. Reheat the sauce in a pot over medium-low heat, stirring frequently until heated through, about 15 minutes. Reheat the asparagus in a microwave-safe container, uncovered, on high, just until warm, about 2 minutes, then continue with Step 5.

From Beverly:

This became the all-time favorite pasta sauce at my house when I served it at an after-the-theater supper for family and friends following my son Sam's stage debut in *The Music Man.* Of course when his sister, Grey, got her turn in the stage version of *The Wizard of Oz,* no other menu would do. The nice thing for a mom whose nerves are shattered by sympathetic stage fright is that the sauce can be made days ahead and refrigerated or months ahead and frozen. With the cooking already done, that's one less thing to fret about.

A blend of artichokes, black olives, and feta cheese, offset by a complex blend of herbs and spices, makes for a memorable sauce. The meat can be any combination of ground turkey and beef so long as you have two pounds total. Serve the sauce over a spinach pasta if you can find it. If not, regular pasta works just fine.

Opening Night Pasta

2 teaspoons olive oil
2 large onions (for about 2 cups chopped)
1 pound ground turkey
1 pound lean ground beef
2 teaspoons garlic powder
1½ teaspoons dried oregano
1 teaspoon dried thyme
1 teaspoon sugar
4 bay leaves
½ teaspoon black pepper
¼ teaspoon ground cloves
1 can (14 ounces) artichoke hearts packed in water
2 cans (2½ ounces each) sliced black olives
2 cans (14½ ounces each) diced tomatoes seasoned with garlic and onion
2 cans (8 ounces each) tomato sauce
1 package (1 pound) pasta of your choice, cooked (see page 88 for cooking instructions), for serving
½ cup already-crumbled feta cheese, or more to taste

START TO FINISH: 20 MINUTES

1. Heat the olive oil in a 4½-quart Dutch oven or soup pot over medium heat. Peel and coarsely chop the onions, adding them to the pot as you chop. Stir occasionally.

2. Add the turkey and beef to the pot, raise the heat to medium-high, and cook, stirring from time to time. While the meat cooks, stir in the garlic powder, oregano, thyme, sugar, bay leaves, pepper, and cloves.

3. While the meat continues to cook, open all of the cans and drain the artichoke hearts and olives. Coarsely chop the artichokes. Add the tomatoes with their juice, the tomato sauce, and the drained olives and chopped artichokes to the pot. Stir well.

4. Let cook, stirring frequently, until the meat is no longer pink, about 5 minutes longer, then reduce the heat to medium. Let cook for about 5 more minutes to blend the flavors. Stir from time to time. Remove and discard the bay leaves. Serve the sauce at once over hot, drained pasta or let simmer until ready to serve. Top each serving with 1 tablespoon feta cheese, or more to taste.

■ *Serves 8*

DO-AHEAD

The sauce can be refrigerated, covered, for up to 2 days or frozen in a microwave-safe container for up to 2 months.
• If the sauce has been frozen, thaw it in the microwave oven on the defrost setting, following the manufacturer's directions.
• To reheat, place the sauce in a pot over medium heat and stir frequently until heated through, about 20 minutes.

THE PASTA POT

From Alicia:

A pasta pot is a big baby, usually 6 quarts or larger, with a full colander insert (frequently called a steamer) and a lid. It's oh so easy to cook large quantities of pasta in one of these and then just lift out the colander insert to drain it. No dumping, no burning yourself with the steam, no need to scream "Hot pot coming through!" as you move from the stove to the sink. Well, okay—with two dogs, a cat, and two kids underfoot at my house, I still have to make sure the path is clear.

Since one of the tricks to cooking a lot of pasta at one time is using a pot that's big enough, having a special one just for the job makes sense. The colander insert makes the draining step and water-bath step almost one continuous move. My mother-in-law got so attached to my pasta pot, she requested one for Christmas.

Pasta pots are available in kitchen stores. If you already own a large (6-quart) pot, check to see if there's a steamer insert that will transform it into a pasta pot. Just be sure the insert is the full depth of the pot or there won't be enough room for the pasta to move around and cook evenly. Whether you decide to invest in a new pot or an insert, you'll find it indispensable, and not just when company is coming.

Phased and Flexible

Pasta with Cabernet Sauce and Sausage

The bold flavors of red wine and Italian sausage take a jar of store-bought tomato sauce to completely new heights. What could be easier? Don't breathe a word and your guests will never know! Spicy food lovers will want to use hot Italian sausage; those with tamer tastes can opt for mild. Since the recipe needs only a little wine, choose a bottle that you enjoy drinking and serve what's left along with dinner. We like this sauce over a tube-shaped pasta such as penne or on spiraled rotini.

1¼ pounds Italian hot or sweet sausage
2 large onions (for about 2 cups chopped)
2 medium-size green bell peppers (for about 2 cups bite-size pieces)
2 teaspoons bottled minced garlic
⅓ cup dry red wine, such as cabernet sauvignon
2 jars (about 26 ounces each) spaghetti sauce
½ teaspoon sugar
¼ teaspoon black pepper
1 package (1 pound) tubular pasta of your choice, cooked (see page 88 for cooking instructions), for serving
Already-grated Parmesan cheese, for serving (optional)

PHASE 1: 20 MINUTES

1. If the sausage has casings, use kitchen shears or a sharp knife to remove them. Place the sausage in an extra-deep, 12-inch nonstick skillet over medium-high heat. Cook, stirring frequently, breaking the sausage into bite-size pieces.

2. While the sausage cooks, peel and coarsely chop the onions, adding them to the skillet as you chop. Rinse, core, and seed the bell peppers. Cut them into bite-size pieces and add to the skillet. Add the garlic. Continue to cook, stirring frequently, until the sausage is no longer pink, about 10 minutes longer. Remove from the heat. Put the meat and vegetables in a colander and drain well. *The sausage mixture can be refrigerated, covered, at this point for up to 24 hours or frozen in a microwave-safe container for up to 3 weeks (see Notes).*

PHASE 2: 6 MINUTES MOSTLY UNATTENDED COOKING TIME

3. Place the sausage mixture back in the skillet over high heat. Add the wine. Add the spaghetti sauce, sugar, and black pepper. Stir well. Bring the mixture to a boil, reduce the heat to low, and simmer 5 minutes or until ready to serve. Serve over hot, drained pasta. Pass grated Parmesan at the table to sprinkle on top, if desired. *The sauce can be served at once or refrigerated, covered, for up to 24 hours. If the sausage was not frozen following Phase 1, the completed sauce can be frozen in a microwave-safe container for up to 1 month (see Notes).*

■ *Serves 8*

Notes: If the sausage mixture or completed sauce has been frozen, thaw it in the microwave oven on the defrost setting, following the manufacturer's directions.

To reheat cold sauce, place it in a skillet over medium heat and stir frequently until heated through, about 20 minutes.

From Beverly:

Do-ahead means I can do it, especially on those occasions when we're having guests on a regular weeknight. This entire casserole can be assembled in three phases, which means I can do the first part the day before and come back to my creation the morning I plan to serve it. Then when I hit the kitchen after work, the casserole just pops in the oven for about 20 minutes to warm through. That's realistic even for desperate nights.

To save time, try to buy ground sausage, not links. Either the Alfredo-style sauce from the refrigerator section of the grocery store or the one that comes in jars, found on the aisle beside the spaghetti sauce, can be used. If you're using the kind in a jar, measure out one cup and refrigerate the remaining sauce for another meal.

Rotini Bake with Sausage and Sautéed Vegetables

1 package (1 pound) rotini
1 pound hot or sweet Italian sausage
1 large onion (for about 1 cup chopped)
1 large red bell pepper (for about 1 cup bite-size pieces)
1 large orange or yellow bell pepper (for about 1 cup bite-size pieces)
Cooking oil spray
1 tablespoon olive oil
1 container (10 ounces; about 1 cup) refrigerated Alfredo-style pasta sauce (see Notes)
½ cup milk
2 teaspoons dried basil
1 tablespoon bottled minced garlic
Salt and black pepper
¼ cup already-grated Parmesan cheese

PHASE 1: 20 MINUTES

1. Place the rotini in 4 quarts of boiling unsalted water and cook until tender, following the directions on the package, 10 to 11 minutes.

2. Meanwhile, if the sausage has casings, use kitchen shears or a sharp knife to remove them. Place the loose sausage in a 12-inch nonstick skillet over medium heat and let brown, 12 to 15 minutes. Stir from time to time, breaking the sausage into bite-size pieces.

3. While the sausage cooks, peel and coarsely chop the onion. Rinse, core, and seed the bell peppers and chop them into bite-size pieces.

4. When the sausage is done, put it in a colander and drain well. Pat with paper towels to remove as much fat as possible. Spray a 13 × 9-inch glass or ceramic baking dish with cooking oil spray. Put the drained sausage in the baking dish. Drain the rotini in the same colander. Pour the rotini over the sausage and toss. *The cooked pasta and sausage and chopped vegetables can be refrigerated, covered, for up*

*to 24 hours. Refrigerate the sausage mixture in the baking dish
(see Notes). Refrigerate the onions and bell peppers in separate small
containers.*

PHASE 2: 15 MINUTES

5. Heat the olive oil in a 12-inch nonstick skillet over medium-high
heat. Add the chopped onion to the skillet and cook 2 minutes,
stirring from time to time. Add the chopped bell peppers and
cook, stirring from time to time, until the vegetables begin to brown
and soften, about 6 minutes. While the vegetables cook, whisk
together the pasta sauce, milk, and basil in a small mixing bowl until
well combined. Set aside. Add the garlic to the skillet with the vegetables and continue to cook for 2 minutes longer.

6. Add the cooked vegetables and the sauce mixture to the baking
dish with the cooked pasta and sausage. Stir until the pasta is coated
with sauce. Season with salt and black pepper to taste. Spread the
pasta-meat-vegetable mixture evenly in the baking dish and sprinkle
the Parmesan evenly over it. *The casserole can be refrigerated, covered,
at this point for up to 12 hours.*

PHASE 3: 20 MINUTES UNATTENDED BAKING TIME

7. Remove the casserole from the refrigerator and preheat the oven
to 350°F.

8. Bake the casserole, uncovered, until heated through and just
beginning to brown on top, about 20 minutes. Serve at once.

■ *Serves 8*

Notes: Several companies make Alfredo-style sauces. They may be
found in cartons in the dairy section of the supermarket or in jars
alongside the other pasta sauces. We don't recommend the reduced-
fat versions unless you are accustomed to cooking with them.

If you do not have room to store a large baking dish in your
refrigerator, place the sausage mixture in a large zipper-top plastic
bag or mixing bowl to store, then transfer it to a baking dish sprayed
with cooking oil spray before continuing with the recipe.

SANITY SAVER

*With today's hectic
schedules, if
you're trying to get
more than two couples
together, the date often
needs to be reserved a
month or more in
advance. But you don't
want your invitation to
be forgotten. When the
date is crucial, such as
a birthday or going-
away celebration, use a
two-part strategy. First,
telephone six weeks to a
month in advance to
announce the event and
set the date. Say you'll
call back closer to the
time with all of the
details. Then, ten days
to a week beforehand,
call again to fill your
guests in on everything
they need to know. This
also serves as a subtle
reminder.*

The first time we zipped through this lasagna recipe, we couldn't believe it. Who would think you could get lasagna ready for the oven in less than half an hour. And what a lasagna it is! Thanks to a shot of Madeira, one of our favorite secret weapons, there's a depth of flavor as if the sauce had simmered all day. (Madeira is a fortified wine; you'll find it near the sherries in the wine section of the supermarket or liquor store. Once opened, it will keep for several months for use in cooking.) We're always thankful for a fail-safe recipe to serve our vegetarian friends, and this one is at the top of our list.

Lazy Spinach Lasagna

9 lasagna noodles (see Notes)
1 box (10 ounces) frozen chopped spinach
1 container (about 16 ounces) Alfredo-style pasta sauce
    (see Notes)
½ cup Madeira
Cooking oil spray
1 container (15 ounces) fat-free ricotta cheese
½ cup already-grated or -shredded Parmesan cheese
1 large egg
1 package (8 ounces) already-sliced, fresh button
    mushrooms
¾ cup (3 ounces) already-shredded, part-skim
    mozzarella cheese

PHASE 1: 25 MINUTES

1. Place the lasagna noodles in 3½ quarts of boiling unsalted water. Cook according to the directions on the package, 8 to 10 minutes, and then drain.

2. Meanwhile, unwrap the spinach and place it in a medium-size microwave-safe bowl. Microwave the spinach, uncovered, on high, until thawed, about 5 minutes.

3. While the spinach thaws, pour the pasta sauce into a small mixing bowl. Add about 1 tablespoon of water to the emptied container and shake, then pour this into the bowl. Add the Madeira and stir until well blended.

4. Spray a 13 × 9-inch glass or ceramic baking dish with cooking oil spray. Spread about 1 cup of the sauce mixture evenly in the bottom of the baking dish. Place 3 cooked lasagna noodles in the baking dish so that they cover the sauce mixture.

5. Remove the spinach from the microwave and drain it in a colander. Press the spinach with a large spoon to remove any excess moisture (the spinach shouldn't be completely dry). Put the spinach back into

the bowl used for microwaving. Add the ricotta, Parmesan, and egg to the bowl with the spinach. Stir well to blend. Spread half of the spinach mixture over the lasagna noodles in the baking dish.

6. Microwave the mushrooms in a covered medium-size microwave-safe dish for 2 minutes on high. Drain off any moisture. Scatter the mushrooms over the spinach mixture in the baking dish.

7. Place 3 lasagna noodles so that they cover the vegetables in the baking dish. Pour half of the remaining sauce mixture over these noodles. Spread the remaining spinach mixture over the sauce in the baking dish. Place 3 lasagna noodles so that they cover the top layer of the spinach mixture. Pour the remaining sauce mixture evenly over the noodles on top. *The assembled lasagna can be refrigerated, covered, for up to 24 hours or frozen for up to 1 month. If the lasagna has been frozen in a glass baking dish, thaw it in a microwave oven on the defrost setting, about 15 minutes or following the manufacturer's directions. If the lasagna has been frozen in a metal baking dish, place it in the refrigerator to thaw 24 hours before you plan to bake it.*

PHASE 2: 50 MINUTES MOSTLY UNATTENDED BAKING TIME

8. Preheat the oven to 350°F.

9. Bake the lasagna, uncovered, until bubbly, about 40 minutes. Remove from the oven and sprinkle the mozzarella over the top. Return the lasagna to the oven and bake until the mozzarella is melted on top, about 10 minutes more. Serve at once or let the lasagna rest until ready to serve.

■ *Serves 8*

Notes: You will need 9 lasagna noodles and most 8-ounce packages contain a few more than that. Since some of the noodles inevitably tear while cooking, we prepare the whole box to better our chances of getting 9 perfect ones.

Several companies make Alfredo-style sauces. They may be found in jars alongside the other pasta sauces or in the dairy section of the supermarket. The refrigerated containers usually hold only 10 ounces, so you'll need a container and a half here. We don't recommend the reduced-fat versions unless you are accustomed to cooking with them.

SANITY SAVER

Since so many people are vegetarians or have special dietary needs, we always ask ahead whether there are foods our guests can't eat. Who wants to present a luscious beef stew to someone who doesn't eat meat or a shrimp dish to a friend with high cholesterol?

THE BOSS IS COMING

From Beverly:

Having the boss over for dinner can strike terror in the heart of the host, and for good reason. Never mind that the story is generations old. The fear rises anew each and every time.

My turn to cook for the boss is a month away, and already I'm nervous. I'm trying out menus and imagining everything that could go wrong. The combinations are endless—on both fronts.

Time to get a grip and call my therapist. Oh, that's right, I don't have a therapist. Alicia will have to do. I telephone her instead.

"Just relax." I hear Alicia's butter-smooth voice, the one she uses when I'm hysterical. "Don't you remember our rules?"

It can't be that bad if there are rules. My mind, however, is blank.

"What rules?" I squeak into the phone. "Remind me. Quick."

So, here they are, the Rules for Rescue When the Boss Is Bearing Down. I suggest making a copy, laminating it, and carrying it close at all times during the dreaded week before. Recite as many times as necessary.

Rules for Rescue When the Boss Is Bearing Down

1. Remember the boss is just a person.

2. Plan a realistic menu. If you don't know anything about the boss's eating habits, it's probably best to avoid red meat.

3. Stick with recipes you know. If you do choose something new, practice ahead of time.

4. Pick a setting for the meal where you'll be most comfortable because a comfortable host makes for comfortable guests. The dining room with your fine china or the deck with your best plastic? You can decide.

5. Do as much cooking as humanly possible before the boss arrives.

6. Since there's a chance you'll be skittish, make a reminder sheet listing all duties in detail.

7. Remember the boss is just a person.

It's not going to feel like a cliché when it happens to you.

Mushroom Lasagna Alfredo

9 lasagna noodles (see Notes)
1 tablespoon olive oil
2 large onions (for about 2 cups chopped)
1 package (8 ounces) already-sliced, fresh button mushrooms
1 package (6 ounces) already-sliced portobello mushroom caps
1 tablespoon bottled minced garlic
½ cup sweet Marsala (see Notes)
2 large, ripe tomatoes, or 6 ripe plum tomatoes
1 container (15 ounces) fat-free ricotta cheese
1 large egg
1 teaspoon dried Italian-style seasoning
Cooking oil spray
1 container (about 16 ounces) Alfredo-style pasta sauce (see Notes)
2 cups already-shredded, part-skim mozzarella cheese
½ cup already-grated or -shredded Parmesan cheese

PHASE 1: 25 MINUTES

1. Place the lasagna noodles in 3½ quarts of boiling unsalted water. Cook according to the directions on the package, 8 to 10 minutes, and then drain.

2. Meanwhile, heat the olive oil in an extra-deep, 12-inch nonstick skillet over medium-high heat. Peel and coarsely chop the onions, adding them to the skillet as you chop. Coarsely chop the button and portobello mushrooms, adding them to the skillet as you chop. When all the mushrooms have been added, add the garlic and cook until the mushrooms release their liquid and the onions are tender, about 3 minutes. Add the Marsala and cook until almost all of it has evaporated, about 4 minutes more. Remove from the heat.

We knew we had a winner when our friend asked if she could keep a copy after testing this recipe. She prepared the rich vegetarian dish for her in-laws during one of the busiest times of the year, Christmas. Her response: "This is one of the most impressive lasagnas I've ever made, and yet it's one of the easiest."

All you have to do is cook the mushrooms, onions, and garlic while the lasagna noodles are cooking, which is almost a no-brainer. Then assemble the lasagna—you're done in less than 25 minutes.

Perfect for those occasions when you want to serve a meat-free meal, the lasagna is so filling it won't leave anyone wanting more. For an even fancier fare, substitute assorted gourmet mushrooms for some of the button mushrooms. If fresh tomatoes are in sad shape due to the season, or outrageously expensive, you can substitute two 14½-ounce cans of chopped tomatoes after draining them well.

3. While the mushrooms are cooking, rinse and cut the tomatoes into ¼-inch slices. Mix the ricotta, egg, and Italian-style seasoning in a medium-size bowl until well blended.

4. Spray a 13 × 9-inch glass baking dish with cooking oil spray. Spread about ¾ cup of the pasta sauce evenly in the bottom of the dish. Place 3 cooked lasagna noodles in the dish so that they cover the sauce. Spread half of the onion-and-mushroom mixture over the lasagna noodles in the dish. Sprinkle with about 1 cup of mozzarella.

5. Place 3 lasagna noodles so that they cover the layer of mozzarella. Spread the ricotta mixture over these, then add the tomatoes (cutting them to fit, if necessary). Top this layer with 3 more noodles. Spread the remaining onion-and-mushroom mixture over these noodles. Top with the remaining pasta sauce, spreading to cover the mushroom mixture well. Sprinkle on the remaining mozzarella. *The assembled lasagna can be refrigerated, covered, for up to 1 day.*

PHASE 2: 50 MINUTES MOSTLY UNATTENDED BAKING TIME

6. Preheat the oven to 350°F.

7. Bake the lasagna, uncovered, until bubbly, about 45 minutes. Remove from the oven and sprinkle with the Parmesan. Return the lasagna to the oven and bake until the Parmesan is melted on top, about 5 minutes more. Remove from the oven and let rest for 10 to 15 minutes before slicing and serving.

■ *Serves 8 to 10*

Notes: You will need 9 lasagna noodles and most 8-ounce packages contain a few more than that. Since some of the noodles inevitably tear while cooking, we prepare the whole box to better our chances of getting 9 perfect ones.

Look for Marsala, a fortified wine, near the sherries in the wine section of the supermarket or liquor store.

Several companies make Alfredo-style sauces. They may be found alongside the other pasta sauces or in the dairy section of the supermarket. The refrigerated containers usually hold only 10 ounces, so you'll need a container and a half here. We don't recommend the reduced-fat versions unless you are accustomed to cooking with them.

TIME SAVER

Arrange your grocery shopping list according to the layout of the aisles of the supermarket. This will cut down on time spent in the store.

From Beverly:

It seems like all of my friends have cut meat out of their diets at one time or another. I used to fret over what to serve them, and so when I saw a version of this recipe in the newspaper a few years ago, I paused. Ordinarily I would have passed it by—lentils over pasta? With sesame oil, no less? I have to admit it sounded odd, but the fact that the recipe came from the Moosewood folks, coupled with the fact that I was desperate for some new vegetarian ideas, made me decide to try it. Boy, was I surprised. This sauce quickly becomes addictive, and even if you're not usually a lentil lover, the sweet-and-sour combination is sure to convert you.

Over the years I have changed the recipe around to make it faster, using convenient ingredients like baby carrots and bottled garlic and ginger. All of the prep work can be done a day ahead, and the entire sauce can be fixed up to two days in advance or frozen for up to a month. Just pull it out and heat it up before your guests arrive. We like to serve the sauce over penne or other tubular pasta.

Sweet-and-Sour Lentil Sauce for Pasta

2 teaspoons vegetable oil
2 large onions (for about 2 cups chopped)
2 cups (about 24) already-peeled baby carrots
2 teaspoons bottled minced garlic
2 teaspoons bottled fresh ginger (see Note)
1 can (14½ ounces) vegetable broth or chicken broth
1 medium-size green bell pepper (for about
    1 cup chopped)
2 cups lentils
⅔ cup rice wine vinegar or white vinegar
½ cup honey
½ cup reduced-sodium soy sauce
1 tablespoon Asian (dark) sesame oil
½ teaspoon crushed red pepper flakes (optional)
¼ cup cornstarch
1 package (1 pound) penne or tubular pasta of your
    choice, cooked (see page 88 for cooking instructions),
    for serving

PHASE 1: 11 MINUTES

1. Heat the vegetable oil in a 4½-quart Dutch oven or soup pot over medium heat. Peel and coarsely chop the onions, adding them to the pot as you chop. Stir from time to time. Cut the carrots into ¼-inch slices. Add the carrots to the pot. Cook, stirring from time to time, until the onions are soft, about 2 minutes.

2. Add the garlic and ginger to the onions and carrots and stir. Add the vegetable broth and 2 cups of water.

3. Rinse, core, seed, and coarsely chop the bell pepper. *The onion mixture can be refrigerated, covered, at this point for up to 24 hours. Refrigerate the diced bell pepper separately in a covered container.*

BUY A BIG HAM

I t's like cheating, it's so easy. When you need to feed a crowd, think ham. It comes already cooked, in giant hunks, and sometimes, already sliced. If the mainstay of the meal practically takes care of itself, you're free to concentrate on other things. Just add some side salads and sandwich rolls—almost like magic, a picture-perfect buffet will spread before your very eyes.

When shopping for a ham at the supermarket, you'll have lots of choices: bone-in or boneless, sliced or unsliced, glazed or not. Unless you're feeding an army, half a ham will be a gracious plenty. We prefer the hams that are sold in heavy-duty plastic rather than the canned variety. For ultimate ease, buy the ham sliced, although you'll have no control over how thick the slices will be. If we buy an unsliced ham, we often place the meat on a platter, cut a few slices, then leave the knife and meat fork at the table and let guests carve as much as they'd like.

It used to be that specialty stores were the only places to buy spiral-sliced hams, and the hefty price tags could be a barrier. These days, supermarkets and price clubs have jumped on to the ham wagon. The competition means lower prices and maybe even the chance to grab a ham on sale. Since the sell-by dates don't expire for weeks, we especially like to keep an eye out for markdowns on hams left over after Easter and Christmas. We've been lucky enough to snag them for as little as a dollar a pound.

One advantage to a glazed ham is that you can let it come to room temperature and serve it immediately, with no cooking at all. However, we also like to buy plain hams that come with packets of glaze since we find the already-glazed hams can sometimes be too heavy on the sugar—although you *can* just scrape some of the glaze off. If there's no glaze included with your ham, it's easy to make your own. Just melt together a cup of brown sugar and two tablespoons of butter, stir, pour the mixture over the ham, stud it with a few whole cloves, and bake it at 325°F until heated through (about 45 minutes for a 9-pound ham just out of the refrigerator). Buying a disposable aluminum pan to hold the ham makes cleanup a breeze.

No matter how you slice it, a ham makes the host look good.

PHASE 2: 40 MINUTES MOSTLY UNATTENDED COOKING TIME

4. Return the onion mixture to the pot, cover, and bring to a boil over high heat. Meanwhile, rinse, pick over, and drain the lentils. When the onion mixture comes to a boil, add the lentils. Reduce the heat to medium-low or enough heat to maintain a slow boil. Cover and cook until the lentils are tender but still hold their shape, about 30 to 35 minutes.

5. When the lentils are done, add the diced bell pepper, and the vinegar, honey, soy sauce, sesame oil, and crushed red pepper, if using. Raise the heat to medium, stir well, and continue to cook, uncovered, just until the green pepper wilts, about 5 minutes. Mix the cornstarch with ¼ cup of water in a jar that has a lid. Shake well to break up any lumps. Pour a little of the cornstarch mixture evenly over the lentil sauce. Stir gently, adding more cornstarch mixture as necessary, until the sauce thickens slightly, 3 to 5 minutes (you may not need all of the cornstarch). Serve at once over hot, drained pasta. *The sauce can be refrigerated, covered, for up to 2 days or frozen in a microwave-safe container for up to 1 month. Do not thicken the sauce before freezing. If the sauce has been frozen, thaw it in the microwave oven on the defrost setting, following the manufacturer's directions. To reheat, place the sauce back in the cooking pot over medium heat and stir frequently until heated through, about 20 minutes. When the sauce is hot, proceed to thicken it as described in Step 5.*

■ *Serves 8*

Note: Bottled fresh ginger is the perfect replacement for time-consuming fresh ginger. Called minced, chopped, crushed, or ground, depending on the brand, bottled fresh ginger is available in the produce section of larger supermarkets. Finely minced fresh ginger can be substituted.

TIME SAVER

If you let guests serve themselves straight from the pots on the stove, you won't have to spend hours washing a slew of serving bowls. (The pots have to be cleaned anyway.) A good friend of ours, a proper Southern belle at that, lends dignity to the practice by calling it a "Carolina buffet."

No matter how many traditional meat loaf recipes I try, my mom's is still the best. I've loved it for as long as I can remember, and without fail, every child I've served it to becomes an immediate fan, too. When we "desperized" the original recipe in our first book, *Desperation Dinners!*, I was surprised by how many people wanted not only the quick 20-minute version we featured there, but the original recipe, too. We make the meat loaf in a glass baking dish because it's prettier for serving. If you use a metal one, it will take a little longer to bake.

While we never seem to have the time to make this delicious loaf midweek, we enjoy it when we can find an hour to bake the huge loaf. So here is the original meat loaf recipe. It's irresistible.

Mom's Original Meat Loaf

4 slices whole wheat bread
3 large eggs
1 cup milk
2 large onions (for about 2 cups finely chopped)
¼ cup densely packed fresh parsley, or 1 tablespoon
   dried parsley
1 cup already-grated Parmesan cheese
2 tablespoons Dijon or other prepared mustard
1 tablespoon Worcestershire sauce
1 teaspoon salt
½ teaspoon black pepper
3 pounds extra-lean ground beef
Cooking oil spray
2 cups ketchup

PHASE 1: 20 MINUTES

1. Cut the bread into small cubes and set aside.

2. Break the eggs into a large bowl and gently beat them. Add the bread cubes and milk and stir well. Peel and finely chop the onions, adding them to the bowl with the bread cubes as you chop. If using fresh parsley, rinse and finely chop it. Add the parsley, Parmesan, mustard, Worcestershire sauce, salt, and pepper to the bread cubes and mix well.

3. Crumble the ground meat over the bread mixture and then fold together using a spoon or your hands, mixing well (see Note).

4. Spray a 13 × 9-inch glass or metal baking dish with cooking oil spray and transfer the meat mixture to the baking dish. Form into a large loaf, about 3 inches high. *The meat loaf can be refrigerated, covered, at this point for up to 8 hours. Or you can wrap it well in waxed paper, place in an extra-large, freezer-weight zipper-top plastic bag, and freeze for up to a month. Thaw the meat loaf overnight in the refrigerator and then proceed with Phase 2.*

**PHASE 2: 1 HOUR UNATTENDED BAKING TIME,
PLUS 10 MINUTES RESTING TIME**

5. Preheat the oven to 350°F.

6. Pour the ketchup over the entire meat loaf. Bake, uncovered, until cooked through, about 1 hour if using a glass baking dish or 1 hour and 10 minutes if the baking dish is metal. Let rest at room temperature for 10 minutes before slicing and serving.

■ *Serves 8*

Note: If you use your hands to mix and form the meat loaf, wash them thoroughly with antibacterial soap once you have finished.

GAME NIGHT

From Alicia:

I grew up with board games. Monopoly, Clue, and Life were precious parts of my younger years. In college, it was Pictionary, Trivial Pursuit, and Scattergories. And my kids have caught the fever. As a family we started with Candyland and have advanced to Scrabble, Upwords, and even good old Yahtzee.

Game nights don't have to be for just a single family. In fact, the old saying "the more the merrier" is definitely true when it comes to games. Younger children can pair with adults or older children to form teams. When there are more than six of you, teams make play faster and therefore keep the interest of even smaller children.

Have an "I'm not much of a game player" in your midst? Scorekeeper, timer, dice roller, or rules mediator are great roles, too. Not to mention chief drink fetcher for when the play gets really serious.

If you're just starting a game night tradition, be sure to tell your guests about your idea when you invite them. Maybe they have a favorite game they can bring along. Or invite the kids to pick the game and save the adult choices for an adults-only night.

Sharing stories and laughs with friends over a game board is always a treat. Just remember to leave enough time for dinner.

From Alicia:

From Alicia:

My kids call this the meatball meat loaf, and indeed meatballs are what it reminds me of. Imagine the goodness of a perfectly spiced Italian meat sauce and homemade meat-balls conveniently packaged in a family favorite—meat loaf. For serve-along suggestions, see the box opposite.

Italian Meat Loaf

2 large eggs
¾ cup Italian-style bread crumbs
¾ cup already-grated Parmesan cheese
½ cup milk
1½ cups commercially prepared traditional,
    smooth-style spaghetti sauce
2 teaspoons Worcestershire sauce
1 small onion (for about ½ cup finely chopped)
1 cup already-shredded mozzarella cheese
1½ teaspoons dried Italian-style seasoning
1 teaspoon garlic powder
½ teaspoon salt
¼ teaspoon black pepper
3 pounds extra-lean ground beef
Cooking oil spray

PHASE 1: 20 MINUTES

1. Break the eggs into a large bowl and gently beat them. Add the bread crumbs, Parmesan, milk, ¾ cup of the spaghetti sauce, and the Worcestershire sauce. Stir well. Peel and very finely chop the onion, adding it to the bowl with the bread crumbs as you chop. Add ¾ cup of the mozzarella and the Italian-style seasoning, garlic powder, salt, and pepper to the bread crumb mixture. Mix well.

2. Crumble the ground meat over the mixture and then fold together using a spoon or your hands, mixing well (see Note).

3. Spray a 13 × 9-inch glass or metal baking dish with cooking oil spray. Transfer the meat mixture to the baking dish. Form into a large loaf, about 3 to 4 inches thick. *The meat loaf can be refrigerated, covered, at this point for up to 8 hours. Or you can wrap it well in waxed paper, place in an extra-large, freezer-weight zipper-top plastic bag, and freeze for up to a month. Thaw the meat loaf overnight in the refrigerator and then proceed with Phase 2. The remaining spaghetti sauce and mozzarella can be frozen in separate containers and thawed at the same time as the meat loaf.*

SPACE SAVER

Storage idea! A blanket chest can be an almost bottomless pit for stashing all sorts of entertaining gear. It can hold everything from reusable, colorful plastic plates to table-cloths and napkins.

4. Preheat the oven to 350°F.

5. Pour the remaining ¾ cup spaghetti sauce over the meat loaf. Place the meat loaf, uncovered, in the center of the oven and bake for 1 hour if using a glass baking dish or 1 hour and 10 minutes if the baking dish is metal. Just before the last 10 minutes of baking, sprinkle the remaining ¼ cup mozzarella over the top of the loaf.

6. Remove the meat loaf from the oven and let rest for 10 minutes before slicing and serving.

■ *Serves 8*

Note: If you use your hands to mix and form the meat loaf, wash them thoroughly with antibacterial soap once you have finished.

MEAT LOAF— THE PERFECT FAMILY DINNER

What better food for a family-style gathering than one of our favorites from childhood? Nothing is homier or more satisfying than a nice, juicy meat loaf. Choose from a traditional one (see Mom's Original Meat Loaf on page 106) or the up-to-date Italian version here, a sure favorite for any self-respecting meatball lover.

Hearty slices of meat loaf make a satisfying meal served alongside Cheryl's Party Potatoes (see page 265), noodles or rice, and Green-and-White Salad (see page 228). Fastest Fruit Salad (see page 270) rounds out the dinner.

For a perfect evening, rent *Mary Poppins* for the after-dinner entertainment.

From Beverly:

The first cookbook I ever used for entertaining as a newlywed was *Chef Paul Prudhomme's Louisiana Kitchen.* Everything I tried from the book was wonderful, but those days were long before kids and the Desperate Life hit. I would spend hours experimenting in the kitchen, Prudhomme's book by my side. Now that I have to juggle my daughter's Saturday morning tennis lessons with my son's afternoon soccer games and countless other chores, the thought of spending hours cooking from any cookbook gives me a headache. But a few years ago I realized I truly missed my old friend Paul. So I started working to see if I could streamline and shorten the recipes without sacrificing the trademark flavors. This rich dish makes me think of old-fashioned chicken à la king jazzed up to a New Orleans beat. It's amazing served over puff pastry cups, but you could substitute egg noodles, toast points, or rice. The whole dish takes just 25 minutes to pull together, yet the taste is terrific. I believe even Paul Prudhomme himself would be pleased.

Saucy Chicken

3 tablespoons butter
1 large onion (for about 1 cup chopped)
1 package (8 ounces) already-sliced, fresh
    button mushrooms
1 medium-size green bell pepper (for about 1 cup
    bite-size pieces)
1 large red bell pepper (for about 1 cup bite-size pieces)
2⅔ to 3 pounds skinless, boneless chicken breasts
¼ cup dry sherry (not cooking sherry)
1 teaspoon dried basil
1 teaspoon onion powder
1 teaspoon garlic powder
1 teaspoon dry mustard
⅓ cup all-purpose flour
1⅓ cups low-fat chicken broth (from one
    14½ ounce can)
1 cup heavy (whipping) cream
Salt and black pepper
8 frozen puff pastry shells (see Notes)

PHASE 1: 25 MINUTES *(see Notes)*

1. Melt the butter in a 4½-quart Dutch oven or soup pot over medium heat. Meanwhile, peel and coarsely chop the onion, adding it to the pot as you chop. Add the mushrooms to the pot and stir from time to time.

2. Rinse, core, and seed the bell peppers. Cut the bell peppers and the chicken into bite-size pieces. Add the bell pepper and chicken pieces to the pot with the onion and mushrooms. Cook, stirring frequently, until the chicken is no longer pink in the center, 6 to 8 minutes. While the chicken cooks, add the sherry, basil, onion powder, garlic powder, and mustard.

3. In a small jar that has a lid, combine the flour with ⅓ cup of the chicken broth. Shake well to break up any lumps and set aside. Add the remaining 1 cup chicken broth and the cream to the cooking chicken in the pot. Bring the mixture to a boil. Shake the flour mixture again and add most but not all of it to the pot, stirring well, until the liquid begins to thicken, 2 to 3 minutes. Add the remaining flour mixture a little at a time until the sauce is slightly thicker than heavy cream. Season with salt and black peppern to taste. *The chicken mixture can be refrigerated, covered, for up to 24 hours or it can be frozen in a microwave-safe container for up to 1 month. If it has been frozen, thaw it in a microwave oven on the defrost setting, following the manufacturer's directions. To reheat, place the thawed chicken mixture in a pot over medium heat and stir frequently until heated through, about 20 minutes.*

PHASE 2: 25 MINUTES MOSTLY UNATTENDED BAKING TIME

4. Preheat the oven to 400°F.

5. About 25 minutes before you're ready to serve, bake the puff pastry shells until golden brown, according to the directions on the package. Remove the top and inside of each puff pastry shell according to the directions on the package. Serve the chicken and its sauce over the baked puff pastry shells.

■ *Serves 8*

Notes: Frozen puff pastry shells frequently come in packages of 6, which means you'll have 4 left over. Keep these frozen for another use. You can dress up a family meal by baking and filling the shells with beef stew or a creamy chicken dish.

If you want to prepare this dish start to finish, preheat the oven and start to bake the puff pastry shells as described in Steps 4 and 5 *before* beginning Step 1.

SANITY SAVER

Make it a policy to serve company meals buffet style or family style. This means the host doesn't have to stand in the kitchen beforehand and dish up the food.

From Beverly:

If you're a fan of chicken salad, you'll surely enjoy this Southern version. Often served when women gather for lunch, it's a sentimental favorite for me, since my Grandmother Hood prepared it for a bridesmaids' lunch the day before I got married. I hope it becomes a special recipe for your family get-togethers, too.

Hot Chicken Salad

2 pounds skinless, boneless chicken breasts
20 butter-flavored crackers, such as Town House or Ritz
4 large ribs celery (for about 2 cups diced)
1 small onion (for about ½ cup diced)
1½ cups already-shredded carrots (optional; see Notes)
1 small container (8 ounces) sour cream (see Notes)
¾ cup mayonnaise (see Notes)
1 teaspoon Worcestershire sauce
1 teaspoon curry powder
½ teaspoon black pepper
Cooking oil spray

PHASE 1: 20 MINUTES MOSTLY UNATTENDED COOKING TIME

1. Place the chicken breasts in a 4½-quart Dutch oven or soup pot. Add just enough cold water to cover the chicken, about 1 quart. Cover the pot and bring to a rolling boil over high heat, about 5 minutes.

2. While the water comes to a boil, place the crackers in a 1-quart zipper-top plastic bag and seal. Crush the crackers to crumbs.

3. As soon as the water boils, remove the pot from the heat and let stand, covered, until the chicken is no longer pink in the center, about 15 minutes. Remove the chicken from the pot. Discard the broth or reserve it for another use. *The cooked chicken can be refrigerated, covered, for up to 24 hours. Set the bag of cracker crumbs aside until you assemble the casserole.*

PHASE 2: 20 TO 25 MINUTES

4. Cut the cooked chicken into bite-size chunks and place them in a large mixing bowl. Rinse the celery and dry it thoroughly. Dice the celery and add it to the bowl with the chicken. Peel and finely dice the onion; add it to the bowl.

5. If using the carrots, coarsely chop the already-shredded pieces. Add them to the bowl with the chicken. Add the sour cream, mayonnaise, Worcestershire sauce, curry powder, and pepper. Stir until well combined.

6. Spray an 11 × 8-inch glass or ceramic baking dish with cooking oil spray. Pour the chicken mixture into the dish and spread evenly. Sprinkle the cracker crumbs evenly over the top. *The casserole can be refrigerated, covered, at this point for up to 8 hours.*

PHASE 3: 25 TO 30 MINUTES UNATTENDED BAKING TIME

7. Preheat the oven to 350°F.

8. Bake the casserole, uncovered, until the vegetables are just crisp-tender, 25 to 30 minutes.

■ *Serves 8*

Notes: Can't find already-shredded carrots? Just peel and shred 2 medium-size carrots instead.

Low-fat sour cream and low-fat mayonnaise may be used in this dish without changing the flavor. However, the lighter sour cream will release liquid. Just serve the chicken salad with a slotted spoon and leave the extra liquid behind in the dish.

From Alicia:

My family really enjoys an evening planned around a Mexican-inspired menu. Chips with Guiltless Guacamole (see page 48) and Roasted Garlic Salsa (see page 50 are just the tickets for starting the night. Then move on to this snappy casserole. It goes together quickly, then waits until you're ready to pop it in the oven and enjoy. (Do-ahead directions are sprinkled throughout the recipe.) You drench big, overstuffed flour tortillas in a cheesy cream sauce just before baking and they come out of the oven moist and bubbling, with a mellow flavor. Those with smaller appetites will only want half, but the heftier eaters will enjoy the whole enchilada. Serve this with Cuban Black Beans (see page 255) and Red Rice (see page 248).

Enchanting Chicken Enchiladas

2 teaspoons vegetable oil
1 large onion (for about 1 cup chopped)
2 teaspoons bottled minced garlic
2 pounds skinless, boneless chicken breasts
2 large red or yellow bell peppers (for 2 to 2½ cups chopped)
2 cans (14½-ounces each) Mexican-style stewed tomatoes (see page 51) or diced tomatoes seasoned with jalapeño or chile peppers
Cooking oil spray
8 large flour tortillas (10 to 12 inches each; see Note)
2 teaspoons chicken bouillon crystals, or 2 chicken bouillon cubes
1½ cups half-and-half
1 package (8 ounces) already-shredded Mexican blend cheese
Sour cream, for serving

PHASE 1: 20 MINUTES

1. Heat the oil over medium heat in an extra-deep, 12-inch nonstick skillet. Peel and coarsely chop the onion, adding it to the skillet as you chop. Add the garlic and stir from time to time. Cut the chicken into bite-size chunks, adding the chunks to the skillet as you cut. After the first breast has been added to the pan, raise the heat to medium-high. Continue to cut and add the remaining chicken chunks. Cook the chicken, stirring from time to time, until it is no longer pink outside, 4 to 6 minutes.

2. Meanwhile, as the chicken cooks, rinse, core, seed, and coarsely chop the bell peppers, adding them to the skillet as you chop. When the chicken is no longer pink, add the cans of tomatoes with their juices and stir until well mixed. Remove from the heat. *The chicken mixture can be refrigerated, covered, at this point for up to 12 hours.*

PHASE 2: 10 MINUTES

3. Spray two 13 × 9-inch baking dishes with cooking oil spray. Using a slotted spoon to drain off as much of the liquid as possible, place about ½ cup of the chicken mixture in the center of a tortilla. Wrap enchilada style, folding in two sides of the tortilla, leaving the enchilada open on both ends. Place the filled tortilla in one of the prepared baking dishes seam side down. Repeat until all the tortillas are filled, arranging them in the baking dishes in a single layer. *The filled tortillas can be refrigerated, covered, at this point for up to 3 hours.*

PHASE 3: 10 MINUTES, PLUS 40 MINUTES MOSTLY UNATTENDED BAKING TIME

4. Preheat the oven to 350°F.

5. Crush the bouillon cubes, if using, with the back of a spoon. Put the half-and-half and bouillon crystals or crushed cubes and ¾ cup of the cheese in a 2-cup glass measure. Microwave on high until heated through, about 2 minutes. Stir until the bouillon dissolves and the mixture is well combined.

6. Pour the cheese mixture evenly over the enchiladas, making sure each one is moistened. Bake for 30 minutes, covered with aluminum foil. Then remove the foil and sprinkle on the remaining 1¼ cups of cheese. Bake, uncovered, until the cheese is melted and bubbly, about 10 minutes more. Serve immediately with sour cream on the side.

■ *Makes 8 large enchiladas*

Note: Although enchiladas are traditionally made with corn tortillas, flour tortillas (usually used for burritos) work best for this recipe.

SPACE SAVER

*S*torage idea! *Transform a hall closet into "Entertaining Central" to store every-thing from extra wine-glasses to your slow cooker.*

Paella is a rich Spanish dish that's made on top of the stove in a special pan also called a *paella*. But in the traditional method you have to cook at the last minute, hovering close by the pan. That's not for us. Instead, we slide a casserole into the oven, then head off to dress before our guests arrive. Our oven version adds a whole new dimension to this Spanish classic without compromising any of the flavors we've come to love.

Spanish paellas are made with saffron, but it's an expensive spice that most cooks don't keep on hand. We rely on paprika to give the characteristic golden color, but if you happen to have saffron, feel free to add a pinch in place of the paprika. This casserole makes a generous amount of food, so it's a good choice when you're feeding folks with hearty appetites.

Baked Party Paella

1 fish-flavored bouillon cube, such as Knorr
1 large onion (for about 1 cup chopped)
1 pound chorizo or kielbasa
2 pounds skinless, boneless chicken breast halves
Cooking oil spray
2 cans (6½ ounces each) minced or
    chopped clams
1 can (14½ ounces) diced tomatoes
    seasoned with garlic and onion
3 bay leaves
1 tablespoon Worcestershire sauce
2 teaspoons dried basil
2 teaspoons bottled minced garlic
2 teaspoons paprika
1½ teaspoons dried thyme
1 teaspoon Tabasco sauce, or more to taste
    (optional)
2 tablespoons olive oil
2 cups converted rice (see Note)
1 cup frozen green peas

PHASE 1: 8 MINUTES

1. Place 2 cups of water in a glass measuring cup, add the bouillon cube, and microwave, uncovered, on high, until the cube almost dissolves, about 3 minutes. Stir until the bouillon cube dissolves.

2. While the bouillon is in the microwave, peel and coarsely chop the onion. Then cut the sausage into ¼-inch slices. Cut each half breast into 4 roughly equal pieces. *The fish bouillon and the onion, sausage, and chicken pieces can be placed in separate, covered containers and refrigerated at this point for up to 8 hours.*

**PHASE 2: 12 MINUTES, PLUS 1 HOUR AND 15 MINUTES
MOSTLY UNATTENDED BAKING TIME**

3. Preheat the oven to 375°F.

4. Spray a 15 × 10-inch roasting pan with cooking oil spray. Place the chicken pieces in the prepared pan. Pour the fish bouillon, ½ cup of water, and the clams with their juice and tomatoes with their juice into the pan. Add the bay leaves, Worcestershire sauce, basil, garlic, paprika, thyme, and Tabasco sauce, if using. Evenly drizzle the olive oil over the other ingredients and sprinkle the rice evenly over all. Scatter the chopped onions and sliced sausage evenly over the rice.

5. Cover the pan snugly with extra-wide, heavy-duty aluminum foil. Bake for 1 hour. Remove the pan from the oven, uncover, and scatter the still-frozen peas over the top. Cover the pan again and continue to cook the paella until the rice is tender, about 15 minutes. Serve at once or let stand, covered, until ready to serve. Remove and discard the bay leaves before serving.

■ *Serves 8 generously*

Note: The firmer texture of converted (parboiled) rice works better than long-grain rice in this recipe.

Cajun Catfish Gumbo

2 large onions (for about 2 cups chopped)

1 large green bell pepper (for about
  1½ cups bite-size pieces)

2 large ribs celery (for about 1 cup bite-size pieces)

1 pound andouille sausage or kielbasa (see Notes)

2 pounds skinless, boneless catfish fillets

4 tablespoons (½ stick) butter

2 teaspoons vegetable oil

2 fish-flavored bouillon cubes, such as Knorr

¼ cup all-purpose flour

2 cans (14½ ounces each) stewed tomatoes

1 tablespoon bottled minced garlic

1 tablespoon Cajun seafood seasoning blend, such as
  Chef Paul Prudhomme's Seafood Magic

1 teaspoon dried thyme

½ teaspoon black pepper

1 tablespoon Worcestershire sauce

¼ teaspoon Tabasco sauce, or more to taste

2 cups frozen sliced okra (see Notes)

6 cups hot cooked rice (from 2 cups uncooked
  converted rice; see page 120 for cooking
  instructions), for serving

PHASE 1: 15 MINUTES

1. Peel and coarsely chop the onions. Rinse, core, and seed the bell pepper. Rinse the celery. Cut the bell pepper and celery into bite-size pieces.

2. Cut the sausage into ¼-inch slices. Cut the catfish into bite-size pieces. *The vegetables, sausage, and catfish can be refrigerated at this point for up to 24 hours. Store the onions in a covered container or in a zipper-top plastic bag. Refrigerate the bell pepper and celery together in another covered container or plastic bag. Refrigerate the sausage and the catfish separately in covered containers or plastic bags.*

When Sharon Thompson, who writes about food for the *Lexington Herald-Leader* in Lexington, Kentucky, told us gumbo is one of her favorite Desperate meals, our eyebrows shot up. Gumbo's got to be hard to make, we thought. Think of all those ingredients. Think again. Thanks to Sharon, we started to experiment with gumbos of our own. We've divided the preparation into two parts to make things easier to schedule. Zip through all the cutting and dicing up to a day ahead, then pull out your pot to actually make the soup the next day. This gumbo is hearty enough for even stout appetites and relies on the sweet, farm-raised catfish now readily available in most supermarkets. As is traditional, the gumbo is served over rice.

PHASE 2: 20 MINUTES

3. Melt the butter in the oil in a 6-quart soup pot over medium-high heat. Add the onions; cook until slightly soft, about 3 minutes.

4. Meanwhile, place 2 cups of water in a glass measuring cup, add the bouillon cubes, and microwave on high until the cubes begin to dissolve, about 3 minutes.

5. Add the flour to the soup pot and stir constantly until it starts to brown, 1 to 2 minutes, then add 4 cups of water. Remove the bouillon from the microwave, stir to finish dissolving, and add to the pot. Raise the heat to high and stir to loosen any brown bits from the bottom of the pot. Add the bell pepper and celery pieces. Add the tomatoes with their juice and the garlic, Cajun seasoning, thyme, black pepper, and Worcestershire and Tabasco sauces and cover the pot.

6. When the gumbo comes to a boil, after about 3 minutes, add the sliced sausage to the pot. Add the still-frozen okra and cover the pot again. Let the soup return to a boil, then add the catfish pieces. Reduce the heat to medium and let simmer, uncovered, until the okra is thawed and the fish is opaque and flakes easily with a fork, about 3 minutes. Taste the soup and add more Tabasco sauce, if desired.

7. To serve, place about ¾ cup of hot, cooked rice into each of 8 large soup bowls. Ladle the gumbo over the rice and serve, passing additional Tabasco sauce at the table. *The gumbo can be refrigerated, covered, for up to 24 hours or frozen in a microwave-safe container for up to 1 month. If the gumbo has been frozen, thaw it in a microwave oven on the defrost setting, following the manufacturer's directions. To reheat, place the gumbo in a pot over medium heat and stir frequently, until heated through, about 20 minutes.*

■ *Serves 8*

Notes: Substitute turkey kielbasa for a lower-calorie dish. Turkey kielbasa often comes in 12-ounce packages, which is enough for the gumbo. However, package weights vary from brand to brand and using up to a pound is fine.

Buy frozen okra in a plastic bag rather than a box. It's easier to measure and thaws faster, too.

SANITY SAVER

After cutting onions, rinse your cutting board with bottled lemon juice to remove the onion aroma.

BASIC WHITE RICE

Provided you keep a few guidelines in mind, cooked rice can be refrigerated for up to 24 hours and then reheated. When preparing rice in advance, we prefer to use converted (parboiled) rice since the grains are firmer after cooking and don't clump if a little oil is mixed in. Although conventional wisdom calls for cooking converted rice for 20 minutes, we find it needs to steam for 25 minutes in order to be tender. This recipe serves eight people, allowing for servings of three-quarters of a cup per person as a bed of rice.

2 cups converted rice
¼ teaspoon salt (optional)
2 teaspoons vegetable oil

START TO FINISH: 30 MINUTES

1. Place 4 cups of water in a 3-quart or larger saucepan over high heat, cover, and bring to a boil, about 5 minutes. Add the rice and salt, if using, cover the pot, and reduce the heat to low.

2. Cook the rice for 25 minutes. When done, pour the oil into the pot and fluff the rice with a fork, mixing in the oil.

3. Refrigerate the rice in a microwave-safe container, covered with microwave-safe plastic wrap, for up to 24 hours.

4. To reheat the rice, cut a 1-inch slit in the plastic wrap for a vent. Microwave, covered with the plastic wrap, on high, until the rice is heated through, about 4 minutes, stopping once halfway through to fluff with a fork. Reheating times may vary from microwave to microwave.

■ *Makes 6 cups; serves 8*

Cooking rice is not difficult, still it's a convenient step to get out of the way long before your guests mob the kitchen.

Shrimp Creole à la Beverly

2 large onions (for about 2 cups chopped)

*2 large green bell peppers (for about 3 cups
    bite-size pieces)*

3 large ribs celery (for about 1½ cups chopped)

1 tablespoon butter

1 tablespoon olive oil

4 teaspoons bottled minced garlic

2 bay leaves

1 teaspoon dried thyme

*1 teaspoon Cajun seasoning blend, such as Paul
    Prudhomme's Seafood Magic, or more to taste*

1 teaspoon Worcestershire sauce

¼ teaspoon black pepper

¼ teaspoon Tabasco sauce, or more to taste

1 large can (28 ounces) diced tomatoes

1 large can (15 ounces) tomato sauce

½ cup ketchup

*2 pounds already-peeled medium-size raw shrimp,
    thawed if frozen*

*6 cups hot steamed rice (from 2 cups uncooked
    converted rice; see opposite for cooking instructions),
    for serving*

PHASE 1: 10 MINUTES

1. Peel and coarsely chop the onions. Rinse, core, and seed the bell
peppers. Cut into bite-size pieces. Rinse and coarsely chop the celery.
*The vegetables can be refrigerated, covered, at this point for up to 24
hours. The celery and bell peppers may be stored in the same container.*

PHASE 2: 12 MINUTES

2. Melt the butter in the olive oil in a heavy 4½-quart Dutch oven or
soup pot over medium-high heat. Add the chopped onions and cook,

From Beverly:

Some sauces improve
with freezing or being
refrigerated for a day, and
shrimp Creole sauce is a star
in this category. I like to
make double batches to
freeze for entertaining on the
spur of the moment. It's my
favorite secret weapon.

Don't let looks deceive.
This recipe has several phases,
but it is not a difficult dish.
Flexibility is the main reason
for these phases. If you make
the sauce ahead and reheat it,
dinner can be ready to serve
just 10 minutes after your
guests arrive. In keeping with
custom, the Creole is served
over hot rice.

MONEY SAVER

Stretch fancy foods
such as shrimp
by serving them in a
sauce over rice or pasta.
Add extra vegetables,
too, and think of the
expensive item almost
as a garnish.

stirring frequently, until the onions soften and begin to brown, about 6 minutes. (If the onions begin browning very fast, reduce the heat to medium.)

3. Add the chopped bell peppers and celery and reduce the heat to medium, if you have not already done so. Continue to cook, stirring frequently, until the celery softens, about 5 minutes. Meanwhile, add the garlic, bay leaves, thyme, Cajun seasoning, Worcestershire sauce, black pepper, and Tabasco sauce. *The vegetable mixture can be refrigerated, covered, at this point for up to 24 hours.*

PHASE 3: 25 MINUTES MOSTLY UNATTENDED COOKING TIME

4. Return the vegetable mixture to the pot. Add the diced tomatoes with their juice, the tomato sauce, and ketchup to the vegetable mixture. Place the pot over medium-high heat, bring the sauce to a boil, then reduce the heat to medium-low. Let simmer, uncovered, stirring frequently, until the vegetables are soft and the flavors are well blended, about 20 minutes. Taste the sauce and add more Cajun seasoning or Tabasco sauce, if desired. *The sauce can be refrigerated, covered, at this point for up to 24 hours or frozen for up to 1 month. If the sauce has been frozen, thaw it in a microwave oven on the defrost setting, following the manufacturer's directions. To reheat, place the sauce over medium heat and stir frequently, until it comes to a moderate boil, about 20 minutes.*

PHASE 4: ABOUT 10 MINUTES

5. Bring the sauce back to a boil. Add the shrimp. Cook at a moderate boil, stirring frequently, until the shrimp are pink and opaque throughout, 7 to 10 minutes depending on the size of the shrimp. Remove and discard the bay leaves. Serve the shrimp Creole at once over hot steamed rice.

■ *Serves 8*

SANITY SAVER

Deck and patio safety should always be observed. Especially when children are included, plastic ware is the best bet, avoiding the chance of a broken plate or glass. Discount and mart stores carry reuseable plastic ware in a wide variety of colors with stemware to match.

PICK A PLACE TO EAT

Choosing a menu for guests is a lot easier if you first decide where you'll eat the meal. Got a tiny dining room but a spacious deck? Plan to invite friends over during temperate seasons and serve casual dinners outside.

Even if your dining room is mammoth, you may not want to use it. Some of our friends never use theirs except on Thanksgiving. The atmosphere is just too formal for them, and the hosts tend to feel impelled to make the food match the surroundings. Instead, if a big game on TV is the evening's entertainment, they offer up lap trays in the living room. They say it's easier and a lot more fun.

Once you've chosen a space for dining, let it dictate the menu. Eating spaghetti on a bamboo tray wouldn't be the wisest choice, but a bowl of chili will work just fine. Entrées that don't need cutting and are easy to transport from the plate to the mouth, foods that don't drip or slosh, and things that don't generate many crumbs fit the general guidelines when guests are balancing trays as they eat.

When you're eating on the porch or deck, grilled sausages or chicken enchiladas take on a festive feel. Even if you don't have a deck, colorful blankets spread on the lawn create excitement. Everyone loves a picnic, and you don't need a park to throw one.

Eating outdoors, however, pits you against the weather. Depending on where you live, you'll want to avoid entertaining in the times of year that bring things like hurricanes, snow, large mosquito populations, and extreme heat. In North Carolina, the combination of all of these means we have only about two optimal months in the fall and two in the spring, but we consciously plan to gather friends on the patio during both those times of year. Particularly when children are involved, entertaining outside can be the easiest way to go. There's a host of menu choices in our salads chapter (beginning on page 188) and cookout chapter (beginning on page 150) that would be easy to serve outdoors.

No matter where you choose to dine, when you match the menu to the surroundings, you can serve up a fabulous feast that will please everyone.

Pick your season, pick your space, and the menu will fall into place.

Sometimes called Frogmore stew, this South Carolina Lowcountry classic is a delicious, informal, easy-on-the-cook dinner that company always enjoys. Make it during the summer when the corn is sweet and fresh. The shrimp boil calls for big paper napkins and cold beer or a friendly white wine, such as a pinot grigio or pinot gris. Since guests peel their own shrimp at the table, nothing fancy is allowed. (We've been known to cover the table with newspapers.) Be sure to put some bowls out for collecting the shrimp shells.

Our friend Felicia Gressette, a South Carolina native and former food editor of *The Miami Herald,* graciously supplied this recipe. She says you can scale the stew up or down according to the number of guests you're having. The "hardest" thing for the cook to do is shuck the corn, so when we're really desperate, we substitute frozen ears. Felicia serves the stew with cocktail sauce, a big green salad, a platter of sliced ripe tomatoes, and crusty garlic bread.

Felicia's Lowcountry Boil

8 ears fresh or frozen corn
16 small red potatoes
2 pounds kielbasa or other spicy smoked sausage
1 or 2 boxes (3 ounces each) crab-and-shrimp boil
  (see Notes)
3 pounds medium-size raw shrimp, unpeeled,
  thawed if frozen

PHASE 1: 15 MINUTES

1. If using fresh corn, shuck the ears and remove the silks. Rinse and scrub the potatoes but do not peel them. Cut the sausage into 2-inch pieces. *The shucked corn, potatoes, and sausage can be refrigerated, covered, at this point for up to 12 hours. Place the corn in a zipper-top plastic bag and store the potatoes and sausage together in a covered container.*

PHASE 2: 25 MINUTES MOSTLY UNATTENDED COOKING TIME

2. About 25 minutes before you plan to begin cooking the stew, fill a 10-quart stock pot with water to a depth of about 5 inches. (Or, about 11 minutes ahead, fill two 6-quart pots to a depth of about 3½ inches.) Add the crab-and-shrimp boil (if you're using 2 pots, you'll need 2 boxes), cover, and bring to a boil over high heat (see Notes).

PHASE 3: 20 MINUTES

3. Add the potatoes to the stock pot, cover, and let boil for about 10 minutes. Add the kielbasa chunks, cover, and cook about 5 minutes more. Add the corn (fresh or frozen), cover, and cook a minute or two longer. Add the shrimp (with the shells still attached) and, using a long-handled wooden spoon, shift the contents so that the shrimp settle into the hot spicy water. Cover the pot and turn off the heat. The shrimp will be done when they are pink and opaque throughout, about 3 minutes. Don't overcook.

4. Remove the crab boil bag, if using, and discard. To serve, use tongs to remove the corn and pile it at one end of a big platter. With a slotted spoon, remove the remaining ingredients and place them on the platter. Serve at once.

■ *Serves 8*

Notes: Although we generally use Old Bay seafood seasoning, Felicia prefers Zatarain's brand of crab-and-shrimp boil for this recipe because it's less peppery. The kind sold in a box has all the spices in a mesh bag, which can be easily removed and discarded before serving.

Some people like to add a bottle of beer to the cooking water; others squeeze in a fresh lemon or lime. If desired, add any of these at the same time you add the crab-and-shrimp boil.

CONTAINERS OF YOUR DREAMS

From Beverly:

If your plate or bowl is interesting enough, no other froufrou is necessary to make food look good. One of my favorite bowls for salsa has a pottery frog perched along the rim, and it never fails as a conversation piece. Likewise, the pattern on a pottery plate my sister-in-law brought me from Italy is so intricate it's a garnish in and of itself. Another sister-in-law gave me an olive bowl that has a built-in compartment for the pits. Again, it's always eye-catching.

In addition to hinting around just before your birthday, there are several ways to go about collecting interesting serving pieces. Watch for price reductions in department stores; check "junktique" stores and even estate sales and tag sales. (Someone else's cast-off wedding gift may strike your fancy.) Stores that specialize in mass-produced American pottery sometimes yield surprising finds. In addition, check national outlets that carry overstocked and discontinued merchandise and offer substantial discounts.

The wonderful flavors of Frogmore stew, a summertime seafood boil that's traditional in South Carolina, taste even better when you add some chicken and onions to make a soup for all seasons. No need to wait for picnic table weather; pass out the spoons and dig in.

The soup is so flexible that you can add other similar vegetables or omit any of the vegetables, or the kielbasa or chicken, and still be pleased with the result. It's true to its roots, in a Lowcountry "throw it in if you have it" manner. Now that's good eating!

Winter Frogmore Soup

1 tablespoon olive oil
2 large onions (for about 2 cups chopped)
2 pounds red potatoes (for about 4 cups bite-size pieces)
1 pound kielbasa
2 cans or bottles (12 ounces each) light-bodied beer
3 cups frozen corn kernels
2 tablespoons seafood seasoning, such as Old Bay
½ teaspoon salt
¼ teaspoon black pepper
2 skinless, boneless chicken breast halves
  (about ⅔ pound total)
1 pound already-peeled medium-size raw shrimp,
  thawed if frozen
Tabasco sauce

PHASE 1: 30 MINUTES

1. Heat the olive oil in a 4½-quart Dutch oven or soup pot over medium heat. Peel and coarsely chop the onions, adding them to the pot as you chop. Cook for 3 to 4 minutes until slightly soft. Meanwhile, rinse and scrub the potatoes. Cut them into bite-size pieces but do not peel them. Add them to the pot with the onions. Stir from time to time. Slice the kielbasa into ¼-inch thick slices and add them to the pot as you slice.

2. Add the beer and 3 cups of water to the pot. Raise the heat to high, cover, and bring to a boil. Add the still-frozen corn, seafood seasoning, salt, and pepper, removing the lid as briefly as possible. When the mixture returns to a boil, reduce the heat to medium, maintaining a slow boil. Continue to cook until the potatoes are fork tender, about 10 minutes longer. *The soup can be refrigerated, covered, at this point for up to 24 hours. Let cool to room temperature before placing it in the refrigerator.*

PHASE 2: 20 MINUTES

3. Place the chicken breasts in a 3-quart or larger pot. Add just enough cold water to cover, about 1 cup. Cover the pot and bring to a rolling boil over high heat, about 5 minutes. As soon as the water boils, remove the pot from the heat and let stand, covered, until the chicken is no longer pink in the center, about 15 minutes. Remove the chicken from the pot and let cool, then shred using 2 forks. Discard the broth or reserve for another use. *The shredded chicken can be refrigerated, covered, for up to 24 hours.*

PHASE 3: 15 MINUTES

4. Return the soup to the soup pot and bring to a boil over medium-high heat, about 10 minutes. When the soup is boiling, add the shredded chicken and the shrimp and cook until the shrimp are pink and opaque throughout, about 3 to 4 minutes. Remove from the heat. Serve the soup in bowls with Tabasco sauce on the side.

■ *Serves 8*

MONEY SAVER

When calling to invite guests over for dinner, you'll often get the question, "What can I bring?" Your first response may be, "Oh nothing," but some guests will insist. A good suggestion for guests such as these is an interesting hunk of cheese, some in-season fruit, or perhaps a bottle of wine or a six-pack of beer. It makes guests feel better to bring something, it's easy, and it saves on your expenses.

CHAPTER FOUR

The Good Ol'

From Alicia:

When I got married, my wish list included the standard small appliances: a food processor, a blender, a mixer, and a Crock-Pot. After all, Mom had used her slow cooker for years, lugging it to church potlucks and deck parties, filled with hot, ready-to-serve beans, chili, or stews.

Well, I got my requested Crock-Pot, the ultramodern kind with removable crock in a lovely taupe and brown with olive green highlights (this was more than fifteen years ago, mind you). It stayed in the box for years; all sealed up with the packaging still intact and a stray piece of white wrapping paper still taped to the box. I moved it into our first house, then to the next, still in the original box.

Five years later when we were turning the spare bedroom into a nursery, I came across that slow cooker. Should I sell it in a yard sale with other unused wedding presents? Or if I actually put it in my kitchen, would I use it? I called my mom for a few recipes, thinking that since my life was going to include children, I might want to rethink the benefits of slow cooking in a Crock-Pot.

I use the slow cooker the same way my mom did, keeping soup hot for the Teacher Appreciation Day luncheon, carting along chili for the fourth grade hot dog bash, or simmering "baked" beans before the church social and potluck. But once I actually started cooking regularly in the crock, even for

Crock-Pot

guests, I frankly couldn't believe I had managed without it for as long as I did. Now I own two new, sleek stainless steel-looking Crock-Pots I'm not embarrassed to have on the counter top.

The preparations for most of our slow cooker recipes are quick and easy, taking less than 20 minutes. For all of our recipes that include meat, there's no need to brown it first. Chop an onion, measure out a few spices, dump them in the pot, and then it's a matter of putting on the lid and leaving the smart appliance to do the real work. It's the perfect way to get that slow-cooked taste we thought we had to give up. All without stressing out the cook. Now there's no problem making everything from Great-Grandma's Beef Stew to Carolina Crock-Pot Barbecue.

Whether you need to purchase a new Crock-Pot (see page 131 for advice) or you have an old gift you've barely used, we encourage you to experiment and discover the wonders of slow cooking for your guests.

Not selling this precious piece of equipment was one of the best kitchen decisions I have ever made.

From Alicia:

One step through the front door and you know something good is happening in the kitchen when this roast is cooking. But when I asked a group of friends what they thought about pot roast as an entertaining recipe, they almost all said they remembered it as one of their mothers' standby recipes yet hardly ever cooked it themselves. Time constraints or the notion that a simple pot roast was a bit plain for entertaining were the biggest obstacles to sharing this easy-to-prepare dish with friends and family.

The robust flavor of fresh rosemary is reason enough to resurrect this old-fashioned way to feed a crowd. But a Desperate Cook's real salvation is that it takes less than 20 minutes to get the roast into the pot—Crock-Pot, that is. The meat becomes unbelievably tender in the slow cooker and children love the carrots and potatoes. Our thanks go to our friend Julie Realon for turning us on to the amazing flavors of this roast.

Simmered and Sumptuous

New Old-Fashioned Pot Roast

1 chuck roast (4 to 5 pounds)
3 medium-size onions
2 cups (about 24) already-peeled baby carrots
8 medium-size potatoes
½ cup ketchup
¼ cup red wine vinegar
2 tablespoons Worcestershire sauce
1 teaspoon salt
3 tablespoons fresh rosemary leaves, or 1 tablespoon
   dried rosemary

START TO FINISH: 16 MINUTES, PLUS 8 TO 10 HOURS UNATTENDED COOKING TIME

1. Trim off and discard any excess fat from the roast and place it in the bottom of a 5-quart or larger slow cooker. Peel and thinly slice the onions, adding them to the pot as you slice. Add the carrots to the pot. Rinse, peel, and quarter the potatoes, adding them to the pot.

2. In a 4-quart container or glass measure, combine the ketchup, vinegar, Worcestershire sauce, salt, and ½ cup water. Mix well. Pour over the roast and vegetables. Sprinkle the rosemary over the roast and cover the pot. Cook on low for 8 to 10 hours. When done, the roast and vegetables will be very tender. To serve, spoon a portion of meat and vegetables into each of 8 shallow bowls or pasta plates.

■ *Serves 8*

Alternative Cooking Method: If you don't have a slow cooker, heat 1 tablespoon of vegetable oil in an extra-deep, 12-inch nonstick skillet over medium-high heat and brown the roast on both sides. Mix together the sauce ingredients and pour over the roast. Peel and slice the onions and add them and the rosemary to the skillet. Reduce the heat to low and cook, covered, for 2 hours.

Add the carrots to the pot. Rinse, peel, and quarter the potatoes, add them to the pot, and cook for 1 more hour.

DO-AHEAD

The cooked roast and vegetables can be refrigerated for up to 2 days. To reheat, slice the meat into serving portions, place these in a large skillet or Dutch oven, and heat with the vegetables over medium-low heat, stirring occasionally, until heated through, about 30 minutes.

ABOUT BUYING A SLOW COOKER

A slow cooker is one electrical appliance every Desperate Cook should own, and like most appliances, they are being updated all the time. Slow cookers are available everywhere from discount stores to fancy kitchen shops, and you can pay anywhere from $40 to $80 for one.

We like the large, 6-quart capacity, oval-shaped slow cookers for their flexibility with recipe quantities and their ability to hold large cuts of meat. Look for one that has a crock that can be removed from the heating element.

"Programmable" slow cookers will switch to a warm setting after the selected cooking time is finished (for example after 8 hours of cooking on the setting low, the slow cooker switches to warm). It is not recommended that you use the warm setting for longer than 4 hours.

For more information about using slow cookers, see pages 135 and 149.

From Beverly:

I wasn't quite prepared for her answer when I asked my mother, Dot Mills, for the beef stew recipe I had loved as a child. "I don't really have a recipe," Mom explained. "I just make it the way your great-grandmother used to." After some experimenting and several long-distance telephone conferences, we've gotten as close as we can to a recipe for that original flavor.

As always, Alicia and I couldn't resist adding our own modern touches as well as techniques. Great-grandmother and Mom made their beef stew on the stove top (see the alternative cooking method following the recipe). But keeping an eye on a pot for 3½ hours doesn't always fit our schedules, so we added onion soup mix for depth and transposed the recipe into the Crock-Pot. Now, with only 15 minutes of actual work, we can enjoy the dish I remember from childhood.

You'll swear it took a team of cooks to make this meaty stew brimming with the sweet flavor of onions. Serve it over hot steamed rice, just like Great-grandma did.

Great-Grandma's Beef Stew

4 pounds well-marbled beef cubes for stew
4 large onions (for about 4 cups slices)
1 envelope (1 ounce) dry onion soup mix, such as Lipton
1 teaspoon black pepper
½ teaspoon dried sage
½ cup cornstarch
About ¼ cup densely packed fresh parsley
6 cups hot cooked rice (from 2 cups uncooked converted rice; see page 120 for cooking instructions), for serving

START TO FINISH: 15 MINUTES, PLUS 8 TO 10 HOURS UNATTENDED COOKING TIME

1. Place the beef cubes in the bottom of a 5-quart or larger slow cooker. Peel the onions and slice them into crescent-shaped strips, about ¼ inch wide, adding them to the pot as you slice. Add the soup mix, pepper, sage, and 3 cups water and stir to mix well. Cover the pot and cook on low for 8 to 10 hours.

2. Shortly before you are ready to serve, mix the cornstarch with ½ cup of water in a jar with a lid and shake vigorously to mix. Drizzle half of the cornstarch mixture over the stew and stir to thicken. Add more if necessary, until the liquid in the stew is slightly thicker than heavy cream.

3. Rinse the parsley well and shake the leaves to remove any excess water. Remove and discard the tough stems but do not worry about the smaller, upper stems. You should have about ¼ cup of leaves. Chop the parsley and stir into the stew. Serve over hot steamed rice.

■ *Serves 8 generously*

Alternative Cooking Method: If you don't have a slow cooker, peel and slice the onions into ¼-inch wide crescent-shaped strips. Heat 1 tablespoon of vegetable oil in a 5-quart Dutch oven or soup pot over medium-high heat. Brown one quarter of the onion slices and the beef cubes. Add the remaining onions, onion soup mix, pepper, sage, and 3 cups water and stir to mix. Let come to a boil, then reduce the heat to low and simmer until the beef cubes are so tender that they fall apart, about 3½ hours, then proceed with Steps 2 and 3.

Beef Stew Mexicana

4 pounds well-marbled beef cubes for stew
2 teaspoons sugar
1 teaspoon chili powder
½ teaspoon ground cumin
½ teaspoon salt
1 cinnamon stick (3 inches long)
½ lime
1 can (14½ ounces) Mexican-style stewed tomatoes
    (see page 51) or diced tomatoes seasoned with
    jalapeño or chile peppers
1 tablespoon bottled minced garlic
2 large onions
½ large red or green bell pepper (for about ½ cup
    bite-size pieces)
About ½ cup densely packed fresh cilantro
1 can (14½ ounces) fat-free beef broth
¼ cup cornstarch
6 cups hot cooked rice (from 2 cups uncooked
    converted rice; see page 120 for cooking
    instructions), for serving

START TO FINISH: 20 MINUTES, PLUS 8 TO 9 HOURS MOSTLY UNATTENDED COOKING TIME

1. Place the beef cubes in the bottom of a 5-quart or larger slow cooker. Sprinkle the sugar, chili powder, cumin, and salt over the beef. Place the cinnamon stick on top of the beef. Squeeze the juice from the lime half into the pot. Add the tomatoes with their juice.

There are occasions when you'd like to have friends over, but the day's agenda just doesn't allow you to be at home to prepare. That's when it's time to pull out the slow cooker, plug it in, and be on your way. With this recipe, what you'll find when you return (at least a few minutes before your guests arrive, we hope) is a fabulous stew. Regular beef stew is wonderful for entertaining, especially on a weeknight. Spice it up a bit with an international flair and suddenly the ordinary becomes exotic any day of the week. Our blend of chili powder, cumin, and spicy tomatoes makes for a remarkable depth. If you like a real kick in your Mexican dishes, add a chopped fresh jalapeño pepper or some Tabasco sauce. Serve the stew over hot, steamed rice.

133

2. Sprinkle the garlic over the tomatoes. Peel and cut the onions into bite-size pieces. Scatter the pieces evenly over the mixture in the pot. Rinse, core, and seed the bell pepper half; cut it into bite-size pieces. Scatter these evenly over the onions.

3. Rinse the cilantro and shake the leaves to remove any excess water. Remove and discard any tough stems but do not worry about the smaller, upper stems. You should have about ½ cup of leaves. Coarsely chop the leaves and add them to the pot. Add the beef broth. Cover the pot and cook on low heat for 8 to 9 hours.

4. Up to 1 hour before serving the stew, remove and discard the cinnamon stick. Mix the cornstarch and ¼ cup water in a jar that has a lid. Shake well to break up any lumps. Pour a little of the cornstarch mixture evenly over the hot stew. Stir gently from time to time, adding more cornstarch mixture as necessary, until the liquid in the stew is slightly thicker than heavy cream, about 5 minutes. Serve the stew over hot rice.

■ *Serves 8*

Alternative Cooking Method: If you don't have a slow cooker, preheat the oven to 275°F. Prepare the onions, bell pepper, and cilantro as described in Steps 2 and 3. Place all of the ingredients for the stew except the cornstarch in a 5-quart Dutch oven or covered casserole dish. Cover the Dutch oven and place it in the middle of the hot oven. Bake until the beef is fork-tender and cooked through, 4½ to 5 hours. To thicken the stew, heat the Dutch oven over medium-high heat. Bring the stew to a slow boil and proceed with the directions in Step 4. Stir gently from time to time until the stew is thick, about 2 to 3 minutes.

DO-AHEAD

The stew can be refrigerated, covered, for up to 2 days or it can be frozen for up to 1 month in a microwave-safe container. Do not thicken it before freezing.
• If the stew has been frozen, thaw it in a microwave oven on the defrost setting, following the manufacturer's directions.
• To reheat, place the stew in a large pot over medium heat and stir frequently until it is heated through, about 20 minutes. Once the stew is hot, proceed to thicken it as described in Step 4.

ABOUT CROCK-POTS AND THIS BOOK

The slow cooker recipes in this book were tested in a Rival Crock-Pot. The Rival corporation was the first and is the biggest manufacturer of slow cookers, and the name Crock-Pot is its registered trademark. Other brands can have different settings and, therefore, the temperatures the crocks maintain may vary. All of our recipes can be prepared in other slow cookers, but you may have to adjust the cooking time. We've given a time range for each recipe to help you do this.

Each manufacturer provides an instruction booklet that gives you guidelines for cooking. Please read the manufacturer's instructions and warnings carefully before using your slow cooker.

Rival's Crock-Pots generally register 200°F when set on low and 300°F on high. Use this as a point of comparison for your slow cooker. Here's how to test its temperature: Fill the pot with 8 cups of cold water, cover the crock with the lid, and run the cooker on low heat for 8 hours. Then, check the temperature of the water with an accurate thermometer. If the water temperature is about 185°F, the low temperature of your pot is comparable to that of the Crock-Pot. If it is higher than 200°F, you may need to adjust your cooking times to allow for the hotter temperature. It's difficult to overcook a dish in a slow cooker, but check meat dishes after 8 hours to see if they are fork-tender. If your slow cooker runs at a lower temperature than a Rival, you may need to let things cook for the maximum length of time we've indicated in our recipes.

You'll find more pointers on using slow cookers on page 149.

Not all slow cookers are identical. They may cook at different temperatures.

Stifado with Artichokes

In traditional Greek cooking, the *stifado* style refers to using equal amounts of meat and small white onions, often called pearl onions. However, since peeling these tiny onions is extremely time-consuming, we've opted to use small regular onions, either white or yellow. That makes this stew exceptionally easy to put together in just 15 minutes. (Don't worry about the lengthy ingredient list. You just dump everything in. Then you let the Crock-Pot do the rest.) Our *stifado* is not just another ho-hum stew. A jolt of cinnamon, cloves, and red wine makes for an aromatic, delightfully exotic dish. We like to serve it over hot steamed rice, but for a slightly different twist, try it over the rice-shaped pasta called orzo (see page 88 for pasta cooking instructions).

4 pounds well-marbled beef cubes for stew
1 cinnamon stick (3 inches long)
1 bay leaf
3 whole cloves
2 tablespoons raisins
½ cup dry red wine
1 can (6 ounces) tomato paste
1 tablespoon bottled minced garlic
1 tablespoon firmly packed light brown sugar
1 tablespoon red wine vinegar
1 teaspoon black pepper
1 teaspoon ground cumin
1 teaspoon dried oregano
6 small onions
2 cups already-peeled baby carrots
1 can (14½ ounces) diced tomatoes seasoned with garlic and onions
1 can (13¾ ounces) artichoke hearts packed in water, or 1 package (9 ounces) frozen artichoke hearts
Salt
¼ cup cornstarch, if necessary
6 cups hot cooked rice (from 2 cups uncooked converted rice; see page 120 for cooking instructions), for serving

START TO FINISH: 15 MINUTES, PLUS 8 TO 9 HOURS UNATTENDED COOKING TIME

1. Place the beef cubes in the bottom of a 5-quart or larger slow cooker. Place the cinnamon stick, bay leaf, cloves, and raisins on top of the meat. Measure the wine in a 2-cup measure. Add the tomato paste to the wine and whisk to blend. Add the garlic, brown sugar, vinegar, pepper, cumin, and oregano to the tomato paste mixture. Stir to mix well, then pour over the meat.

2. Peel and quarter the onions and scatter them over the tomato paste mixture. Add the carrots and the tomatoes with their juice. Drain the artichokes and scatter them on top of the carrots and tomatoes. (If you are using frozen artichokes, rinse them with warm water just long enough to break apart, then add to the pot.)

3. Cover the pot and cook on low for 8 to 9 hours. Remove and discard the cinnamon stick, bay leaf, and cloves. Season with salt to taste. Stir gently before serving to be sure the tomato paste is well incorporated.

4. The stew should be thick but if it has not reached the desired thickness, mix the cornstarch with ¼ cup of water in a jar that has a lid. Shake well to break up any lumps. Pour a little of the cornstarch mixture evenly over the stew. Stir gently from time to time, adding more cornstarch mixture as necessary, until the liquid in the stew is slightly thicker than heavy cream, about 5 minutes. Serve the stew over hot cooked rice.

■ *Serves 8*

Alternative Cooking Method: If you don't have a slow cooker, preheat the oven to 275°F. Peel and quarter the onions. If using frozen artichokes, rinse them with warm water just long enough to break apart. Place all of the ingredients for the stew except the cornstarch in a 5-quart Dutch oven or covered casserole dish. Cover the Dutch oven and place it in the middle of the hot oven. Bake until the beef is fork-tender and cooked through, 4½ to 5 hours. If you want a thicker sauce, heat the Dutch oven on the stove over medium-high heat. Bring the stew to a slow boil and proceed with the directions in Step 4. Stir gently from time to time until the stew is thick, about 2 to 3 minutes.

DO-AHEAD

The stew can be refrigerated, covered, for up to 2 days or it can be frozen for up to 1 month in a microwave-safe container. Do not thicken it before freezing.
• If the stew has been frozen, thaw it in a microwave oven on the defrost setting, following the manufacturer's directions.
• To reheat, place the stew in a large pot over medium heat and stir frequently until heated through, about 20 minutes. Once the stew is hot, proceed to thicken it as described in Step 4, if necessary.

THE POKER PARTY

From Beverly:

My favorite dinner party of all time got started because my husband's family loves to play poker. At family reunions over the years the rest of us in-laws joined in, and what I learned was a bit surprising.

First of all, after-dinner games of poker—family style anyway—aren't really about gambling. You don't lose the grocery money when you play for nickels, a revelation that came as an enormous relief to me. What mainly happens around our poker table is that, as everyone concentrates on the cards, people let down their usual defenses and start being themselves. You find out exactly who's competitive, who's sly, and who's always lucky. At the same time, you'll get plenty of jokes, good-humored ribbing, and sideline conversations about topics you'd never imagined discussing. By the end of the night, you know all the guests so much better than if you'd just stuck to polite dinner conversation.

Our family poker games worked so well, I started to wonder what it would be like to play with other folks. My husband had been wanting to invite some co-workers for dinner, but I had been resisting because I figured all anybody would talk about the whole night was the office. But what if we invited them over for poker?

The first attempt was so successful we decided to repeat the party—menu and all—a couple of weeks later for another group. Poker parties continue to be one of our favorite ways to entertain folks we want to get to know better. If you'd like to try one, here are a few tricks we've learned along the way.

• The only real requirement for a poker party is that at least one person in the group knows how to play. (If for some reason poker just won't fly with your family or friends, there are lots of other fun card and board games that provide a similar after-dinner atmosphere (see page 107 for more suggestions).

• Make sure you tell guests it's a poker party when you issue the invitation. Expect that at least one or two will protest that they don't know how to play. Promise them it doesn't matter. (It doesn't.)

You'll have a good time together, and it's a lot easier than, say, going hang gliding.

• Prepare a poker cheat sheet for the beginners. This is a list that details in order the combinations of cards that win. Run through a couple of practice rounds at the beginning of the night, and before long everyone will be a card shark.

• If you're not a poker expert, either, but you're game to try, just pick up a book on card game rules. There are lots of quirky poker variations that can keep the evening interesting, and the books explain them all.

• You need four people for a good round of poker but seven at the table is the maximum. If you have eight or more, set up two tables and have folks rotate places halfway through the evening to mix up the conversation opportunities.

• It's nice to have at least two decks of cards at each table so you don't have to sit around waiting for someone to shuffle.

• Plastic poker chips don't cost much, and they're available at game shops and discount stores. If you're not ready to invest, use macaroni noodles or other short pasta. Dried beans and pennies make good poker chips, too.

• If anyone happens to express discomfort at the idea of gambling, suggest that the jackpot be donated to the winner's favorite charity at the end of the night. Or just "forget" to cash in the noodles and then there's no out of pocket expense.

From Alicia:

I'm all for ground beef burritos for midweek family meals. But when I serve guests, I love something a bit beefier. When our Crock-Pot roast turned out so beautifully (see page 130), I knew the answer to my beef burrito dilemma was solved. A large chuck roast is just the thing for that traditional shredded beef texture I crave. Perfectly seasoned, but not too spicy, these burritos will not leave your guests wondering "Where's the beef?"

If tacos are more your style, this recipe is perfect for them, too. Crisp taco shells in the oven at the very last minute and let your guests fill them directly from the pot to avoid soggy shells.

DO-AHEAD

Shredded beef will hold on low in the Crock-Pot for up to 2 hours before serving. Or the beef can be prepared completely up to 24 hours ahead and refrigerated, covered. To reheat, place the shredded beef with its sauce in a pot over medium-low heat until heated through, about 20 minutes. Stir occasionally.

Big Beefy Burritos

1 chuck roast (4 to 5 pounds)
1 tablespoon chili powder
1 teaspoon ground cumin
1 teaspoon onion powder
1 teaspoon garlic powder
2 cans (14½ ounces each) Mexican-style stewed
   tomatoes (see page 51) or diced tomatoes seasoned
   with jalapeño or chile peppers
8 large flour tortillas (10 to 12 inches each)
1 cup already-shredded Mexican blend cheese
Other assorted garnishes, such as sour cream, chopped
   tomato, Guiltless Guacamole (see page 48), Roasted Garlic
   Salsa (see page 50), and/or shredded lettuce

**PHASE 1: 5 MINUTES, PLUS 8 TO 10 HOURS
UNATTENDED COOKING TIME**

1. Trim off and discard any excess fat from the roast and place it in the bottom of a 5-quart or larger slow cooker. Sprinkle the chili powder, cumin, and onion and garlic powders over the roast. Add the tomatoes with their juice and cover the pot. Cook on low for 8 to 10 hours.

PHASE 2: 10 MINUTES

2. Shred the cooked beef using two forks and stir well. Place 1 tortilla on each of 8 serving plates. Spoon some of the meat mixture in the center of each tortilla and top with the garnishes of your choice. Fold the tortillas over the filling, tucking in one end only, and serve.

■ *Serves 8*

Alternative Cooking Method: If you don't have a slow cooker, heat 1 tablespoon of vegetable oil in an extra-deep, 12-inch nonstick skillet over medium-high heat and brown the roast on both sides. Mix together the sauce ingredients and pour over the roast. Reduce the heat to medium-low and cook, covered, for 3 hours. When the roast is very tender, proceed with the directions in Step 2.

KID-FRIENDLY IDEAS

From Alicia:

Have you ever met someone who seems perfectly at peace even when surrounded by complete chaos? My friend Sharon Gustafson is just like that. Whether it's a ninth birthday party for fifteen of her daughter's closest friends or an hors d'oeuvre party for forty during the ACC basketball playoffs, Sharon is in her element when it comes to entertaining. While I really enjoy a big party of adults, the pandemonium kids can create amazes me. I often joke about wanting to be like Sharon when I grow up. But until that time, I can take note and copy her. Imitation is still the highest form of flattery, right?

Sharon's secret, I think, is that she diffuses situations before they get out of hand. So as the kids arrive at her door she immediately directs them to the kitchen table or out to the deck to decorate their drinking cups for the night. Sometimes it's just dressing up a bright-colored Solo cup with assorted stickers to make it that wonderful masterpiece. Or maybe it's using paint pens to make intricate designs on wacky straw cups. Marking the cups for sipping all night is a particularly smart tactic when multiple children are around.

Simple arts and crafts are always a hit with children, and adults can enjoy them, too. Beverly and I threw a Halloween party once where everyone decorated a Mardi Gras-style mask before dinner and then wore it out to trick-or-treat.

Whatever diversion you choose, it's a way to channel the eagerness (or help with the shyness) of the children as they enter the party. Plus, who would think that a few stickers and children's names written for them in permanent marker could make such a difference? But my children always want to take home their special cups whether they last past breakfast the next morning or not.

> *The key with children, we've learned, is to keep it simple.*

Here's a special version of our favorite tomato sauce for midwinter when the fresh tomatoes are only a pale imitation of the real thing. Onions, garlic, and fresh basil infuse canned tomatoes with a bright flavor that's not overly sweet, and the food processor makes quick work of all the chopping. Everything goes into the slow cooker in a flash, then you can be on your way. A long simmer is perfect for producing moist, tender meatballs. The sauce also can be cooked ahead and frozen. When your guests arrive, they'll be greeted with the ultimate in comfort food— spaghetti and meatballs. They'll think they've been transported to Italy. Even though tradition dictates spaghetti, we also love this dish over short pasta, such as penne or rotini, which is easier for kids to manage.

Our Favorite Spaghetti and Meatballs

4 cloves garlic

2 medium-size onions

About ½ cup densely packed fresh basil

2 cans (28 ounces each) crushed tomatoes

1 large can (15 ounces) tomato sauce

1 tablespoon extra-virgin olive oil

½ teaspoon dried oregano

2 teaspoons sugar

¼ teaspoon black pepper

1⅔ pounds frozen meatballs (each about 1¼ inches in diameter)

1 package (1 pound) spaghetti or other pasta of your choice, cooked (see page 88 for cooking instructions), for serving

Already-grated Parmesan cheese, for serving

START TO FINISH: 15 MINUTES, PLUS 7 TO 9 HOURS UNATTENDED COOKING TIME

1. Peel the garlic, drop the garlic cloves 1 at a time through the feed tube of a food processor with the machine running, and finely chop. Peel the onions, cut them into quarters, and drop the pieces through the feed tube with the machine running and finely chop. Put the garlic-onion mixture in a 5-quart or larger slow cooker.

2. Rinse the basil well and shake to remove any excess water. Remove and discard any tough stems. You should have about ½ cup of leaves. Drop the basil through the feed tube of the processor with the machine running and finely chop. Add the chopped basil to the pot with the garlic onion mixture.

3. Add the tomatoes and their juice, tomato sauce, olive oil, oregano, sugar, pepper, and still-frozen meatballs to the slow cooker. Stir to mix well, making sure all of the meatballs are covered with sauce.

4. Cover the pot and cook on low for 7 to 9 hours.

5. Serve the sauce and meatballs over hot, drained pasta. Pass grated Parmesan at the table to sprinkle on top.

■ *Serves 8 generously*

Alternative Cooking Method: If you don't have a slow cooker, prepare the garlic, onions, and basil as described in Steps 1 and 2. Place all of the ingredients for the sauce in a 5-quart or larger pot. Cover the pot, place it over medium-high heat, and bring the sauce to a boil. Uncover the pot, stir well, and reduce the heat to maintain a very slow boil. Simmer, uncovered, until the sauce has thickened, 1 hour to 1 hour and 10 minutes. Stir about every 20 minutes to prevent sticking.

Carolina Crock-Pot Barbecue

1 pork loin roast (3½ to 4 pounds)
1 cup bottled barbecue sauce, plus additional sauce, for serving

START TO FINISH: 5 MINUTES, PLUS 8 TO 10 HOURS UNATTENDED COOKING TIME

1. Trim any visible fat from the pork and cut the roast in half. Place the roast halves side by side in the bottom of a 5-quart or larger slow cooker. Pour the sauce over the pork and cover the pot. Cook on low 8 to 10 hours or until an instant-read meat thermometer inserted in a roast half registers at least 160°F.

2. When the pork is done, use 2 forks to pull the meat into shreds (the meat should be very tender, so this will be easy to do).

3. Serve at once with additional sauce to pass at the table.

■ *Serves 8*

Finally, barbecue for the folks who don't have all day to stand over a wood fire and roast a pig. With the right barbecue sauce, a Crock-Pot does an amazing job of turning out melt-in-your-mouth shredded pork. Boutique bottled sauces abound on supermarket shelves; pick the one you like best. If you're serving children, the sloppy joe flavor of a sweeter sauce will entice everyone to join the clean plate club. Thin, smooth sauces work best in this recipe. If you can't find a substitute for your favorite thick-style sauce, thin it with water to drizzling consistency. Then pass the thick stuff at the table for a bolder flavor.

From Alicia:

Thick and rich, this chili is one of the corner-stones of my entertaining repertoire. If it's even close to chili weather, I serve it, and boy-oh-boy the guests do rave. (I've gotten used to keeping a couple of copies of the recipe in the kitchen to pass out after dinner, which shows just how popular it has become.) The combination of perfect spices and slow-simmered, tender beef chunks makes for a truly outstanding result. I rarely have leftovers.

Steak and Black Bean Chili

3½ to 4 pounds well-marbled beef cubes for stew
4 teaspoons chili powder
2 teaspoons garlic powder
2 teaspoons ground cumin
2 large onions (for 2 cups chopped)
2 large green peppers (for 3 cups chopped)
3 cans (15 ounces each) black beans
3 cans (14½ ounces each) chili-style seasoned
    tomatoes
2 teaspoons sugar
1 can (6 ounces) tomato paste
Salt and black pepper
Sour cream, for serving (optional)
Already-shredded Cheddar cheese, for serving
    (optional)

START TO FINISH: 15 MINUTES PREPARATION, PLUS 8 TO 10 HOURS UNATTENDED COOKING TIME

1. Place the beef cubes in the bottom of a 5-quart or larger slow cooker. Sprinkle the chili powder, garlic powder, and cumin over the beef. Peel and coarsely chop the onions, adding them to the pot as you chop. Rinse, core, seed, and coarsely chop the bell peppers, adding them to the pot as you chop.

2. Put the beans in a colander, rinse well, and drain. Add the beans to the pot. Add the tomatoes with their juice and sprinkle the sugar over the tomatoes. Do not stir. Cover the pot and cook on low for 8 to 10 hours.

3. Uncover the pot and stir in the tomato paste. Season with salt and pepper to taste and stir well. Serve at once, topped with sour cream and cheese, if desired.

■ *Serves 8*

DO-AHEAD

The chili can be prepared and refrigerated, covered, for up to 2 days or frozen for up to 1 month in a microwave-safe container.
• If the chili has been frozen, thaw it in a microwave oven on the defrost setting, following the manufacturer's directions.
• To reheat, place the chili in a large pot over medium heat and stir frequently until it returns to a gentle boil and is heated through, about 20 minutes. Stir only gently to avoid mushy beans.

Alternative Cooking Method: If you don't have a slow cooker, prepare the onions, bell peppers, and beans as described in Steps 1 and 2. Heat 1 tablespoon of olive oil in a 5-quart Dutch oven or soup pot over medium-high heat. Add the beef cubes, onions, and bell peppers and cook until the onions and bell peppers are soft and the meat is lightly browned, about 15 minutes. Add the chili powder, garlic powder, cumin, beans, tomatoes with their juice, sugar, and tomato paste, stir, and let come to a boil. Reduce the heat to low and simmer, stirring occasionally, until the beef is fork-tender and the flavors blend, about 2 hours. Season with salt and pepper and serve with the toppings, if desired.

ABOUT CHILDREN'S BIRTHDAY PARTIES

Anyone who's a parent of young children would probably agree that there isn't a "traditional" type of birthday party for them any longer. Our kids have been invited to or have held parties at the horseback riding stables, at the swimming pool in the local hotel, and in the park for picnics that included rock climbing. Of course, all these parties involved food, one way or another. If you're serving food at home for a birthday party, this book is a spot-on guide to kid-friendly fare. Here are some of our kids' favorites:

- Roasted Garlic Salsa and Blue Chips, page 50
- Roasted Garlic and Mozzarella Pizza, page 78
- Crispy Oven-Baked Chicken Fingers, page 83
- Blue Jay Point Pasta, page 90
- Our Favorite Spaghetti and Meatballs, page 142
- Carolina Chili Dogs, page 163
- Pizza Burgers, page 171
- Stuffed Bacon-Cheddar Burgers, page 172
- Any of the brownie sundaes, pages 318 through 320

Whether you serve these easy recipes before or after a birthday activity or as the main event, you'll have a house full of happy and satisfied kids, guaranteed.

An old wives' tale has it that eating chile peppers will help induce labor when a baby is overdue. Perhaps that's why an impatient pregnant friend of ours invited a group of us for a dinner that featured three different kinds of chili, including one that was made with chicken. While still spicy, chicken chili somehow seems lighter than that made with beef. The white beans here keep with the color scheme, while red bell peppers and corn add a bright accent. By chilling out with this chicken chili you can shorten your kitchen labor.

SANITY SAVER

Make your gatherings fit your home. Got a tiny dining room but a spacious deck? Plan to invite friends over during the temperate seasons and serve casual meals outside.

Chill-Out Chicken Chili

3½ to 4 pounds skinless, boneless chicken breast halves
1 jumbo onion (for about 1½ cups chopped)
2 medium-size red bell peppers (for about 2 cups bite-size pieces)
1 teaspoon olive oil
4 teaspoons bottled minced garlic
2½ teaspoons ground cumin
2 teaspoons chili powder
1 teaspoon sugar
¼ teaspoon Tabasco sauce, or more to taste (optional)
1 can (14½ ounces) fat-free chicken broth
1 can (14½ ounces) diced tomatoes seasoned with garlic and onion
1½ cups yellow corn kernels, frozen or canned
3 cans (15½ ounces each) great Northern beans
2 cans (4 ounces each) chopped green chiles (see Notes)
⅓ cup cornstarch
Already-shredded Monterey Jack cheese or Mexican cheese blend, for serving
Sour cream, for serving

START TO FINISH: 25 MINUTES, PLUS 6 TO 8 HOURS MOSTLY UNATTENDED COOKING TIME

1. Cut the chicken into bite-size chunks and place in a 5-quart or larger slow cooker. (See Notes.)

2. Peel and coarsely chop the onion; add it to the pot. Rinse, core, seed, and cut the bell peppers into bite-size pieces; add to the pot.

3. Add the olive oil, garlic, cumin, chili powder, sugar, and Tabasco sauce, if using, to the pot. Then add the chicken broth, tomatoes with their juice, and the corn. Put the beans in a colander, rinse well, and set aside to drain. If the green chiles have a lot of juice on top, drain it off, then add the chiles to the pot. Stir to mix well. Put the beans on top of the chili mixture but do not stir.

4. Cover the pot and cook on low for 6 to 8 hours.

5. Up to 1 hour before serving, mix the cornstarch and ⅓ cup water in a jar that has a lid. Shake well to break up any lumps. Pour a little of the cornstarch mixture evenly over the hot chili. Stir gently from time to time, adding more cornstarch mixture as necessary, until the chili is slightly thicker than heavy cream, about 5 minutes. Serve in bowls, topped generously with cheese and sour cream.

■ *Serves 8*

Notes: The weight of a can of chiles can vary a bit from brand to brand. It doesn't matter so long as the cans are roughly 4 ounces each.

Be sure to wash your hands with antibacterial soap after handling raw chicken. Also, spray with antibacterial spray any surfaces the raw chicken may have touched.

Alternative Cooking Method: If you don't have a slow cooker, prepare the chicken, onion, and bell peppers as described in Steps 1 and 2. Heat 1 tablespoon of olive oil in a 5-quart Dutch oven or soup pot over medium-high heat. Add the chicken, onion, and bell peppers and cook until the onion and bell peppers are soft and the chicken is no longer pink outside, 8 to 9 minutes. Add the remaining ingredients as described in Step 3. Let come to a boil, reduce the heat to medium-low, and simmer until the chicken is no longer pink in the center and the flavors blend, about 20 minutes. When the chili is cooked through proceed with Step 5.

DO-AHEAD

The chili can be prepared and refrigerated, covered, for up to 2 days or frozen for up to 1 month in a microwave-safe container. Do not thicken it before freezing.

• If the chili has been frozen, thaw it in a microwave oven on the defrost setting, following the manufacturer's directions.

• To reheat, place the chili in a large pot over medium heat and stir frequently until it returns to a gentle boil and is heated through, about 20 minutes. Stir only gently to avoid mushy beans. Once the chili is hot, proceed to thicken it as described in Step 5.

Vegetarian Mushroom-Barley Chili

From Alicia:

Beverly and I have immediate families full of carnivores. So creating a meatless chili that wouldn't leave our crowd feeling let down wasn't easy. But because we have enough friends and extended family members that appreciate a vegetarian alternative, we knew we needed to have a satisfying chili recipe we could all enjoy. With its hearty base of barley, this rich, thick stew made with onion, bell pepper, and mushrooms is perfect. Topped with shredded cheese and sour cream, no one misses the meat.

Pearl barley is found in the same aisle in the grocery store as the dried beans. While we love 10-minute barley as a staple in our desperate weeknight pantries, the superfast variety cooks too quickly for this recipe. But we don't want to be chained to the stove either, so we select the traditional medium barley and cook it in the Crock-Pot. Now everything cooks to perfection with only 12 minutes prep time and no worries that the barley will burn or stick. Just dump in the ingredients, turn on the pot, and let the cooker work its magic.

2 cans (14½ ounces each) vegetable broth
1 cup medium barley
½ teaspoon ground cumin
2 teaspoons chili powder
1 large onion (for about 1 cup chopped)
1 large green bell pepper (for about 1½ cups chopped)
1 package (8 ounces) already-sliced, fresh button mushrooms
2 cans (15½ ounces each) light-red kidney beans
2 cans (14½ ounces each) diced tomatoes seasoned with garlic and onion
1 teaspoon sugar
Already-shredded Cheddar, Monterey Jack, or a cheese blend, for serving (optional)
Sour cream, for serving (optional)

START TO FINISH: 12 MINUTES, PLUS 8 TO 10 HOURS UNATTENDED COOKING TIME

1. Pour the vegetable broth into a 5-quart or larger slow cooker. Add the barley, cumin, and chili powder. Stir well.

2. Peel and coarsely chop the onion; add it to the pot. Rinse, core, seed, and coarsely chop the bell pepper; add it to the pot. Coarsely chop the mushrooms and add them to the pot.

3. Put the beans in a colander, rinse well, and drain. Add the beans to the pot. Add the tomatoes with their juice. Sprinkle the sugar evenly over the tomatoes.

4. Cover the pot and cook on low for 8 to 10 hours. Stir well and then serve with shredded cheese and sour cream, if desired.

■ *Serves 8*

ABOUT USING A SLOW COOKER

No question that a slow cooker is convenient, but to use it wisely, there are things to bear in mind. First, and most important, the benefit of having an appliance you can leave on all day unattended comes with two caveats:

1. You should never leave children unattended in the presence of any electrical appliance.

2. Because the outside of the slow cooker gets quite hot, place it on a heat-resistant surface that is away from other sources of heat (not near a hot gas or electric burner or in a heated oven). Corian and other solid-surface countertops may not be able to withstand extended exposure to the hot temperature of a slow cooker. Nor should you operate a Crock-Pot on a finished wooden surface.

Here are some more things to keep in mind when you are using a slow cooker:

• Slow cookers need no preheating. In fact you should avoid the drastic temperature changes that may occur if you place cold food in a warm slow cooker.

• Always cook with the lid on and avoid lifting it off repeatedly as this changes the temperature within the crock and will make the cooking time longer.

• Do not reheat food in a slow cooker.

• The crock of a slow cooker is not designed to be used for storage; transfer any leftovers to another container.

• When setting a hot crock on a table or countertop, always place it on top of protective padding.

• Never use a slow cooker outdoors.

• Slow cookers do not turn themselves off. Always unplug your slow cooker when you are finished using it.

Some things you should know in order to take best advantage of a slow cooker.

CHAPTER FIVE

The Casual

Selfishly, we have always loved grilling because our husbands enjoy taking over the cooking.

Grilling is about the only time you'll find us encouraging you to cook in front of your guests. While we can't stand the idea of the host facing the stove to ready dinner inside, we love cooking out on the patio or deck with our friends. And, fire, smoke, the sizzle of meat—these all intrigue our men. When they want to take over cooking the main course, we simply smile and hand them the tongs. After all, who are we to stand in the way of genius at the grill?

Grilling outdoors says casual. It says come on out, grab a beer, and chat with us while we fix these dogs (Carolina Chili Dogs, German Bratwurst with Sauerkraut, and State Fair Sausage Dogs, to be exact). And what's a grilling chapter without steaks? We've got Amazing Steaks here. But steak doesn't only mean beef, and there's no more delicious way to describe our portobello mushrooms than as "steak" sandwiches. Of course, the most popular sandwich hot off the grill is a big juicy burger, and we have two dressed-up burgers that are sure to surprise and satisfy.

You'll find Vacation Fish Boats to remind you of the coast and gentle sea breezes, chilled white wine, and the warm glow that comes after spending the day in the sun. Pork Chops with Fruit Sauces will make you wish you had this dish in your repertoire years ago, and the same goes for Chicken with Mustard Glazes. Neither requires marinating, so dinner is ready to serve lickety-split.

Cookout

While some of our recipes *do* require a few hours of marinating for just the right taste, the advance preparation for every one can be done hours before your guests arrive. That's the beauty of marinades—a few minutes of work earlier in the day (or even the day before), then you can walk away until you're ready to grill. We've shared our absolute favorites for everything from the perfect pork tenderloin for a party to our version of chicken satés (chicken grilled on a stick).

Sprinkled throughout the chapter are easy homemade condiments that are simple to prepare ahead and wonderful with grilled food. Finally, we've thrown in a couple of grilled sides, too. If you're heating up the grill for the main, why not toss on a few veggies to go with it?

So, fire up your grill (we prefer a gas one, but all the dishes here can be grilled over charcoal, too). Between the fun and fellowship of cooking outdoors and the sizzling sounds of dinner, appetites will be raring to go in no time at all.

Amazing Steaks

8 boneless rib eye or strip steaks (6 to 8 ounces each)
6 tablespoons (¾ stick) butter
⅓ cup Worcestershire sauce
Microwave Béarnaise, Spicy Chimichurri Sauce, or Madeira
Mushrooms (optional; recipes follow), for serving

START TO FINISH: 20 MINUTES

Nothing satisfies our beef cravings quicker than a thick, juicy, grilled steak. Being the true carnivores we are, we've trained our families to demand no less. The first secret to a superb steak is buying good-quality beef. We especially enjoy New York strip (also known, depending on where you are, as Kansas City strip or top loin) and rib eye steaks. Nice and marbled, these beauties are easy to grill to perfection. They are good on their own and even better with Microwave Béarnaise, Spicy Chimichurri Sauce, or Madeira Mushrooms.

1. Trim the steaks if necessary but leave some fat along the edges for flavor. Place the steaks in a single layer in a baking pan with at least 1-inch sides. Prick the steaks with a fork several times.

2. Place the butter and Worcestershire sauce in a 2-cup or larger glass measure, cover with a paper towel, and microwave on high until the butter is melted, about 45 seconds. Whisk briskly to mix well. Pour the butter mixture over the steaks.

3. Turn on a gas grill to medium-high.

4. Place the steaks on the hot grill and cook for 4 to 6 minutes on the first side. Spread any butter left over in the baking pan on top of the steaks as they grill. Caution: Watch for flare-ups from the butter; these will burn out quickly.

5. Turn the steaks and continue to grill for 4 to 6 minutes for medium-rare, or to your personal preference. Serve immediately with the condiment of your choice, if desired.

■ *Serves 8*

DO-AHEAD

The steaks can be refrigerated, lightly covered, following Step 2 for up to 3 hours.

Microwave Béarnaise

We've enjoyed this truly unbelievable sauce for years and offered up a version of it in our first book. It enhances any cut of beef, but we particularly love the flavors of lemon and tarragon blended with cream spooned over our Amazing Steaks. For an extra-rich version, you can use a half cup of heavy cream instead of the half-and-half and cream mix.

1 small onion (for about ½ cup chopped)
¼ cup distilled white vinegar or white wine vinegar
¼ cup dry white wine
½ teaspoon dried tarragon
4 large eggs
8 tablespoons (1 stick) butter
¼ cup half-and-half
¼ cup heavy (whipping) cream
2 teaspoons fresh lemon juice

START TO FINISH: 20 MINUTES

1. Peel and finely chop the onion, then put it in a small (1-quart) saucepan with the vinegar, wine, and tarragon. Bring to a boil over high heat and continue to boil until only about 1 tablespoon of liquid is left in the pan with the onion, about 3 minutes. Remove from the heat and set aside.

2. Separate the eggs, placing the yolks in a small bowl and setting the whites aside for another use. Beat the yolks well with a fork or whisk. Place the butter in a 4-cup glass measure, cover with a paper towel, and microwave on high until melted, about 1 minute. Remove the butter from the microwave and stir in the half-and-half, heavy cream, lemon juice, and beaten egg yolks. Microwave, uncovered, on high, for 2 minutes, stopping every 15 to 20 seconds to stir with a fork or small whisk. When done, the sauce will be just slightly thickened. Remove the sauce from the microwave and stir in the onion mixture.

3. Serve immediately or cover and refrigerate until ready to use.

■ *Makes about 1⅔ cups*

DO-AHEAD

The béarnaise sauce can be refrigerated, covered, for up to 2 days in a microwave-safe container. To reheat, microwave, uncovered, on high until heated through, about 2 minutes. Stir well and serve.

Spicy Chimichurri Sauce

From Beverly:

While living in Miami, I grew to love *chimichurri*, the garlic-parsley sauce served as a condiment for beef in the local Nicaraguan steak houses. After moving to North Carolina, this was a treat I absolutely missed. Then I spied a recipe for *chimichurri* in Steven Raichlen's book *Miami Spice*. It's just as wonderful as I remembered. As a bonus, it's surprisingly easy to make. Our thanks for this recipe go to Steven, who is most frequently known these days for his popular "Barbecue Bible" cookbooks. Try it with our Amazing Steaks or with grilled pork or chicken.

> *5 cloves fresh garlic*
> *About 1 cup densely packed fresh parsley*
> *½ cup good-quality olive oil*
> *1½ tablespoons fresh lemon juice*
> *½ teaspoon dried red pepper flakes*
> *½ teaspoon salt, or more to taste*
> *⅛ teaspoon black pepper, or more to taste*

START TO FINISH: 5 MINUTES

1. Peel the garlic. Rinse the parsley well and shake the leaves to remove any excess water. Remove and discard the tough lower stems but do not worry about the smaller, upper stems. You should have about 1 cup of leaves.

2. Drop the parsley through the feed tube of a food processor with the machine running. Process until finely minced. Drop the garlic cloves 1 at a time through the feed tube of the processor with the machine running. Process until finely minced.

3. Add the olive oil, lemon juice, red pepper flakes, salt, and black pepper to the bowl of the processor and process until well mixed, 5 to 6 seconds. Taste for seasoning, adding more salt and black pepper if necessary.

■ *Makes about ¾ cup*

DO-AHEAD

The *chimichurri* sauce can be refrigerated, covered, for up to 4 days.

Madeira Mushrooms

Agreat asset to keep in your cupboard, Madeira, a fortified wine from Portugal, adds a marvelous depth to everything it touches. Its flavor is particularly suited to mushrooms. Just add a splash to the pan and suddenly you've got a gourmet treat—the perfect condiment for our Amazing Steaks, grilled chicken breasts, or pork chops.

> *1 tablespoon butter*
> *1 tablespoon olive oil*
> *1 small onion (for about ½ cup chopped)*
> *2 packages (8 ounces each) already-sliced,*
> *   fresh button mushrooms*
> *⅓ cup Madeira or dry sherry*
> *¼ teaspoon salt, or more to taste*

START TO FINISH: 12 MINUTES

1. Heat the butter and oil in a 12-inch nonstick skillet over medium heat. Meanwhile, peel and coarsely chop the onion, adding it to the skillet as you chop. Coarsely chop the mushrooms and add them to the onion.

2. Cook, stirring frequently, until the mushrooms just begin to soften, about 2 minutes. Add the Madeira and stir well. Raise the heat to medium-high. Continue to cook, stirring from time to time, until the mushrooms have released their liquid, about 3 minutes more. Add the salt. Taste for seasoning, adding more salt if necessary. Remove from the heat and serve at once or allow to stand at room temperature for up to 30 minutes before serving.

■ *Serves 8*

DO-AHEAD

Madeira mushrooms can be refrigerated, covered, for up to 2 days in a microwave-safe container. To reheat, cover with a paper towel and microwave on high until heated through, about 2 minutes, stopping once halfway through to stir.

We love plain grilled pork chops during the work week. But when we're serving them to company, we pair them with a delicious topping, such as our Peach Season Salsa or Fast Festive Fruit Sauce. Suddenly everyday chops are transformed into party food.

Pork Chops with Fruit Sauces

8 boneless, center-cut loin pork chops (about ¾-inch
    thick and 4 ounces each)
Vegetable oil
Salt and black pepper
Peach Season Salsa or Fast Festive Fruit Sauce
    (recipes follow), for serving

START TO FINISH: 15 MINUTES

1. Brush each pork chop with oil. Lightly salt and pepper both sides of each pork chop.

2. Turn on a gas grill to high.

3. Place the seasoned pork chops on the hot grill and cook, with the grill covered, 6 minutes on the first side, then turn the chops and continue to grill, uncovered, until the chops are cooked through, 5 to 6 minutes more. Be careful not to overcook. Serve with the Peach Season Salsa or Fast Festive Fruit Sauce.

■ *Serves 8*

DO-AHEAD

The pork chops can be refrigerated, covered, following Step 1 for up to 8 hours.

HANDLING HOT PEPPERS

Adding a hot pepper, such as a jalapeño, to a salsa dip can contribute a certain zip your guests are sure to remember. But you have to be careful not to add a zip to your eyes in the process. We suggest wearing thin household rubber gloves that fit well when handling hot peppers. It's easy to keep a pair labeled "Peppers" in a drawer next to the sink. That way they don't get mixed up with the gloves used for other household jobs.

If you choose not to wear gloves, then be sure to wash your hands well with warm soapy water before going on to other kitchen duties and definitely before touching your eyes or face.

Peach Season Salsa

It's either peach season or it's not. When summer peaches hit the height of juicy splendor, we serve them every chance we get. Not just in pies and cobblers anymore—our zesty salsa combination of sweet, sour, and spicy pairs perfectly with meaty pork chops hot off the grill. The amount of sugar in this recipe is correct for fully ripe peaches. If yours aren't very sweet, you may need a little more sugar to suit your taste. Make the salsa up to 2 hours before serving. The lime juice will keep the salsa from turning dark, but it will not hold for longer than that.

3 large freestone peaches (for about 3 cups diced)
1 lime
½ teaspoon sugar, or more to taste
¼ teaspoon salt
1 large, ripe tomato (for about 1 cup diced)
1 clove fresh garlic
1 fresh jalapeño pepper (for about 1 tablespoon minced)
About ¼ cup densely packed fresh cilantro

START TO FINISH: 15 MINUTES

1. Pit, peel, and dice the peaches. Place in a medium-size serving bowl. Cut the lime in half, squeeze the juice over the peaches, and sprinkle them with the sugar and salt. Stir to coat well.

2. Rinse, core, and dice the tomato, leaving the peel on. Add the diced tomato to the diced peaches.

3. Peel and chop the garlic. Add it to the peach mixture. Rinse and seed the jalapeño (see box at left). Mince the jalapeño finely and add to the salsa.

4. Rinse the cilantro well and shake the leaves to remove any excess water. Remove and discard the tough lower stems but do not worry about the smaller, upper stems. You should have about ¼ cup of leaves. Mince the cilantro. Add it to the salsa and stir well. Taste for seasoning, adding more sugar if necessary.

■ *Makes about 3 cups*

DO-AHEAD

The peach salsa can be refrigerated, covered, for up to 2 hours.

Fast Festive Fruit Sauce

From Beverly:

Our buttery mixture of dried fruits is so pretty it looks like it came right out of a gourmet restaurant. As well as with pork chops, this sauce is also nice with grilled or roasted poultry. By the way, I used to fret when recipes instructed me to "boil the liquid until it is reduced by half." Maybe I'm volume impaired, but I've even gone so far as to pour the dangerously hot broth into a measuring cup to be sure I was on the right track. Trust me, you don't need to take such extreme measures with this sauce. If you're off even by a quarter cup in either direction, the sauce will still turn out great. A little more liquid just yields a slightly thinner sauce.

> 1 can (14½ ounces) fat-free chicken broth
> 15 dried apricots (for about ½ cup chopped)
> ½ cup golden raisins
> ½ cup dried cranberries or dried cherries
> ¼ cup maple syrup (see Note)
> 2 tablespoons balsamic vinegar
> 3 tablespoons cold butter

START TO FINISH: 12 MINUTES

1. Pour the chicken broth into a 2-quart saucepan and bring it to a boil over high heat. Meanwhile, coarsely chop the apricots.

2. When the broth boils, stir in the chopped apricots and the raisins and cranberries. Allow the fruit mixture to cook at a rolling boil until the liquid is reduced by a bit more than half, about 6 minutes. Remove the pan from the heat.

3. Add the maple syrup and vinegar. Stir to mix well. Cut the butter into 3 pieces, add them all to the pan, and swirl the butter in the sauce just until it is dissolved. Serve at once or let the sauce stand at room temperature until ready to serve.

■ *Makes about 2 cups*

Note: Be sure to use real maple syrup in this recipe.

DO-AHEAD

The sauce can stand at room temperature for up to but no longer than 2 hours because the dried fruit continues to absorb liquid as it stands. If you have let the sauce stand and prefer to serve it warm, rewarm it in the microwave oven, uncovered, on high for 1 minute. Stir to mix well and serve.

LITTLE THINGS COUNT

I t's often the little things that push our buttons:

The guests are about to arrive, and you can't find a single match in the entire house.

You'd love to serve that wonderful merlot, but who knows where the corkscrew is?

Coffee after dinner is a must, but you just realized that your seven year old used all the filters for an art project.

This is why we like to keep a drawer for the "little things" we might need. Even if there's no designated drawer available for these little gems, it's still a good idea to have them on hand. Zipper-top bags are great for keeping small items together and make them easier to find in large drawers and cabinets. We take a quick peek a day or so ahead to see if there'll be any need for last-minute purchases. Here's what we find essential:

• **Matches and fire sticks:** A big box of kitchen matches goes a long way. So does a trusty extended lighter, which makes lighting the grill or the candles terrifically easy.

• **Corn picks:** You know, those cute little handles you stick in the ends of corn on the cob. (See our easy recipe on page 260 for Can-Do Corn on the Cob.)

• **A corkscrew**

• **An instant-read meat thermometer:** Wondering if that pork tenderloin is done? Stick one of these thermometers right in the meat and know for sure, instantaneously!

• **Bamboo skewers:** Keep a package on hand for kebabs.

• **A bottle opener:** If you're having a casual get-together and the bottle opener needs to stay with the cooler out on the deck, tie a colorful string around it to secure it to the cooler's handle.

• **Coffee filters and scoop:** Nothing is more annoying than to have to hunt for that scoop.

• **Birthday candles:** You'd be surprised how many times we pull out the little candles to celebrate a recent birthday or anniversary completely spontaneously.

• **Decorative spreaders:** From plain to fancy and back to whimsical, these small spreaders can be great conversation pieces.

Some might call it the kitchen junk drawer. We call it our salvation drawer.

159

When we're surprised by company and need to produce dinner pronto, we're always glad for frozen chicken breasts—but not just any old frozen chicken breasts. Keep bags of individually quick-frozen (IQF) skinless, boneless chicken breasts on hand and you always can grill with no advance notice.

Because the chicken breasts are glazed with a thin coating of ice that keeps them from sticking together, you can pull out the exact number of chicken pieces you need. And, because the chicken doesn't freeze together in a large block, you can grill the breasts without thawing them first. While starting with frozen breasts takes a bit longer than grilling unfrozen ones, you will still be ready to eat in roughly 15 minutes.

Chicken on the grill is always popular, but do you ever wish for an easy alternative to bottled barbecue sauce? Our mustard glazes depend on pantry ingredients that are no trouble to keep on hand, plus the glazes are so delicious and easy to stir together, you'll want to make all three.

Chicken with Mustard Glazes

Plum Spicy Glaze, Orange-Dijon Glaze, and/or
Golden Mustard Glaze (recipes follow)
8 frozen skinless, boneless chicken breast halves
(about 2⅔ pounds total; see Note)
2 tablespoons plus 2 teaspoons olive oil
Salt and pepper (optional)

START TO FINISH: 20 MINUTES

1. Turn on a gas grill to medium-high.

2. Make the mustard glaze(s) of your choice.

3. Brush or rub each piece of chicken all over with about 1 teaspoon olive oil. Place the chicken on the hot grill and cook, with the grill covered, 5 minutes on the first side to partially defrost, then turn and grill, covered, 7 to 8 minutes on the second side.

4. Turn the chicken back to the first side and brush each piece with a mustard glaze. Continue to grill, uncovered, for 1 minute. Turn the chicken and brush the second side with glaze. Continue to grill, uncovered, until the breasts are no longer pink in the center, 1 to 2 minutes more. Remove from the grill and serve at once or hold at room temperature for up to 30 minutes.

■ *Serves 8*

Note: You may notice that of all the chicken recipes in this book, this is one of the few that calls for a specific number of chicken breast halves as opposed to a total weight. That's because we've found that chicken breast sizes are not uniform from brand to brand or even from package to package, and in recipes calling for cut-up chicken pieces, the important factor is total weight. This recipe calls for a breast half per serving, and so we specify 8 breast halves. If possible, choose breast halves that weigh about 5 to 6 ounces each. If you are using chicken breasts that aren't frozen, you'll need to grill them for 3 to 5 minutes on each side, turning only once. (All chicken cooking times may vary somewhat depending on your grill and the thickness of the meat.) Be sure to wash your hands with antibacterial soap after handling raw chicken. Also, spray with antibacterial spray any surfaces the raw chicken may have touched and discard any leftover glaze.

Plum Spicy Glaze

Slightly hot thanks to the mustard, this glaze is a perfect choice for those who like a zing in every bite. Just two ingredients from the Asian foods section of the supermarket, Chinese plum sauce and Chinese mustard give it an exotic flair that belies its simplicity.

> ½ cup Chinese plum sauce
> ¼ cup Chinese mustard

START TO FINISH: 3 MINUTES

Put the plum sauce and mustard in a small mixing bowl. Stir to mix them well.

■ *Makes ¾ cup*

Orange-Dijon Glaze

Here again, a mere pair of ingredients can transform a plain chicken breast into a company specialty. It's hard to pick a favorite, but Beverly says this sweet-and-sour blend may well be hers when she's really pushed for time.

> 1 cup all-fruit orange marmalade
> ¼ cup Dijon mustard

START TO FINISH: 3 MINUTES

Put the marmalade and mustard in a small mixing bowl. Stir to mix them well.

■ *Makes 1¼ cups*

DO-AHEAD

The plum and orange-mustard glazes can be refrigerated, covered, for up to 3 days.

Golden Mustard Glaze

Choose any grainy or brown mustard, such as Gulden's, that you find in the supermarket. Plain Dijon mustard would work well in the glaze, too.

1 cup spicy brown prepared mustard
⅓ cup firmly packed light brown sugar

START TO FINISH: 3 MINUTES

Put the mustard and brown sugar in a small mixing bowl. Stir to mix them well.

■ *Makes about 1⅓ cups*

DO-AHEAD

The brown sugar and mustard glaze can be refrigerated, covered, for up to 3 days.

GAS GRILLS

We've long been fans of gas grills. Their last-minute efficiency has saved us many a desperate weeknight. But we find we like them even better for company. Most gas grills don't require more than a few minutes of preheating, if any at all. (Check the instructions.) This means any time you'd otherwise spend readying the grill can be spent preparing for your guests in other ways. Even the simplest gas grill can be lit in an instant and ready to cook minutes later.

Control of the heat setting—just like on your stove top—is another big advantage. Many grills have thermostats on the cover and will indicate what the temperature inside the grill is when the lid is closed. (All of the recipes in this chapter were tested with gas grills, but of course, if you prefer to grill with charcoal, check the instruction book of your grill for timing guidelines.)

If you find that you have a space that lends itself to outdoor gatherings, such as a deck or patio, and live in a part of the country where an investment in a grill would pay off, consider looking into a gas grill. We wouldn't give ours up for anything and even during the work week enjoy a little alfresco dining.

Carolina Chili Dogs

1 cup Carolina Chili (recipe follows)
8 hot dogs (see Note)
8 hot dog buns
Your choice of additional condiments, such as prepared
*   mustard, ketchup, diced onions, pickle relish, and/or*
*   a southern-style creamy cole slaw like Louise's Big*
*   Bowl Slaw (see page 226), for serving*

START TO FINISH: 22 MINUTES

1. Begin making the Carolina Chili.

2. While the chili simmers and about 12 to 15 minutes before you plan to serve the chili dogs, turn on a gas grill to medium-high.

3. Place the hot dogs on the hot grill and cook until heated through and just beginning to brown all over, about 5 minutes. Heat the buns on the grill, if desired. To serve, place each hot dog in a bun. Pass the chili and other condiments separately.

■ *Serves 8*

Note: We prefer all-beef hot dogs. Several brands make "bun-length" hot dogs, and we like the way they truly do fill up the bun and the tummy, too.

Carolina Chili

From Beverly:

A quart of hot dog chili might seem like a lot, but since my mother's version is good enough to win a blue ribbon at the state fair, it won't last long. Besides, the recipe is based on a can of tomato paste, and it's just as easy and quick to make a quart as it is to make a pint. It freezes for weeks, too, so why not? My family eats Carolina Chili Dogs so frequently that we never use the chili for anything else, but I'll bet if you spoon some over hamburger buns, sloppy-joe style, your kids will be grateful.

We've served these franks at Girl Scout and neighborhood picnics, to out-of-town friends and family alike. Nobody says no to these hot-diggity chili dogs. Our thanks go to Beverly's mother, Dot Mills, for sharing her grand-children's favorite chili recipe, which as Eastern North Carolina style dictates, is mildly sweet and does not contain any beans.

Over the years I've noticed that a serving of chili tends to be about 2 tablespoons per hot dog at my house, so I freeze my chili in small batches, say about a half cup for the family or a cup for company dinners. Notice how much chili your family typically uses and freeze it in batches accordingly.

> *1¼ pounds extra-lean ground beef (see Notes)*
> *1 large onion (for about 1 cup chopped)*
> *1 can (6 ounces) tomato paste*
> *½ cup ketchup*
> *1 tablespoon chili powder*
> *2 teaspoons Worcestershire sauce*
> *1 teaspoon cider vinegar or distilled white vinegar*
> *1 teaspoon salt*
> *¼ teaspoon black pepper (optional)*

START TO FINISH: 22 MINUTES

1. Place the beef and 2 cups of water in a 4½-quart Dutch oven or soup pot over high heat. Bring the water to a boil while peeling and coarsely chopping the onion. Add the chopped onion to the beef. When the water boils, reduce the heat to medium. Stir to begin breaking up the meat.

2. Add the tomato paste, ketchup, chili powder, Worcestershire sauce, vinegar, salt, and pepper, if using. Stir well until the tomato paste has dissolved and the meat is mostly broken up.

3. Continue to cook the chili at a slow boil, stirring about every 5 minutes or so, until the mixture is thick, about 15 minutes. As the mixture thickens, you may need to reduce the heat to medium-low or low to prevent sticking. Serve on hot dogs (see Notes).

■ *Makes 1 quart*

Notes: To avoid greasy chili, be sure to choose a very lean ground beef since the beef is not browned and drained in this recipe.

Many Southerners prefer chili that is finely ground (roughly the consistency of cooked oatmeal) because it's easier to spread on a hot dog and easier to eat as well. To try it this way, place the chili (cooled at least 20 minutes) in a blender or food processor and blend on high until finely ground, 30 to 45 seconds.

DO-AHEAD

The chili can be refrigerated, covered, for up to 2 days or it can be frozen for up to 2 months.
• If the chili has been frozen, thaw it in a microwave oven on the defrost setting, following the manufacturer's directions and stirring after each 1-minute interval, then reheat.
• To reheat, place the chili in a microwave-safe container, cover with a paper towel, and microwave on high until heated through, 2 to 3 minutes for 1 cup, stopping once halfway through to stir.

German Bratwurst with Sauerkraut

2 teaspoons olive oil
2 large onions (for about 2 cups sliced)
1 pound bag refrigerated sauerkraut (see Note)
8 already fully cooked bratwurst
8 hero rolls
Brown mustard, for serving

START TO FINISH: 20 MINUTES

1. Turn on a gas grill to high. Put the olive oil in a 12-inch cast iron skillet and place the skillet on one side of the grill.

2. While the skillet heats, peel the onions, cut them in half lengthwise, and cut each half into crescent-shaped slices about ¼ inch wide. Put the sauerkraut in a colander and drain well.

3. Add the onions to the hot skillet and grill, stirring frequently, until soft, about 10 minutes.

4. While the onions cook, place the bratwurst on the hot grill and cook, turning frequently, until plump, with browned grill marks on all sides, 5 to 6 minutes. Remove from the grill.

5. When the onions are done, stir in the sauerkraut and cook long enough to heat through and thoroughly mix, about 2 minutes.

6. If your rolls are not already cut, slice them along the top, being careful not to cut all the way through. Heat the rolls on the grill, if desired. To serve, place each sausage in a roll and pass the mustard and the onion-sauerkraut sauce separately.

■ *Serves 8*

Note: We prefer to use refrigerated sauerkraut instead of canned because of its fresh, mild taste.

Nothing quite satisfies our cookout cravings like a smoky bratwurst right off the grill. Top it with sauerkraut and we're in heaven. Or at least Oktoberfest heaven. Grab a beer and join us!

DO-AHEAD

If you want to make the onion-sauerkraut sauce ahead, on the grill or on the stove, it can stand at room temperature for up to 1 hour. Or cover and refrigerate it for up to 2 days. To reheat, place it in a microwave-safe container, cover with a paper towel, and microwave on high until the sauce is heated through, about 3 minutes, stopping at least once halfway through to stir.

The livestock exhibits are great, but the real reason we make the yearly pilgrimage to the state fair is to eat the grilled sausages just dripping with onions and peppers. Special enough for company? You bet. The only drawback is that these dressed-up dogs are messy to eat, so serve them in substantial buns with plenty of paper napkins.

State Fair Sausage Dogs

1 tablespoon vegetable oil
3 large onions (for about 3 cups sliced)
2 large green bell peppers
   (for about 4 cups sliced)
2 tablespoons bottled minced garlic
¼ teaspoon black pepper
2 pounds smoked, already fully cooked beef sausage or
   already fully cooked kielbasa
8 hero rolls
2 tablespoons balsamic vinegar
Your choice of condiments, such as yellow or
   spicy brown prepared mustard and ketchup,
   for serving

START TO FINISH: **30 MINUTES**

1. Turn on a gas grill to high. Put the oil in a 12-inch cast iron skillet and place the skillet on one side of the grill.

2. While the skillet heats, peel the onions, cut them in half lengthwise, and cut each half into crescent-shaped slices about ¼ inch wide. Rinse the bell peppers, then cut in half, core, and seed them. Cut each half into ¼-inch strips, then cut the strips in half crosswise.

3. Add the onions, bell peppers, garlic, and black pepper to the skillet and grill, stirring occasionally, until soft, about 15 minutes.

4. While the vegetable mixture cooks, cut the sausages into 8 equal pieces. Place the sausages on the hot grill and cook, turning frequently, until plump, with browned grill marks all over, about 12 minutes. Remove from the grill and cut each piece in half lengthwise.

5. If your rolls are not already cut, slice them along the top, being careful not to cut all the way through. Heat the rolls on the grill, if desired. Remove the skillet from the grill, add the balsamic vinegar,

DO-AHEAD

The onion-pepper mixture can be cooked on the stove top; it will take about 10 minutes. The cooked mixture can be refrigerated, covered, in a microwave-safe container for up to 2 days. To reheat, cover with a paper towel and microwave on high until heated through, 2 to 3 minutes; stir after every minute.

and toss with the vegetables. To serve, place 2 sausage halves in each roll, overlapping to fit. Pass the condiments and the onion-pepper mixture separately.

■ *Serves 8*

HOT DOGS FOR ALL

From Beverly:

At a recent dinner party, we served hot dogs. A few years ago the mere idea would have seemed ludicrous. No longer. Here's what happened:

We wanted to throw a farewell dinner for some dear old friends, but between vacation schedules and the quickly approaching move, it had been hard to pin down a date. Finally, if the party was going to happen, it had to happen now.

We decided to keep it simple. Alicia jokingly suggested grilling hot dogs. I didn't laugh. We knew the six children on the guest list would embrace hot dogs with gusto, but somehow it didn't seem quite right for the adults. Then we thought about the different kinds of sausages now available in supermarkets. We'd still serve grilled hot dogs, just a slightly more sophisticated version.

With sauerkraut, some sautéed onions and peppers, a little homemade chili, and a variety of grilled bratwursts, smoked sausages, and kielbasa served on crusty hero rolls, we could enjoy the simplicity of hot dogs without feeling guilty. To add an even more home-cooked and long-planned feel to the meal, we concocted our recipe for Quick Bean Medley for a Crowd (see page 254), which lives up to its name.

This easy menu was such a hit, we've repeated it at everything from plain-old cookouts to the annual Halloween party. The kids can have their old favorite, the adults will appreciate the variety, and the host gets to forget the stress.

Phased and Flexible

London Broil with Molasses Marinade

2 limes
¼ cup vegetable oil
¼ cup molasses (see Note)
¼ cup Worcestershire sauce
1½ teaspoons garlic powder
1 teaspoon onion powder
2 flank steaks (about 1½ pounds each), or 3 pounds
    top round or sirloin

PHASE 1: 5 MINUTES

1. Make the marinade: Cut the limes in half and squeeze the juice into a 2-cup or larger glass measure or bowl. Add the oil, molasses, Worcestershire sauce, garlic powder, and onion powder. Use a wire whisk to mix well. *The marinade can be refrigerated, covered, for up to 12 hours.*

PHASE 2: 6 TO 24 HOURS MOSTLY UNATTENDED MARINATING TIME

2. Place the meat in a gallon-size, freezer-weight, zipper-top bag. Whisk the marinade to recombine. Pour the marinade over the meat. Seal the bag and gently shake to coat the meat with marinade. Lay the bag flat in the refrigerator to marinate for at least 6 hours. Turn over once halfway through marinating. *The meat can marinate for up to 24 hours.*

From Beverly:

The first time I ever served this steak at a party, it was for a small gathering of close friends of ours, some of whom didn't all know each other. By the end of the night, bonding was well on the way, we'd decided to make the dinner an annual event, and of course everyone agreed, "We've gotta have the London broil." Well, if you want an easy party that's sure to actually happen, lock in the next menu and set the date before the guests leave.

As for the London broil, many supermarkets label top round steaks that way. For medium or well-done meat, flank steak would be a moister choice. In either case, the sugar from the molasses in the marinade caramelizes on the meat as it grills and gives it just the right burnished taste.

PHASE 3: 14 TO 20 MINUTES, OR TO PERSONAL PREFERENCE

3. Turn on a gas grill to medium-high.

4. Remove the meat from the bag and discard the marinade. Place the meat on the hot grill and cook to the desired degree of doneness, about 7 to 10 minutes per side for medium-rare, depending on the thickness. Do not overcook. Remove from the grill and thinly slice across the grain. Serve at once or let stand until ready to serve.

■ *Serves 8*

Note: If you prefer, the London broil is just as good made with an equal amount of honey in place of the molasses.

Burgaw Beef Kebabs

½ cup vegetable oil
⅓ cup reduced-sodium soy sauce
2 lemons
¼ cup Worcestershire sauce
2 tablespoons yellow prepared mustard
1 teaspoon black pepper
2 cloves fresh garlic
2½ to 3 pounds beef sirloin already cut into
*   1¼- to 1½-inch cubes*
10 to 12 small (10-inch) bamboo skewers (see Note)

PHASE 1: 6 MINUTES

1. Make the marinade: Pour the oil into a 2-cup glass measure, then add the soy sauce. Cut the lemons in half and squeeze the juice through a small strainer (to catch the seeds) into the measuring cup. Add the Worcestershire sauce, mustard, and pepper. Whisk to blend well.

From Beverly:

This has been one of my favorite recipes for marinated beef since my childhood days in Burgaw, North Carolina, and I crave it still. Few foods other than hot dogs call for plain-old ballpark mustard these days, but in this recipe, the yellow stuff from way back when adds an essential flavor. The heavenly smell that fills your kitchen while you make the marinade lets you know it's going to be something special!

2. Peel and coarsely chop the garlic. Add it to the oil mixture and stir. *The marinade can be refrigerated, covered, for up to 2 days.*

PHASE 2: 8 TO 24 HOURS MOSTLY UNATTENDED MARINATING TIME

3. Place the beef cubes in a 1-gallon or larger, freezer-weight, zipper-top plastic bag. Whisk the marinade to recombine. Pour the marinade into the bag with the beef. Seal the bag and gently shake to coat the meat with marinade.

4. Place the bag flat in the refrigerator to marinate for at least 8 hours. Turn the bag over once halfway through marinating. *The beef cubes can marinate for up to 24 hours.*

PHASE 3: 3 MINUTES

5. Place about 4 cubes of beef on a soaked skewer (depending on the size of the cubes), leaving a little space between the cubes for even cooking. Repeat with the remaining beef cubes. Place the kebabs on a plate or tray. Discard the marinade. *The kebabs can be refrigerated, covered, at this point for up to 6 hours.*

PHASE 4: 7 TO 8 MINUTES, OR TO PERSONAL PREFERENCE

6. Turn on a gas grill to medium-high.

7. Place the kebabs on the hot grill and cook, turning frequently, to the desired degree of doneness. Cooking times will vary depending on the size of the meat cubes and on the grill. In testing, we found grilling 1¼-inch to 1½-inch cubes for 7 to 8 minutes produced medium-rare meat. Serve at once.

■ *Serves 8*

Note: Soak the bamboo skewers in water for at least 20 minutes before assembling the kebabs. This will keep them from burning on the grill. The number of skewers you will need depends on the size of the meat cubes. Our cubes weighed about 1 ounce each. We serve 4 cubes per person for typical appetites, then make several extra skewers to serve as second helpings.

TIME SAVER

To round out a summer menu in a real hurry, copy one of our favorite tricks and buy potato salad from the supermarket deli, stir in some finely chopped onion, and sprinkle paprika on top. Hard to believe, but this transforms that supermarket stuff into what will pass as a close cousin of homemade.

Pizza Burgers

2 pounds extra-lean ground beef
1½ to 2 ounces (about 20 slices) pepperoni
½ cup commercially prepared pizza sauce
½ cup Italian-style dry bread crumbs
8 thin slices mozzarella cheese (about ⅓ pound)
8 hamburger buns
Your choice of condiments, such as prepared mustard,
*   mayonnaise, and/or ketchup, for serving*

PHASE 1: 20 MINUTES

1. Place the ground beef in a large mixing bowl. Coarsely chop the pepperoni and add it to the ground beef. Add the pizza sauce and bread crumbs. Using your hands, wearing disposable plastic gloves, if desired, or using a sturdy plastic spoon, mix until the sauce is fully incorporated into the meat.

2. Shape the meat mixture into 8 patties, using a hamburger press, if possible, or roll into balls and then press firmly between 2 sheets of waxed paper. If you handled the meat, wash your hands well with antibacterial soap. *The patties can be refrigerated, covered, in a single layer or separated by a piece of waxed paper for up to 8 hours.*

PHASE 2: 15 MINUTES

3. Turn on a gas grill to medium-high.

4. Place the prepared patties on the hot grill and cook for 5 minutes, then turn. Grill until the meat is no longer pink in the center, 5 to 6 minutes more. Place a slice of cheese over each burger and continue to cook just until the cheese melts, 1 to 2 minutes more.

5. Heat the hamburger buns on the grill, if desired. Place each burger on a bun and serve with the condiments of your choice.

■ *Serves 8*

"Wow! Pizza *and* hamburgers. My two favorite things all in one! Mom, this is the best recipe you've ever done." That's what Beverly's twelve-year-old son, Sam, said when he agreed to taste test our latest burger creation. That one vote was enough for us to add Pizza Burgers to our Desperate Repertoire. An added bonus is how easy they are to make.

Stuffed Bacon-Cheddar Burgers

Super stuffed burgers bursting with the bold flavors of bacon, cheese, and onion are sure to be crowd pleasers. These burgers are unbelievably easy to put together using already-cooked bacon and already-shredded cheese, which speed you right through the first phase. And, if you aren't ready to fill the backyard with the savory aromas of burgers on the grill just yet, they can wait for up to 8 hours until you are.

14 to 16 slices already-cooked bacon
   (see box on page 218)
2 pounds extra-lean ground beef
1 envelope (¼ cup) onion soup mix,
   such as Lipton
2 cups already-shredded sharp Cheddar cheese
1 cup milk
8 hamburger buns
Lettuce and tomato slices (optional)
Your choice of condiments, such as spicy brown
   prepared mustard, ketchup, and/or mayonnaise,
   for serving

PHASE 1: 15 MINUTES

1. Microwave the bacon until very crisp following the directions on the package, about 10 seconds per slice. Pat with paper towels and let cool for 1 minute. Crumble into bite-size pieces.

2. Meanwhile, place the ground beef in a large mixing bowl. Add soup mix, Cheddar, crumbled bacon, and milk. Using your hands, wearing disposable plastic gloves, if desired, or using a sturdy plastic spoon, mix until everything is incorporated into the meat.

3. Shape the meat mixture into 8 patties, using a hamburger press, if possible, or roll into balls and then press firmly between 2 sheets of waxed paper. If you handled the meat, wash your hands well with antibacterial soap. *The patties can be refrigerated, covered, in a single layer or separated by a piece of waxed paper for up to 8 hours.*

PHASE 2: 15 MINUTES

4. Turn on a gas grill to medium-high.

SPACE SAVER

You're going to need extra space in the refrigerator and freezer the week before your gathering. So go ahead and clean out the vegetable bin—you'll be glad you did!

5. Place the prepared patties on the hot grill and cook for 5 minutes, then turn. Grill until the meat is no longer pink in the center, 5 to 6 minutes more.

6. Heat the hamburger buns on the grill, if desired. Place each burger on a bun and serve with lettuce and tomato slices, if desired, and the condiments of your choice.

■ *Serves 8*

GADGETS: BURGER PRESSES

Whether you are serving sizzling Pizza Burgers (see page 171) or juicy, delicious Stuffed Bacon-Cheddar Burgers (see opposite), you'll want to form your burgers into nice, even round patties. Easier said than done, right? Not if you use a burger press.

This handy little kitchen tool is available in the kitchen utensil section of variety stores or in kitchen supply stores. Most hamburger presses are safe to wash in the top rack of a dishwasher, making cleanup a breeze.

The shaping is only half of it, though. It's when you're flipping the burgers on the grill that you'll come to really appreciate what this inexpensive kitchen helper does. Because it compacts the meat (and any extra ingredients you add) into a neat firm patty, your burgers won't fall apart. Plus, you'll end up with patties that fill the buns instead of puffed-up little balls that leave everyone asking, "Where's the beef?"

THE YARD OLYMPICS

From Beverly:

Some of the most solid, age-old friendships are based on a little healthy competition. After thinking about it, I realized how easy it would be to put that all-too-human drive to work in forging new friendships. That's how the Yard Olympics came to be.

I'm talking about transforming a simple backyard barbecue into a memorable event that helps people loosen up and get to know each other. If you want to entertain a group that includes both preschoolers and preteens, a plain-old afternoon on the deck probably won't work. But if you attach a grand title, like the Yard Olympics, suddenly a simple length of rope for tug-of-war, a few burlap bags for a sack race, and some watermelon seeds for spitting add up to Kodak moments and lots of laughs.

The same concept works with croquet, volleyball, badminton, horseshoes, Ping-Pong, boccie ball, or whatever outdoor sports equipment you happen to have. Just call a simple game a tournament, have a bunch of blue ribbons on hand to award, and watch what happens. Authentic fun, guaranteed.

Here are our favorite tips for tournaments without tears.

• **Include everyone.** Junior might not be able to toss heavy horseshoes, but he'll score every time if he throws a hula hoop.

• **Blow bubbles.** They break all age barriers.

• **Have an award for everyone.** Construction paper can become a blue ribbon in no time, so imagination is the only limit. Categories can range from Best Attitude to Most Improved and Best Jokes on the Court.

• **No time for construction paper cutouts?** Make the blue ribbons a party activity and invite your guests to help. Or, school supply sections often stock awards certificates and ribbons.

• **The hosts' attitudes set the tone.** Let everyone know the real sport is having fun and fostering friendship. A few well-placed jokes and a jovial demeanor should do the trick.

• **No yard?** Transport your crew to the park instead (see pages 232 and 233 for tips on packing picnics and other moveable feasts).

• **Rain?** It's bound to happen sometime. Dust off those board games just in case (see page 107 for suggestions).

Be sure that everybody is a winner, especially all the kids.

Perfect Party Pork

2 limes
2 tablespoons rice wine vinegar or white wine vinegar
2 tablespoons vegetable oil
1 tablespoon reduced-sodium soy sauce
1 tablespoon honey
2 cloves fresh garlic
½ teaspoon dried red pepper flakes (optional)
2 pork tenderloins (about 1 pound each)

PHASE 1: 10 MINUTES, PLUS 6 TO 24 HOURS MOSTLY UNATTENDED MARINATING TIME

1. Cut the limes in half and squeeze the juice into a 2-cup glass measure. Add the vinegar, oil, soy sauce, and honey. Peel and mince the garlic and add it to the lime juice mixture. Add the red pepper flakes, if using. Whisk well to blend in the honey.

2. Place the pork in a zipper-top plastic bag and pour the marinade over it (scrape out any honey that clings to the measure). Seal the bag and lay it flat in the refrigerator to marinate for at least 6 hours. Turn the bag over 2 to 4 times while marinating. *The pork can marinate for up to 24 hours.*

PHASE 2: 20 MINUTES

3. Turn on a gas grill to high.

4. Place the marinated pork on the hot grill and cook 6 minutes. Rotate the meat by a third (pork tenderloins tend to be shaped like triangles). Cook 6 minutes more. Rotate the tenderloin a second third of a turn so that all sides brown. Cook until the internal temperature reaches 160°F on an instant-read meat thermometer, about 8 minutes more. Serve at once or refrigerate, covered, until ready to serve. Let return to room temperature before serving. *The grilled pork can be refrigerated, covered, for up to 24 hours.*

■ *Serves 8*

The easiest way to marinate pork tenderloins is in a large, freezer-weight, zipper-top bag. Pour the marinade over the meat, seal the bag, and throw it in the refrigerator. Turning the bag over every few hours to distribute the marinade evenly eliminates the need for stirring. When it's time to grill, just pull out the pork and throw away the bag and leftover marinade. The intense flavor of lime juice and garlic will have sufficiently seeped into the pork here, so no basting is needed. After 20 minutes on the grill, you've got perfectly cooked pork tenderloin.

From Alicia:

A family favorite for years, this chicken dinner, based on satés, an Indonesian favorite, was nicknamed by my children very early on. When they were younger, I did not marinate their skewered chicken but grilled it at the same time as the rest. When we sat down to dinner, the kids enjoyed their own plain version of the grown-ups' zesty satés. Now that my kids are older and have an appreciation for stronger flavors, I fix everyone's the same way. The red pepper flakes are optional, though, if you want to keep it a little tamer. For those who really like it hot, add the red pepper with gusto and enjoy.

Satés can be made from any type of meat threaded on wooden skewers and grilled or broiled. Our Chicken on a Stick is hearty enough for a main dish, although satés are usually a snack or appetizer. The easy marinade will surprise you—its depth and bold flavors come from just a few ingredients. Pair the satés with Warm Ginger-Peanut Sauce and your guests will feel as though they've been transported to an exotic Indonesian location.

Chicken on a Stick

½ cup Asian (dark) sesame oil
½ cup reduced-sodium soy sauce
¼ cup honey
2 tablespoons red wine vinegar
2 tablespoons bottled fresh ginger (see Notes)
½ small onion (for about ¼ cup chopped)
2 teaspoons bottled minced garlic
1 teaspoon dried red pepper flakes (optional)
¼ teaspoon cayenne pepper
2½ pounds skinless, boneless chicken breasts, thawed if frozen
16 to 24 (10-inch) bamboo skewers (see Notes)
Warm Ginger-Peanut Sauce, for serving (optional; see page 178)

PHASE 1: 10 MINUTES

1. Put the sesame oil, soy sauce, honey, vinegar, ginger, onion, garlic, red pepper flakes, if using, and cayenne in a food processor or blender. Pulse until the onion is chopped fine and all the ingredients are well blended. *The marinade can be refrigerated, covered, for up to 3 days.*

PHASE 2: 20 MINUTES, PLUS 4 TO 8 HOURS MOSTLY UNATTENDED MARINATING TIME

2. Cut the chicken breasts into roughly 1-inch cubes. Thread 4 to 5 pieces of chicken on a soaked skewer. Repeat with the remaining chicken. Place the skewered chicken in a shallow oblong dish (in a layer no more than 2 deep) and pour the marinade over it. Cover and refrigerate for at least 4 hours. *The chicken breasts can marinate for up to 8 hours.*

PHASE 3: 15 MINUTES

3. Turn on a gas grill to high.

4. Remove the chicken from the bag and discard the marinade. When the grill is hot, after about 4 minutes, place the chicken skewers on the grill and cook until the chicken is lightly browned and cooked through, 6 to 10 minutes in all, turning frequently. Serve immediately with the ginger-peanut sauce, if desired.

■ *Serves 8*

Notes: Bottled fresh ginger is the perfect replacement for time-consuming fresh ginger. Called crushed, ground, minced, or chopped, depending on the brand, bottled fresh ginger is available in the produce section of larger supermarkets. Finely minced fresh ginger can be substituted.

Soak the bamboo skewers in water for at least 20 minutes before threading the chicken onto them. This will keep them from burning when you grill the chicken. The number of skewers you will need depends on the size of the chicken cubes.

COOKOUT ESSENTIALS FOR A SMOOTH EVENING

From Alicia:

All it takes is for the bugs to start biting and my night is fairly ruined. That's why when we cook out, I depend on a few items that make for a more pleasant and bug-free evening.

• Tiki torches with citronella-scented oil or candles not only add ambience to the deck or patio but also are great at bug control. They're usually available in the spring at home-and-garden stores and are not very expensive. It only takes two or three to do the trick—just don't forget to pick up the fuel as well.

• Child-safe bug spray. Give a few squirts on those tender ankles to keep the bugs at bay.

• Light baskets or mesh-covered domes for covering the food on the table. Let's face it, even the bugs want to sample the delectable dinner you've prepared. So don't tempt them—give all foods a quick cover.

Warm Ginger-Peanut Sauce

From Beverly:

My troubles started when Alicia dropped by before leaving on vacation. "I've cleaned out my refrigerator," she said, "and I couldn't bear to waste this peanut sauce. Use it as a dip for chicken." That's exactly what I did the first night. But, there was sauce left over, and every time I passed the refrigerator, what got dipped in was my little finger. Forget chicken. The peanut sauce was going straight from the Tupperware into my greedy mouth. By the third day I was guarding my supply. With Alicia away and the recipe for the sauce locked in her house, panic was bearing down.

There are times when one must admit powerlessness in the face of temptation. I caved in to the dirty truth: I was addicted to Warm Ginger-Peanut Sauce. You and your guests will love it, too. Don't be intimidated by the long list of ingredients! Just throw everything into the blender. In a mere 10 minutes you'll have a sauce that's perfect not only for our Chicken on a Stick but also with Crispy Oven-Baked Chicken Fingers (see page 83).

> *4 cloves fresh garlic*
> *1 tablespoon onion powder*
> *2 tablespoons vegetable oil*
> *1 tablespoon Asian (dark) sesame oil*
> *1 tablespoon bottled fresh ginger (see Note)*
> *1 tablespoon red wine vinegar*
> *¼ cup firmly packed light brown sugar*
> *½ cup smooth peanut butter*
> *¼ cup ketchup*
> *¼ cup soy sauce*
> *½ lemon*
> *½ teaspoon ground coriander*
> *1 teaspoon ground turmeric*
> *½ teaspoon crushed dried red pepper flakes, or more*
>   *to taste*

START TO FINISH: 10 MINUTES

1. Peel the garlic cloves and drop them 1 at a time through the feed tube of a blender or food processor with the machine running and finely chop. Add the remaining ingredients one at a time, squeezing the lemon juice through a small strainer (to catch the seeds) directly into the blender or processor bowl. Pulse on high to combine well.

DO-AHEAD

The sauce can be stored covered for up to 2 days.

2. To serve, place in a microwave-safe bowl and microwave, covered with plastic wrap, on high until heated through, 1 to 2 minutes

■ *Makes 1½ cups*

Note: Bottled fresh ginger is the perfect replacement for time-consuming fresh ginger. Called crushed, ground, minced, or chopped, depending on the brand, bottled fresh ginger is available in the produce section of larger supermarkets. Finely minced fresh ginger can be substituted.

LET'S HEAR IT FOR THE GARLIC PRESS

I t's hard to beat a garlic press for mincing peeled cloves quickly. This metal gadget has a slot for the garlic clove and uses a lever and manual pressure to force the garlic through a bunch of tiny holes, mincing it instantly. There's only one caution. By all means, spend a dollar or two more at a kitchen equipment shop or department store to get a self-cleaning press. Otherwise you'll find yourself standing beside the sink poking garlic out of the holes with a toothpick. Then all the time you've saved goes right down the drain. For tips on peeling garlic quickly, see page 259.

Serving shrimp is such a treat that when we do splurge, we want to be sure the flavor shines through. If you slather on a thick sauce and all you can taste is that sauce, you may as well cook something cheap. Fortunately, in this case a light brush of lime butter and a hint of Old Bay seasoning is not only the perfect combination, it's also easy.

Citrus Shrimp Kebabs

2 pounds already-peeled large raw shrimp, defrosted
    if frozen (see Notes)
About 12 to 16 small (10-inch) bamboo skewers
    (see Notes)
8 tablespoons (1 stick) butter
1 lime
2 teaspoons seafood seasoning, such as Old Bay

PHASE 1: 20 MINUTES

1. Curl each shrimp to form a **C** shape and skewer twice, through the body and above the tail section. Don't put too many shrimp on any one skewer. Place the skewered shrimp on a plate or tray. *The skewered shrimp can be refrigerated, covered, for up to 6 hours.*

PHASE 2: 7 TO 10 MINUTES

2. Turn on a gas grill to medium-high.

3. Put the butter in a microwave-safe bowl, cover with a paper towel, and microwave on high until melted, about 1 minute. Cut the lime in half, squeeze the juice into the melted butter, and stir well with a whisk or fork.

4. Brush the shrimp lightly on both sides with some of the butter mixture. Sprinkle the seafood seasoning lightly over both sides.

5. Place the shrimp on the hot grill (this may need to be done in 2 batches, depending on the size of your grill). Cook until pink on the first side, about 2 minutes. Turn and continue cooking until pink and opaque throughout, 2 to 3 more minutes, depending on the size of the shrimp. Do not overcook. Serve at once.

■ *Serves 8*

SPACE SAVER

Storage idea! An old chest of draws is the perfect place to tuck away platters and serving pieces that you don't use very often.

Notes: The definition of "large" shrimp can vary. Stores often size shrimp based on a count of shrimp per pound. For this recipe, choose the very largest shrimp you can afford, but choose shrimp that are no more than 26 to 30 count per pound.

Soak the bamboo skewers in water for at least 20 minutes before using to prevent burning. The larger the shrimp, the less time it will take to skewer them. The number of skewers you will need will depend on the size of your shrimp. It will also depend on whether you want to serve the shrimp still on skewers or remove them behind the scenes and serve on a platter. If you're going to serve the shrimp on skewers, make sure they are evenly distributed.

BABY-SITTER SALVATION, SORT OF

When groups of families gather, it's nice to strike a balance between everyone socializing together and the grown-ups enjoying adults-only conversation. Doing this can be challenging, particularly when preschoolers are involved. One option that helps is to hire a teen or two to play with the kids.

The idea is not to sequester the children to a spot where they're neither seen nor heard. Rather, the idea is to provide an energetic extra pair of hands to help keep your smallest guests happy by initiating games, serving endless cups of juice, and encouraging everybody to share. Be sure to provide any instructions, all the supplies, and whatever safety guidelines you think are necessary.

When it comes time to serve the meal, you'll need all the hands you can get. And if the children eat and run for the swing-set while the adults want to linger over dessert and coffee, the "sort-of" sitter watching over the herd will help everyone relax.

If you happen to have guests younger than two, the sitter can provide another much-needed service. We've hosted several parties where the parents never got a chance to sit down and eat because their youngster got fussy at the table and needed to walk. (We've all been there, right?) The sitter can stroll, jostle, and play with the tyke, and peace will be restored.

From Alicia:

Several years ago we started a summer vacation tradition—fish boats. It's the perfect way to grill any kind of fish, no matter where you are or what kind of grilling equipment you have. When the fish prepared this way became so popular with everyone who dined with us on vacation, we decided it was the perfect way to prepare fish at home for company, too. Choose a flaky white fish for the best texture. We suggest flounder, grouper fillets, or farm-raised tilapia fillets.

TIME SAVER

The quickest way to chop parsley is actually to snip it. Kitchen shears make fast work of snipping parsley leaves. You can rinse the parsley, shake it dry, and then snip the leaves directly over the container you will store them in. Snipped parsley will keep for 24 hours, covered and refrigerated.

Vacation Fish Boats

8 tablespoons (1 stick) butter
1 head already-roasted garlic (for about ¼ cup cloves; see recipe page 262)
1 cup dry white wine
8 white fish fillets (about 6 ounces each)
2 lemons
¼ cup chopped fresh parsley, for garnish (optional)

PHASE 1: 8 MINUTES

1. Place the butter in a 2-cup or larger glass measure, cover with a paper towel, and microwave on high until melted, about 1 minute.

2. Peel and coarsely chop the garlic and add it to the melted butter. Add the wine and whisk to mix well. *The sauce can be refrigerated, covered, for up to 24 hours. If the butter congeals, let it sit at room temperature until it can be stirred again or heat in the microwave for 15 seconds to soften.*

PHASE 2: 12 MINUTES

3. Prepare the fish boats: Tear off 4 sheets of heavy-duty aluminum foil each roughly 20 inches long. (Or use 8 sheets of regular aluminum foil, stacking 2 on top of each other for strength.)

4. Place 2 fish fillets side by side, without overlapping, on the center of a piece of foil. Fold up the edges, crimping to form a 1-inch lip all the way around the fish. Crush the foil lip tight against the fish, working carefully to avoid tearing the foil. (The tops of the fillets will be exposed.) Transfer the fish boat to a baking sheet for easier transport to the grill. Repeat with the remaining fillets and pieces of aluminum foil.

5. Whisk the sauce and spoon it over the fish, dividing it equally among them. *The fish boats can be refrigerated, covered, at this point for up to 4 hours.*

6. Turn on a gas grill to medium-high.

7. Cut the lemons in half and, using a strainer to catch the seeds, squeeze the juice of half a lemon evenly over each fish boat.

8. Transfer the boats to the hot grill and cook, with the grill cover closed, until the fish is opaque and flakes easily with a fork, 10 to 12 minutes.

9. Use a wide metal spatula to transfer the fish boats back to the baking sheet for easier transport to the table. Carefully remove each fish fillet from the foil to a serving plate. Top with the parsley, if using, and serve immediately, spooning any juices remaining in the boats over the fillets.

■ *Serves 8*

FISH FOR COMPANY? BUILD A BOAT

No matter what kind of fish you choose to grill for company, it makes good sense to build a boat. Most white fish fillets are delicious, tender, and flaky. Before you can enjoy them, you need to take care that the fragile fillets don't fall through the grate on the grill. Sure you could buy one of those fancy baskets to grill in, but our desperate solution is fish boats.

Boats are easy to assemble, so children can help, and the only equipment you need is heavy-duty aluminum foil and a cookie sheet to help transport the fish boats to the grill. (You'll find a complete how-to for making fish boats at left.) The best part is the lovely flavors—garlic, butter, and wine—that cook right into the fillets. Don't just think fillets, though. While you don't need a boat for fish steaks, such as salmon or tuna, they'll taste more special fixed this way.

So next time you grill fish for company, build a boat.

Flavorful and meaty enough to star as the main dish at dinner, portobello mushrooms take well to a simple marinade and are particularly yummy when grilled. The portobello is the mature version of another favorite member of the mushroom family, the crimini mushroom. While a crimini is modest in size, a portobello cap can measure from 3 to 8 inches in diameter (although the really large specimens are harder to find). These beauties are appearing in even the smallest grocery stores these days, verifying their popularity.

It's best to buy any fresh mushrooms within a few days of when you plan to eat them. If a 'shroom starts to lose moisture, that means it's losing flavor. The texture is also compromised. Portobellos come as whole mushrooms, as caps, or even already sliced. For this recipe, buy whole mushrooms or caps. Because mushrooms are porous, they absorb the flavor of our savory glaze of oil, vinegar, and basil in no time.

Portobello Mushroom "Steak" Sandwiches

8 large fresh portobello mushroom caps
¼ cup balsamic vinegar
2 tablespoons extra-virgin olive oil
2 teaspoons dried basil
8 slices (about ⅛ inch thick; 8 ounces total) Provolone cheese
8 kaiser rolls or large, crusty buns
8 slices large, ripe tomato (optional)
8 lettuce leaves (optional)
Your choice of condiments, such as Dijon mustard and/or mayonnaise, for serving

PHASE 1: 7 MINUTES, PLUS 2 TO 8 HOURS UNATTENDED MARINATING TIME

1. If the mushroom caps have stems attached, remove and discard them. Rinse and dry the mushroom caps and place them in a large zipper-topped plastic bag. In a small mixing bowl or glass measure, whisk together the vinegar, olive oil, and basil. Drizzle the mixture over the mushroom caps. Seal the bag and shake. Refrigerate for at least 2 hours. *The mushrooms can marinate for up to 8 hours.*

PHASE 2: 7 MINUTES

2. Turn on a gas grill to medium-high.

3. Place the marinated mushroom caps on the hot grill, smooth-side down and cook 3 minutes, then turn the caps over. Place a slice of Provolone on each cap and continue to cook until the cheese melts, about 2 minutes more.

4. Heat the rolls on the grill, if desired. Place each cap on a roll and serve with a tomato slice and lettuce leaf, if desired, and the condiments of your choice.

■ *Serves 8*

Sesame Vegetable Medley

2 large onions (for about 2 cups sliced)
1 large red bell pepper (for about 1 cup sliced)
4 cups (about 12 ounces) fresh broccoli florets
1 package (8 ounces) already-sliced, fresh button mushrooms
¼ cup reduced-sodium soy sauce
2 tablespoons peanut oil or other salad oil
1 tablespoon sesame seeds

PHASE 1: 8 MINUTES

1. Peel the onions and cut them in half. Slice each half into crescent-shaped slices ¼ inch thick. Place the slices in a large-size aluminum foil grilling bag (see box, page 187). Rinse, cut in half, core, and seed the bell pepper. Cut each half into ¼-inch strips and add them to the aluminum foil bag. Rinse the broccoli florets and cut any large ones into bite-size pieces. Add the broccoli florets and mushrooms to the foil bag. Seal the bag loosely. *The filled bag can be refrigerated at this point for up to 12 hours.*

PHASE 2: 12 MINUTES

2. Turn on a gas grill to high.

3. Pour the soy sauce and oil into a 2-cup glass measure and whisk to combine. Pour the mixture into the aluminum foil bag and sprinkle in the sesame seeds. Fold the top of the foil bag to close it securely and gently shake to mix the contents.

4. Place the aluminum foil bag flat on the hot grill, making sure vegetables are evenly distributed. After cooking 8 to 10 minutes the broccoli will be crisp-tender. Remove the bag to a pan to support it and, wearing oven mitts, cut open the top of the foil bag with a sharp knife. Carefully fold back the top of the foil bag, allowing steam to escape. Serve at once.

■ *Serves 8*

Simple vegetables turn exotic with the addition of sesame seeds. A good sprinkling of soy sauce will season the vegetables to perfection. Sealing them in aluminum foil ensures that they will be done just right.

MONEY SAVER

Plan menus around vegetables and fruits when they are in season or on special sale at the supermarket. Not only is seasonal produce cheaper, it's likely to be more flavorful, too.

If you're grilling the main course, you might as well grill the vegetables, too. A handy aluminum foil bag gives a smoky grill flavor without all the fuss of spearing vegetables on skewers. Our combination of squash and bell pepper strips is colorful, and the fresh basil adds the bright taste of summer.

Grilled Squash Mix with Basil Butter

1 large onion (for about 1 cup sliced)
1 medium-size red bell pepper (for about 1 cup sliced)
1 medium-size yellow bell pepper (for about 1 cup sliced)
2 medium-size zucchini (for about 2 cups sliced)
2 large yellow squash (for about 3 cups sliced)
6 tablespoons (¾ stick) butter
About 1 cup densely packed fresh basil
2 teaspoons seasoning salt

PHASE 1: 12 MINUTES

1. Peel the onion and cut it in half lengthwise. Slice each half into crescent-shaped slices ¼ inch thick. Place the slices in a large-size aluminum foil grilling bag (see box opposite). Rinse, cut in half, core, and seed the bell peppers. Cut each half into ¼-inch strips and add them to the aluminum foil bag.

2. Rinse the zucchini and yellow squash. Trim the ends and then cut the zucchini and squash crosswise into slices about ¼ inch thick and add to the foil bag.

3. Place the butter in a 2-cup or larger glass measure, cover with a paper towel, and microwave on high until melted, about 45 seconds. Rinse the basil well and shake to remove any excess water. Remove and discard any tough stems. You should have about 1 cup of leaves. Coarsely chop the basil and add it to the foil bag. Pour the melted butter into the foil bag. Sprinkle the seasoning salt over the vegetables in the foil bag. Fold the top of the foil bag to close it securely and gently shake to mix the contents. *The filled bag can be refrigerated at this point for up to 8 hours.*

PHASE 2: 10 MINUTES MOSTLY UNATTENDED GRILLING TIME, PLUS 10 MINUTES UNATTENDED RESTING TIME

4. Turn on a gas grill to medium-high.

5. Place the aluminum foil bag flat on the hot grill, making sure the vegetables are evenly distributed, cover the grill, and cook 10 minutes. Remove the bag to a pan to support it and, with the bag sealed, let the vegetables stand to finish steaming, for at least 10 minutes or up to 20 minutes (be aware that some of the vegetable juices will leak into the pan). When ready to serve, wearing oven mitts, cut open the top of the foil bag with a sharp knife. Carefully fold back the top of the foil bag, allowing steam to escape. Put the vegetables into a serving dish and serve at once.

■ *Serves 8 generously*

FOIL BAGGIN' IT

We love the full flavors of grilled vegetables but our desperate schedules don't allow for chopping *and* skewering all those pieces. When we saw aluminum foil bags at the supermarket, we knew we'd never have to do without grilled veggies again.

These jumbo bags are made of heavy-duty aluminum foil (Reynolds makes ones called Hot Bags). They have seams that won't open with the slightest of jostling like homemade foil bags sometimes do. It's quick work to chop your vegetables and throw them into the bag, mix your seasoning, and toss it in on top. Seal the bag, give it a shake, and pop the package on the grill. We suggest using the large size, 17 by 15 inches.

Still, if you can't find commercial aluminum foil bags, by all means, make your own pouch using heavy-duty aluminum foil. You'll need two pieces of the extra-wide kind, each roughly 18 by 16 inches. Double over the side seams and crimp the edges on three sides, leaving one side open until filled.

CHAPTER SIX

Standout

There's nothing like a stress-free salad to make easy work of entertaining.

I t's hard to imagine planning an entertaining menu without salads. Want contrast, something fresh, something colorful? Look no further. When you're working ahead, salads are patient. They're versatile, easy to execute, and pretty much adored by all.

Sometimes salad is the star, taking center stage on the plate, but more often than not, salad stands to the side. If a main-dish salad is in order, turn to ones like Chunky Chicken Salad with Macadamia Nuts, Asparagus and Ham Platter Salad, or Party Shrimp Salad with Thai Lime Splash.

When you're serving one-dish entrées that include both vegetables and starch, our philosophy calls for side salads that make an elegant statement. They're built around terrific home-made dressings splashed over leafy greens. To speed preparation we use bags of prewashed salad greens, which are widely available in supermarkets (for more tips on these greens, see the box on page 213). As is the case with our Cilantro-Basil Salad with Mushrooms, Marietta's Mandarin Salad, Awesome Apricot Salad, and Russian Beet Salad, we often rely on distinctive ingredients to liven things up.

For those occasions when you need salad to be a heartier presence, consider our recipes for Greek Greens with Potato Salad, Pretty Pasta Salad with Peas and Carrots, or Red and Black Bean Salad. Salads like these round out a meal handily.

Salads

Nearly all of the work on our salads can be done well in advance, helping you remain calm and collected as the countdown to mealtime approaches. However, you won't always be able to plan ahead, which brings us to matters of the moment—spur-of-the-moment to be precise. If you've found yourself with a true entertaining emergency (as in you're treating guests to take-out pizza due to circumstances beyond your control), a homemade salad dressing poured over a simple bowl of greens can be the little extra touch that pulls everything together. It might convince you to ignore the fact that tonight's menu isn't exactly what you had envisioned. You can make most of our vinaigrettes—everything from Balsamic Vinaigrette and Sweet Red-Wine Vinaigrette to Marietta's Marvelous Dressing and Greek Dressing—in 5 minutes or less with the help of pantry staples. Given a bit more time, say 7 to 10 minutes, you can go for a different kind of salad and whip up Curried Confetti Coleslaw or Unbelievable Broccoli Slaw.

A standard tossed salad certainly has its place, but if you can just as easily serve an out of the ordinary salad your guests will remember, so much the better.

MAIN-DISH SALADS

fast and fabulous

Chunky Chicken Salad with Macadamia Nuts

From Alicia:

This fast salad has quickly become one of my company favorites. Using already-roasted chicken, found right in the supermarket meat case or from the deli counter rotisserie, you can whip the salad up in no time. But leftover turkey, grilled chicken breasts, or your own oven-roasted chicken are good, too.

If you can't find already-chopped macadamia nuts on the baking aisle, check the nuts on the beverage aisle. Or try using already-shelled pistachios or walnuts. And low-fat sour cream and mayonnaise will work fine.

With toasted bagels, Fastest Fruit Salad (see page 270), and tomato slices, the salad makes a light lunch. It's also nice on lettuce leaves with grape clusters.

1 cup already-chopped macadamia nuts
1 small container (8 ounces) sour cream
1 cup mayonnaise
4 cups already-roasted and -sliced chicken, such as
    Perdue Short Cuts carved chicken breast (see Notes)
1 bunch scallions (for about 1 cup chopped, white and
    green parts)
2 large ribs celery (for about 1 cup chopped)
⅓ cup sweet pickle relish (see Notes)
½ teaspoon black pepper, or more to taste
Salt, if macadamia nuts are unsalted

START TO FINISH: 18 MINUTES

1. Spread the macadamia nuts in a single layer on a microwave-safe plate and microwave, uncovered, on high, until fragrant and lightly toasted, about 2 minutes, stirring halfway through. Using oven mitts, remove from the microwave and set aside to cool.

2. Meanwhile, in a medium-size bowl, mix together the sour cream and mayonnaise. Chop the chicken into chunks, if necessary, and add to the mayonnaise mixture. Stir until the chicken is well coated.

3. Rinse and chop the scallions; sprinkle them over the chicken mixture as you chop. Repeat with the celery. Drain the sweet pickle relish well and add it to the salad. Add the toasted nuts and the pepper and stir to mix well. Taste for seasoning, adding salt and pepper if necessary.

■ *Serves 8*

Notes: If you are using Perdue Short Cuts, pick the plain, not the seasoned, variety.

Sweet pickle relish is sometimes called sweet pickle cubes or salad cubes.

DO-AHEAD

The chicken and macadamia nut salad can be refrigerated, covered, for up to 24 hours.

Soda Fountain Chicken Salad

2 to 2⅓ pounds skinless, boneless chicken breasts
4 large eggs
3 to 4 large ribs celery (for about 2 cups diced)
1¼ cups sweet pickle relish with its liquid (see Note)
1 cup mayonnaise
½ teaspoon salt
¾ teaspoon black pepper

PHASE 1: 25 MINUTES

1. Place the chicken in a 4½-quart Dutch oven or soup pot. Add just enough cold water to cover the chicken, about 1 quart. Place the eggs in a 2-quart or larger saucepan and add just enough cold water to cover them. Cover both pots and bring to a boil over high heat.

Back when the very best drug stores all had soda fountains, you could always count on them serving a marvelous chicken salad at lunchtime. We've re-created this Southern classic with lots of sweet pickles. "I had just enough time for the first phase before rushing off to my daughter's school choir performance," our friend Julie Realon reported when she tried out the dish. "The next morning I finished and packed it up to take to a football game picnic lunch. I'm sure we had the best tailgate food anywhere near the stadium."

2. When the water in the pan with the eggs comes to a boil, uncover the pan and let boil for 3 minutes. Remove the pan from the heat, cover it, and let stand, covered, for 15 minutes or up to 1 hour.

3. As soon as the chicken boils, after about 5 minutes, remove the pot from the heat and let it stand, covered, until the chicken is no longer pink in the center, about 15 minutes. Remove the chicken from the pot. Discard the broth or reserve it for another use.

4. While the chicken and eggs stand, rinse and dice the celery. *The cooked chicken and diced celery can be refrigerated separately, covered, for up to 24 hours. The hard-boiled eggs can be refrigerated for up to 4 days.*

PHASE 2: 15 MINUTES

5. Fit a food processor with the steel blade. Cut whole cooked chicken breasts in half. Cut 1 breast half into 4 pieces, process for about 5 seconds, then pulse the motor 3 to 4 more times just until the breast is shredded but not finely ground. Put the shredded chicken into a large mixing bowl. Repeat with the remaining breasts.

6. Peel the hard-boiled eggs, place them in the same processor bowl, and pulse on and off 3 to 5 times or until the eggs resemble coarse crumbs (don't process the eggs too much or you'll have a paste). Add the eggs to the bowl with the chicken.

7. Add the diced celery, pickle relish, mayonnaise, salt, and pepper to the bowl with the chicken. Stir very well until all of the chicken is coated with mayonnaise. Serve at once or refrigerate until ready to serve. *The salad can be refrigerated, covered, for up to 24 hours.*

■ *Serves 8*

Note: Sweet pickle relish is sometimes called sweet pickle cubes or salad cubes.

MONEY SAVER

We love having dinner on the deck. The more casual the setting, the less fancy everything needs to be. Formal meals are by definition more costly, so think informal settings when you want to save money.

BACK HOME AND HUNGRY? THINK SALADS

We're big fans of cold food. Our families seem to be always on the go, and when we finally make it home with guests in tow, we want to eat right away. That's when having a meal's worth of salads waiting in the refrigerator comes in handy. Sure it requires a little forethought, but when the big moment arrives, all that needs to be done is to take out the bowls and remove the plastic wrap. Every now and then there's a last minute tossing of some lettuce with dressing, but that's as complicated as it gets.

Easy, advance preparation is a feature of many of our salads. We wouldn't be true to our North Carolina roots if we didn't have the urge to brag about our amazing recipe for traditional Southern chicken salad (with eggs and pickle relish, of course, see page 191). But we don't dig our heels in at the state border. We've branched out as far as Miami with a show-stopping shrimp salad (see page 204) and veered over to California for an easy wrap-style salad sandwich that's festive and fun (see page 200). We like to choose at least one hearty offering with seafood or meat and one with a starch, such as our Cheese Tortellini Salad (see page 235) or Denise's Vinaigrette Potatoes with Asparagus (see page 242).

When rounding out the menu, it's important to think about time. Because a salad buffet requires a few more dishes than you might ordinarily make, you'll need a dish or two that whips together in just minutes. Over and over again we turn to Picnic Corn Relish (see page 210), Carrot Salad with Fresh Pineapple (see page 222), or one of our easy recipes for coleslaw (see pages 223 through 227). Adding a few loaves of French bread from the bakery or an assortment of crackers is a snap. For a finishing touch that can even double as dessert, Fastest Fruit Salad (see page 270) can't be beat.

The trick to a successful salad-only menu is diversity.

Whether it's a potluck for the year's last PTA meeting, a bridesmaid's lunch, or a baby shower, here's a dependable standby. We've found it's a particular favorite of women. The tomato "cups" are so attractive and rich tasting, guests always assume you worked a lot harder than you did. To make things especially easy, purchase already-cooked chicken, which is widely available in the meat case or supermarket deli. Leftover cooked turkey breast works equally well. Be sure to choose the largest, ripest tomatoes you can find. The salad tastes best hot—it bakes for half an hour. The result is even prettier garnished with a sprinkle of paprika, a sprig of basil or parsley, some snipped chives, or a chive flower.

Chicken Salad-Stuffed Tomatoes

2 pounds skinless, boneless chicken breasts
2 large ribs celery (for about 1 cup chopped)
⅔ cup already-chopped walnuts
⅔ cup mayonnaise (see Note)
⅔ cup already-shredded sharp Cheddar cheese
1½ teaspoons onion powder
Salt and black pepper
8 large, ripe tomatoes (¾ to 1 pound each)

PHASE 1: 20 MINUTES MOSTLY UNATTENDED COOKING TIME

1. Place the chicken breasts in a 4½-quart Dutch oven or soup pot. Add just enough cold water to cover the chicken, about 1 quart. Cover the pot and bring to a rolling boil over high heat, about 5 minutes. As soon as the water boils, remove the pot from the heat and let stand, covered, until the chicken is no longer pink in the center, about 15 minutes. Remove the chicken from the pot. Discard the broth or reserve it for another use. *The cooked chicken can be refrigerated, covered, for up to 24 hours.*

PHASE 2: 15 MINUTES

2. Rinse and dice the celery and put it in a large mixing bowl. Cut the cooked chicken into bite-size pieces and add these to the bowl. Add the walnuts, mayonnaise, Cheddar cheese, and onion powder. Stir until well combined. Season with salt and black pepper to taste. *The salad can be refrigerated, covered, at this point for up to 12 hours.*

PHASE 3: 20 MINUTES

3. Rinse the tomatoes. Cut a ¼-inch slice off the stem end of each but do not peel. Cut out the core and enough flesh to make a bowl, leaving the wall of the tomato intact. Using your fingers or a small spoon, remove the tomato seeds. (Rinse away any seeds that remain and shake the tomatoes to remove any excess water, if necessary.) Lightly salt and pepper each tomato cavity.

4. Place the tomatoes in an 11 × 8-inch glass baking dish. Spoon a heaping ½ cup of the chicken mixture into each tomato cavity. *The stuffed tomatoes can be refrigerated, covered, for up to 12 hours or up to 24 hours if the cooked chicken has not been previously refrigerated.*

PHASE 4: 30 MINUTES UNATTENDED BAKING TIME

5. Preheat the oven to 350°F.

6. Bake the tomatoes, uncovered, until the chicken salad is warm throughout, about 30 minutes.

■ *Serves 8*

Note: You can use low-fat mayonnaise here, if you like.

Chicken-Pesto Pasta Salad

16 ounces tricolored corkscrew pasta or other short pasta
Ice cubes
2 tablespoons olive oil
1 large onion (for about 1 cup chopped)
3 carrots (for about 1½ cups sliced)
1½ pounds skinless, boneless chicken breasts
1 package (8 ounces) already-sliced, fresh button
  mushrooms
½ cup mayonnaise (see Note)
⅓ cup commercially prepared pesto
1 cup already-grated Parmesan cheese

Some things you just have to taste to believe. Sautéed onion, carrots, and mushrooms make for a mellow salad that gives you a different twist on the same-old pasta salad. Don't worry if you can't find the time to make pesto from scratch. In this recipe, commercially prepared pesto, particularly the kind found in the refrigerator section of the supermarket, is a made-in-heaven match for the harried host.

PHASE 1: 20 MINUTES

1. Bring 3 quarts of unsalted water to a boil. When the water boils, add the pasta and cook according to the directions on the package until firm-tender, 9 to 11 minutes.

2. When the pasta is done, put it in a colander to drain and throw in 2 handfuls of ice cubes. Rinse the pasta under cold running water and toss with the ice cubes until the pasta is cool, about 2 minutes. Drain well, shaking to remove as much water as possible. Remove any unmelted ice cubes. *The cooked pasta can be refrigerated, covered, for up to 24 hours. If doing so, before refrigerating, toss the pasta with just enough olive oil to coat it lightly.*

PHASE 2: 20 MINUTES

3. Heat the 2 tablespoons of olive oil in an extra-deep, 12-inch nonstick skillet over medium heat. Peel and coarsely chop the onion, adding it to the skillet as you chop. Peel the carrots and cut them into ¼-inch slices. Add them to the skillet and raise the heat to medium-high.

4. Cut the chicken into bite-size pieces, adding each breast to the skillet as you cut it. Stir frequently. Coarsely chop the mushrooms, add them to the skillet, and cook, stirring frequently, until the mushrooms release their liquid and the chicken is no longer pink, about 5 minutes longer. *The cooked chicken and vegetables can be refrigerated, covered, for up to 24 hours.*

PHASE 3: 3 MINUTES

5. Put the cooked pasta, chicken, and vegetables in a large bowl. Add the mayonnaise, pesto, and Parmesan cheese, and stir well to coat the pasta with sauce. *The pasta salad can be refrigerated, covered, for up to 24 hours.*

■ *Serves 8 generously*

Note: You can use low-fat mayonnaise here, if you like.

TIME SAVER

T*hink polyester before you buy that attractive all-cotton tablecloth and napkins. No matter how spiffy they may be, how much are you willing to iron?*

PRETTY FOOD IN A PINCH

From Beverly:

Fixing food fast is our specialty, and we make sure it darn well tastes good. But when you're pressed for time in general, and you throw a dinner party into the mix, figuring out how to make the food look attractive can be a challenge. Here are some of our favorite simple garnishes for producing pretty food quickly and easily.

• **Paprika:** This is not a spice I use often in cooking, but it's one I use all the time on top of food. The trick is to lightly dust it over white or beige dishes like hummus or chicken salad so the color attracts the eye but doesn't dominate the flavor of the dish.

• **Lemons:** A simple yellow wedge or slice of lemon (seeds removed) alongside a mound of shrimp salad or a piece of fish is both elegant and flavor enhancing. But there is one other quick decoration requiring a knife that isn't difficult. Cut a roughly ¼-inch-thick slice of lemon. Cut the slice through one side of the peel, continuing to cut through the center of the slice and stopping just before the other edge of peel. Take one side of the cut peel in each hand and bend the sides in opposite directions until you end up with a lemon slice curved into an attractive twist. Try this with limes and oranges, too.

• **Cucumbers:** This easy trick requires a sturdy dinner fork. Take the tines of the fork and, using enough pressure to cut through the peel, rake them down the side (top to bottom) of an unpeeled cucumber. Repeat, rotating the cucumber until you have ridges all the way around. It takes about a minute. Now slice the cuke crosswise for an artful effect. Use the slices to enhance a vegetable tray, or place a slice in the middle of a bowl of dip.

• **Mexican-style dollops:** There's a host of foods from South of the Border that can be dressed up with a dash of sour cream, guacamole, or salsa—then there are always canned sliced black olives. Don't like the atomic aftermath of cutting jalapeños? Use them whole to decorate the platter. They pack a wallop, but anyone who likes extra heat won't be shy about absconding with one.

What we've found over the years is that a sprinkle here, an artful dollop there, can make all the difference.

Looking for kudos? Look no further. The exotic mix of bok choy and lettuce coupled with an Asian-inspired sweet-and-sour dressing is practically addictive. Individual portions make a delicious light lunch, or you can toss the entire salad in a big bowl and serve it as part of a salad buffet.

Asian Chicken Salad

2 pounds skinless, boneless chicken breasts
½ cup already-sliced almonds
1 head (about 1½ pounds) bok choy (for about 8 cups chopped)
Asian Dressing (recipe follows)
3 scallions (for about ½ cup chopped, white and green parts)
8 cups medium-packed, prewashed romaine lettuce leaves
1 can (5 ounces) chow mein noodles

PHASE 1: 20 MINUTES

1. Place the chicken breasts in a 4½-quart Dutch oven or soup pot. Add just enough cold water to cover the chicken, about 1 quart. Cover the pot and bring to a rolling boil over high heat, about 5 minutes. As soon as the water boils, remove the pot from the heat and let stand, covered, until the chicken is no longer pink in the center, about 15 minutes.

2. While the chicken cooks, spread the almonds in a pan and toast in a toaster oven at 350°F until light brown, about 5 minutes. Set aside. Rinse and drain the bok choy. Make the Asian Dressing.

3. Remove the chicken from the pot. Discard the broth or reserve it for another use. Rinse the chicken with cool running water until cool enough to handle or refrigerate. *The cooked chicken can be refrigerated, covered, for up to 24 hours. The toasted almonds can be stored at room temperature, covered, for up to 2 days. The rinsed bok choy can be wrapped in paper towels, placed in a plastic bag, and refrigerated for up to 2 days. The salad dressing can be refrigerated, covered, for up to 1 week.*

PHASE 2: 15 MINUTES

4. Cut the cooked chicken into bite-size pieces. Coarsely chop the bok choy into bite-size pieces. Rinse and chop the scallions. *The* *chicken pieces and chopped bok choy and scallions can be prepared up to this point and refrigerated, in separate covered containers, for up to 8 hours.*

PHASE 3: 10 MINUTES

5. Divide the bok choy among 8 plates or place it in a large salad bowl. Evenly divide the lettuce mix, chopped scallions, and chicken pieces among the plates or put in the salad bowl. Drizzle roughly 2½ tablespoons salad dressing over each serving (or all of it over the salad in the bowl). Serve at once or allow the salad to stand at room temperature until ready to serve. Top with the chow mein noodles and toasted almonds just before serving. *The salad can be kept at room temperature for up to 1 hour.*

■ *Serves 8*

Asian Dressing

Soy sauce and a shot of toasted sesame oil make this a flavorful dressing any time you'd like an Asian accent for a salad or shredded cabbage.

> 6 tablespoons rice wine vinegar or
>   white wine vinegar
> ¼ cup sugar
> 3 tablespoons soy sauce
> ½ cup vegetable oil
> 2 teaspoons Asian (dark) sesame oil
> Salt (optional)

START TO FINISH: 5 MINUTES

Put the vinegar, sugar, and soy sauce in a small bowl or 1-pint jar with a lid. Whisk or cover and shake until the sugar begins to dissolve. Add the vegetable oil and sesame oil. Whisk or shake well to blend. Taste for seasoning, adding salt if desired.

■ *Makes 1¼ cups*

DO-AHEAD

The salad dressing can be refrigerated, covered, for up to 1 week. Whisk or shake to recombine before using.

Wraps are simply sandwiches made by tucking a filling inside flour tortillas. They got their start in California, and lucky for us, tortillas have become so popular they are available even in ordinary super-markets. You can buy flour tortillas plain or flavored with various combinations of sun-dried tomatoes, herbs, and vegetables.

The only thing you need to know to put together a wrap is that it's the fat in the tortilla that makes it pliable enough to bend around the ingredients—so don't use fat-free flour tortillas. More specifically, the fat needs to be warm. No more than a few seconds in the microwave does the trick.

As for fillings, don't stop with the one you see here—anything goes. Take a lovely, light-green spinach tortilla flecked with garlic, fill it with plain-old deli ingredients—or even leftover, sliced grilled chicken—and somehow the result doesn't end up ordinary at all. Whether you're headed to the park or out to the back deck, wraps make a flexible, stylish meal.

California Salad Sandwiches

¼ cup Dijon mustard
¼ cup mayonnaise (see Notes)
½ teaspoon garlic powder
4 medium-size, ripe tomatoes (about 1½ pounds total)
2 very ripe California avocados (optional; see Notes)
8 flavored 10-inch flour tortillas
16 slices (about 12 ounces total) Provolone cheese
1 pound thinly sliced smoked deli turkey
1½ cups already-shredded carrots (see Notes)
2 cups alfalfa sprouts or broccoli sprouts (optional)

PHASE 1: 5 MINUTES

1. Stir together the mustard, mayonnaise, and garlic powder in a small mixing bowl. Cover and refrigerate the mustard mixture until ready to use. Rinse and thinly slice the tomatoes but do not peel or seed them. *While the mustard-mayonnaise can be refrigerated, covered, for up to 2 days, the tomatoes should be used within 2 hours of slicing.*

PHASE 2: 25 MINUTES

2. If using the avocados, cut them in half, twisting the halves to remove the seeds. Discard the seeds. Cut the avocado halves in half. Peel the skin away from the flesh. Cut each piece into 4 slices.

3. Microwave 2 tortillas, uncovered, on high for 30 seconds. Spread about 1 tablespoon of the mustard-mayonnaise over the entire surface of each tortilla. In the center of each tortilla, leaving a ½-inch edge, place 2 slices of cheese and one eighth of the turkey, 4 avocado slices, if using, and one eighth each of the tomato slices, carrots, and sprouts, if using. Fold each of the two tortillas over their fillings, tucking in on end only. Repeat with the remaining ingredients.

4. Cut the sandwiches in half, then serve.

■ *Serves 8*

Notes: You can use low-fat mayonnaise in this recipe, if you like.

Make sure the avocados are soft when gently pressed, indicating that they are very ripe.

Can't find the already shredded carrots? Just peel and shred 2 medium-size carrots instead.

DO-AHEAD

The sandwich halves can be wrapped in plastic wrap and refrigerated for up to 2 hours.

SALAD IN A SANDWICH

Entire books have been written about trendy wrap sandwiches, which are simply variations on the Mexican burrito. Large flour tortillas fold around fillings that branch out beyond Mexico to about as far as the culinary imagination cares to reach. But, trendy or not, we like them as an entertaining tool. They're easy to handle and cut down on the utensil anxiety syndrome (you know, the "Did I remember the forks and are my disposable plates strong enough to hold the food?"). They're also attractive and easy to transport. When our party is on the go, we think salads in sandwiches. Whether we're gathering with a group at the symphony in the park or a tailgate dinner before the game, wraps are the ticket.

Here are some of our favorite wrap fillers. Just add lettuce and tomato . . . *mmm!*

- Black Bean "Hummus," page 47
- Chunky Chicken Salad with Macadamia Nuts, page 190
- Joe's Shrimp Salad, page 204
- Riviera Tuna Spread, page 56
- Soda Fountain Chicken Salad, page 191

And, of course, our California Salad Sandwiches (opposite) provide the complete how-to on wrapping.

Serve leftovers to guests? Why not? I created this salad to take care of the Easter ham that lurks in my refrigerator every spring. But if you are starting from scratch, it's still a breeze to put together using a pound of ham from the deli. And it makes a wonderful lunch platter salad for weekend guests.

The Honey-Mustard Vinaigrette is a perfect complement to the salad, but feel free to substitute a bottled poppy seed vinaigrette or any other sweet salad dressing you fancy.

MONEY SAVER

End-of-the-season sales offer great opportunities to catch deals on entertaining essentials. Watch for clearances on tablecloths, plastic chairs, candles, cocktail napkins, baskets, and the like.

Asparagus and Ham Platter Salad

Honey-Mustard Vinaigrette, (optional; recipe follows)
1½ pounds small red potatoes (see Note)
1 to 1½ pounds fresh asparagus, preferably pencil-thin stalks
1 pound Virginia baked or other good-quality deli ham, sliced about ¼ inch thick
Ice cubes
8 cups medium-packed, prewashed Italian-blend salad greens

PHASE 1: 5 MINUTES

1. Make the Honey-Mustard Vinaigrette, if using. *The salad dressing can be refrigerated, covered, for up to 2 weeks.*

PHASE 2: 20 MINUTES

2. Scrub the potatoes (leave the skins on) and cut them into quarters. Carefully add the potatoes to 2 quarts of already-boiling water in a 4½-quart Dutch oven or soup pot over high heat. Cook for 6 minutes.

3. Meanwhile, snap the tough ends off the asparagus where they naturally break and discard the ends. Rinse the asparagus spears well and drain. After the potatoes have cooked for 6 minutes, add the asparagus, cover the pot, and boil until the spears are crisp-tender, about 5 minutes more.

4. While the asparagus cooks, cut the ham into strips about ¼-inch wide and 2 inches long. Cover and refrigerate.

5. When done, put the potatoes and asparagus in a colander to drain (be careful of the steam) and throw in 2 handfuls of ice cubes. Rinse the vegetables with cold running water and toss gently with the ice cubes until the vegetables are cool, about 2 minutes. Drain the vegetables well, removing any unmelted ice cubes. *The cooked vegetables and the ham strips can be refrigerated separately, covered, for up to 24 hours.*

PHASE 3: 5 MINUTES

6. Assemble the salad: Scatter the salad greens over a large serving platter. Top the salad greens with the cooked potatoes and asparagus and the ham strips. *The salad platter can be refrigerated, covered, for up to 4 hours.*

PHASE 4: 2 MINUTES

7. Just before serving, drizzle the Honey-Mustard Vinaigrette or salad dressing of your choice over the salad or pass the dressing at the table.

■ *Serves 8*

Note: The packaged Simply Potatoes cook in the same amount of time as fresh but have a softer texture. The benefit is you don't have to scrub or cut them into quarters. Use 2 packages (1 pound, 4 ounces each) for this salad.

Honey-Mustard Vinaigrette

Mild and slightly sweet, this dressing is just as good on mixed salad greens or fresh spinach leaves as it is on our Asparagus and Ham Platter Salad.

> 1 cup vegetable oil
> ¼ cup honey mustard
> 2 tablespoons white or red wine vinegar
> ½ teaspoon salt
> ½ teaspoon black pepper

START TO FINISH: 5 MINUTES

Put the oil, mustard, vinegar, salt, and pepper in a small bowl or 1-pint jar with a lid. Whisk or cover and shake well to combine.

■ *Makes about 1¼ cups*

DO-AHEAD

The vinaigrette can be refrigerated, covered, for up to 2 weeks. Whisk or shake to recombine before using.

Joe's Shrimp Salad

There's nothing like the stone crab claws at the famous Miami Beach restaurant Joe's Stone Crab. But if you don't live in Florida, this delicacy can be hard to find. That doesn't stop us from craving the flavors of seafood and the restaurant's signature mustard sauce. We snagged the dipping sauce recipe when it was printed in *The Miami Herald*, so we decided to experiment. The result is a wonderful twist on traditional shrimp salad, with spicy overtones from the mustard. You'll think you're on the beach.

4 large eggs
Joe's Stone Crab Mustard Sauce (recipe follows)
4 large ribs celery (for about 2 cups diced)
½ small onion (for about ¼ cup minced)
2 pounds already-cooked and -peeled medium or large
  shrimp, thawed if frozen
Salt and black pepper
Red or green leaf lettuce leaves, for serving

PHASE 1: 15 MINUTES MOSTLY UNATTENDED COOKING TIME

1. Place the eggs in a 2-quart or larger saucepan and add just enough cold water to cover them. Cover the pan, place it over high heat, and bring to a boil. When the water comes to a boil, uncover the pan and let boil for 3 minutes. Remove the pan from the heat, cover it, and let stand for 15 minutes or up to 1 hour. *The boiled eggs can be refrigerated for up to 4 days.*

PHASE 2: 18 TO 20 MINUTES

2. Peel and finely chop the hard-boiled eggs. Place them in a medium-size mixing bowl. Make the mustard sauce and add it to the bowl with the eggs. Rinse and dice the celery and add it to the egg mixture. Peel and mince the onion and add it to the egg mixture. Cut the shrimp in bite-size pieces and add them to the egg mixture. Stir well. Season with salt and pepper to taste. *The salad can be refrigerated, covered, for up to 24 hours at this point.*

PHASE 3: 2 MINUTES

3. Shortly before serving the salad, rinse the lettuce leaves and pat dry. Serve the shrimp salad over the lettuce leaves.

■ *Serves 8*

Joe's Stone Crab Mustard Sauce

To ensure duplicating the famous flavor, we recommend using the brand names specified in this recipe. If you're not so worried about being exact, any brand of dry mustard will do. Our version omits the salt. You may want to add an eighth of a teaspoon. The sauce is also excellent mixed with crab meat and used as a dip for steamed shrimp and, of course, stone crab claws.

½ cup Hellmann's mayonnaise
1½ teaspoons Colman's dry English mustard
1 teaspoon Worcestershire sauce
½ teaspoon A.1. steak sauce
1 tablespoon half-and-half

START TO FINISH: 5 MINUTES

Put the mayonnaise, dry mustard, Worcestershire sauce, steak sauce, and half-and-half in a small bowl and whisk until the dry mustard is completely incorporated.

■ *Makes about ½ cup*

Party Shrimp Salad with Thai Lime Splash

Thai Lime Splash (recipe follows)
8 cups medium-packed, prewashed mixed field greens
2 pounds already-cooked and -peeled large shrimp,
   thawed if frozen
1 large hothouse cucumber, or 2 large Kirby cucumbers
   (see Note)

PHASE 1: 10 MINUTES

1. Make the Thai Lime Splash dressing. *The salad dressing can be refrigerated, covered, for up to 3 days.*

DO-AHEAD

The mustard sauce can be refrigerated, covered, for up to 2 days. Whisk the sauce again before using, if necessary, to recombine.

We have served this salad to raves all around at an after-graduation buffet. The preparation can be done ahead, and then the salad can be dressed at the last minute. If you choose to serve the dressing on the side, double the recipe to allow for individual preferences in serving size.

205

2. Assemble the salad: Place the greens on a large serving platter. Scatter the shrimp evenly over the greens. Rinse but do not peel the cucumber(s). Cut the cucumber(s) into thin slices and scatter these evenly over the salad. *The salad platter can be refrigerated, covered, for up to 4 hours.*

PHASE 3: 2 MINUTES

3. Just before serving, pour the salad dressing evenly over the salad or pass the dressing at the table.

■ *Serves 8*

Note: If you use a hothouse (seedless English) cucumber or Kirby cucumbers, there's no need to peel. Other varieties should be peeled.

Thai Lime Splash

With just the right hint of heat, this sweet-and-sour dressing is the perfect complement to the shrimp in Party Shrimp Salad.

6 cloves fresh garlic
4 limes
2 tablespoons sugar
2 tablespoons Asian fish sauce (see Note)
½ teaspoon dried red pepper flakes
¼ cup peanut oil or vegetable oil

START TO FINISH: 10 MINUTES

1. Peel the garlic cloves and drop them 1 at a time through the feed tube of a food processor or blender with the machine running to chop them.

2. Stop the machine, halve the limes, and squeeze the juice into the processor bowl or blender. Add the sugar, fish sauce, and red pepper flakes. Pulse to mix.

DO-AHEAD

The salad dressing can be refrigerated, covered, for up to 3 days. Whisk to recombine before using.

3. With the machine running, pour the oil slowly in a thin stream through the feed tube, until completely added. Stir just before using.

■ *Makes about 1 cup*

Note: Asian fish sauce or *nam pla* is available in Asian grocery stores and in the Asian section of large supermarkets. The brand A Taste of Thai calls it a seasoning sauce, while the KA-ME brand labels it fish sauce. No matter what you call it, the sauce provides the salty depth necessary for the Thai influence in this dressing.

ABOUT BUYING SHRIMP

Shrimp are more widely available than they used to be, but unless you live in a fishing community, the shrimp you buy are most likely frozen—or were frozen just a few hours before your fishmonger thawed them. However, that's not all bad. Most shrimp are flash frozen at sea, so provided they have been handled properly, they retain their flavor and texture amazingly well. The question at the fish counter these days is not so much "Are the shrimp fresh?" but "How long have they been thawed?" Previously frozen shrimp are best used within 48 hours of thawing.

Just like boneless, skinless chicken breasts, shrimp are usually individually quick frozen (IQF) so that they remain separate in the bag. This means you can pull out as many shrimp as you need for a recipe and pop the leftovers back in the freezer. Just rinse the frozen shrimp under cool tap water for a few minutes to thaw and proceed with your recipe.

In many supermarkets, the individually frozen shrimp are stored in a huge bin, and shoppers can scoop out the amount they need. In most markets, IQF shrimp are available in bags in the frozen foods section, but if you don't find them, ask the fishmonger if there are any on hand and then thaw them yourself at home.

In another timesaving treat for Desperate Cooks, with the exception of fantails, you can almost always find shrimp that are already peeled. Many times they are cooked as well. You'll find that shrimp can be one of a Desperate Cook's best friends.

When the heat of the summer starts to affect our appetites, we turn to main-dish salads for dinner. There's nothing easier to put together after a hot, busy day than a composed or platter salad, and the vegetable bin overflows with fresh produce at this time of year.

A classic *niçoise* salad has another benefit. Even the traditional recipe relies on one of our pantry staples—canned tuna. We suggest premium white albacore packed in spring water for its pure tuna flavor and firm texture. It's a bit more expensive than the other canned tuna varieties, but it's worth it.

Composed salads are simple to serve to crowds. Striking in their layered appearance, they make stunning centerpieces for salad buffets. Our take on the *niçoise* salad is inspired by the flavors of the French Riviera, but we've left out the anchovies and made the eggs optional. Feel free to add anchovies if you wish, but even without them, this salad is still filled with flavor.

Niçoise Salad with Dijon Vinaigrette

4 large eggs (optional)
2 pounds small red potatoes (see Note)
1 pound fresh green beans
Dijon Vinaigrette (recipe follows)
Ice cubes
8 ripe plum tomatoes
1 large red onion
8 cups medium-packed, prewashed salad greens of
   your choice
1 large can (12 ounces) white tuna packed in water
24 already-pitted imported black olives, such as
   niçoise or kalamata

PHASE 1: 15 MINUTES MOSTLY UNATTENDED COOKING TIME

1. If using the eggs, place them in a 2-quart or larger saucepan and add just enough cold water to cover them. Cover the pan, place it over high heat, and bring to a boil. When the water comes to a boil, uncover the pan and let boil for 3 minutes. Remove the pan from the heat, cover it, and let stand for 15 minutes or up to 1 hour. *The boiled eggs can be refrigerated for up to 4 days.*

PHASE 2: 20 MINUTES

2. Scrub the potatoes (leave the skins on) and cut them into quarters. Rinse and drain the green beans and trim and discard the stem ends only. Carefully add the potatoes and green beans to 2 quarts of already-boiling water in a 4½-quart Dutch oven or soup pot over high heat. Let boil, uncovered, until the potatoes are just tender, about 7 to 9 minutes.

3. While the vegetables cook, make the Dijon Vinaigrette.

4. When done, put the potatoes and green beans in a colander to drain and throw in 2 handfuls of ice cubes. Rinse the vegetables with cold running water and toss with the ice cubes until the vegetables are cool, about 2 minutes. Drain the vegetables well, removing any unmelted ice cubes. *The cooked vegetables can be refrigerated, covered, for up to 24 hours. The vinaigrette can be refrigerated, covered, for up to 2 weeks.*

PHASE 3: 15 MINUTES

5. Rinse the tomatoes and cut off the stem ends. Cut each tomato into 4 wedges but do not peel or seed these. Peel the hard-boiled eggs, if using, and cut each into 4 wedges. Peel the onion and slice it into thin rings.

6. Assemble the salad: Scatter the salad greens over a large platter. Arrange the tomato wedges and the cooked potatoes and green beans on top. Open the can of tuna and drain it. Flake the tuna evenly over the salad. Top with the olives, hard-boiled egg wedges, if using, and onion slices. Serve with the vinaigrette on the side. *The salad can be refrigerated, covered, for up to 2 hours before serving.*

■ *Serves 8 to 10*

Note: The packaged Simply Potatoes cook in the same amount of time as fresh but have a softer texture. The benefit is you don't have to scrub or cut them into quarters. Use 2 packages (1 pound, 4 ounces each).

Dijon Vinaigrette

A generous amount of Dijon mustard added to a simple vinaigrette changes both the flavor and appearance dramatically. It makes a terrific dressing for mixed salad greens as well as for the *niçoise* salad.

> *1 cup extra-virgin olive oil*
> *¼ cup Dijon mustard*
> *2 tablespoons white or red wine vinegar*
> *½ teaspoon salt*
> *½ teaspoon black pepper*

START TO FINISH: 5 MINUTES

Put all of the ingredients in a small bowl or 1-pint jar with a lid. Whisk or cover and shake well to combine.

■ *Makes about 1⅓ cups*

DO-AHEAD

The vinaigrette can be refrigerated, covered, for up to 2 weeks. Allow it to return to room temperature and whisk or shake to recombine before serving.

SIDE SALADS

fast and fabulous

Picnic Corn Relish

This recipe is a version of the corn salad our friend Sally Pike of Surf City, North Carolina, brought to a Memorial Day pig pickin' celebration. The perfect side dish to prepare ahead, its flavor actually intensifies after a couple of days in the refrigerator. It's become a favorite take-along dish of ours, too, and every time we share it we get requests for the recipe.

4 cups frozen yellow corn kernels
1 small sweet onion (for about ½ cup chopped)
1 medium-size (about ½ pound) zucchini (for about 1 cup chopped)
1 medium-size green bell pepper (for about 1 cup bite-size pieces)
About ½ cup densely packed fresh cilantro
⅓ cup sugar
⅓ cup distilled white vinegar or white wine vinegar
2 tablespoons vegetable oil
½ teaspoon black pepper
Salt

START TO FINISH: 15 MINUTES

1. Put the corn in a colander and rinse thoroughly with cool water to thaw. Drain well, then place in a large serving bowl. Peel and finely chop the onion and add it to the corn. Rinse and coarsely chop the zucchini and add it to the corn. Rinse, core, and seed the bell pepper. Cut it into bite-size pieces and add it to the corn. Rinse the cilantro well and shake the leaves to remove any excess water. Remove and discard the tough lower stems but do not worry about the smaller, upper stems. You should have about ½ cup of leaves. Mince the cilantro leaves and add to the vegetables.

DO-AHEAD

The relish can be refrigerated, covered, for up to 2 days.

2. Put the sugar and ⅓ cup water in a 2-cup glass measure and microwave, uncovered, on high for 45 seconds. Whisk the mixture until the sugar dissolves. Whisk in the vinegar, oil, and black pepper. Taste for seasoning, adding salt as necessary. Pour the salad dressing over the vegetables and stir to coat well.

■ *Serves 8*

Maw Maw's Pickled Cucumbers

½ cup distilled white vinegar or cider vinegar
3 tablespoons sugar
1 tablespoon vegetable oil
½ teaspoon salt
¼ teaspoon black pepper
1 hothouse cucumber, or 2 medium Kirby cucumbers
*   (see Note)*

START TO FINISH: 10 MINUTES

1. Make the salad dressing: Whisk together the vinegar, sugar, oil, salt, and pepper with ½ cup water until the sugar dissolves.

2. Rinse but do not peel the cucumber(s), then thinly slice. Put the cucumber slices in a shallow serving bowl and pour the salad dressing over the slices. Serve with a slotted spoon or fork to drain off the salad dressing.

■ *Serves 8*

Note: If you use a hothouse (seedless English) cucumber or Kirby cucumbers, there's no need to peel. Other varieties should be peeled.

From Alicia:

I never once sat down to eat Sunday dinner (that's lunch in the South) at my grandmother's in the summer without seeing a bowl full of pickled cucumbers. When sandwiched with a slice of tomato between the steaming halves of a hot-out-of-the-oven biscuit, someone would inevitably declare, "I could make a meal out of just this!"

You can serve Maw Maw's cucumbers immediately, but the longer they marinate, the more intense the flavor. Be aware, though, that after a day the cucumbers will lose their crunch.

DO-AHEAD

The salad dressing can be kept, covered, at room temperature for up to 1 week. The cucumbers can marinate, in the refrigerator, covered, for up to 2 days.

Sometimes all you need is a simple salad to round out the perfect dinner. We turn to this very easy combination again and again. Mushrooms, tomatoes, and a yellow bell pepper are our favorites for the veggies, but you could easily add a green or red bell pepper, cucumber, carrots, radishes, or any other salad vegetables. Just remember to keep it simple and choose vegetables that will keep well if prepared a few hours ahead. We enjoy this salad with everything from old-fashioned pot roast to spaghetti and meatballs.

Simple Salad with Balsamic Vinaigrette

Balsamic Vinaigrette (recipe follows)
8 cups medium-packed, prewashed Italian-blend salad
* greens, such as romaine and radicchio*
1 package (8 ounces) already-sliced, fresh button
* mushrooms*
5 to 6 ripe plum tomatoes
1 large yellow bell pepper (for about 1 cup chopped)

START TO FINISH: 12 MINUTES

1. Make the Balsamic Vinaigrette.

2. In a large salad or serving bowl, toss the greens with the mushrooms. Rinse the tomatoes and cut off the stem ends. Slice the tomatoes lengthwise into ¼-inch strips but do not peel or seed them. Add them to the greens. Rinse, core, seed, and coarsely chop the bell pepper and add it to the salad.

3. Serve on plates or in bowls, with the vinaigrette on the side.

■ *Serves 8*

DO-AHEAD

The salad can be refrigerated, covered, for up to 8 hours.
• The vinaigrette can be kept, covered, at room temperature for up to 1 week. Whisk or shake the vinaigrette to recombine before using.

Balsamic Vinaigrette

The bold flavor of this dressing comes from an ordinary packet of Good Seasons Italian dressing mix. But mixed with balsamic vinegar and extra-virgin olive oil, it's anything but humdrum.

> ⅓ cup balsamic vinegar
> 1 package (0.7 ounce) Italian salad dressing mix,
>   such as Good Seasons
> ⅔ cup extra-virgin olive oil

START TO FINISH: 3 MINUTES

Put the vinegar, salad dressing mix, and olive oil in a small bowl or 1-pint jar with a lid. Add ¼ cup water and whisk or cover and shake well to combine.

■ *Makes about 1¼ cups*

SALAD GREENS

• Use bags of prewashed salad greens to speed you on your way. Greens come already torn in lots of combinations under lots of brands these days, making salads easier than ever.

• Depending on the variety and the brand, the amount of prewashed greens in each bag differs. So we've given a cup measure, based on one cup per person for side salads and slightly more for our platter salads. We've also given cup measures for broccoli coleslaw mix, since those packages vary, too.

• Don't feel as though you must use the greens we've suggested. Be flexible and thrifty. Buy what's on special. We've made note when a particular green plays a starring role in the salad, such as in our Spinach Salad with Sweet Poppy Seed Dressing (see page 229). But you can mix and match other greens and dressings to suit your taste.

• If it's turning out to be a really desperate week, forgo the homemade dressing and use your favorite commercial one. Bear in mind, though, that almost all of our speedy dressings can be prepared up to a week in advance.

Iceberg lettuce has fallen out of favor in this trendy age, so when we saw that our favorite, very hip, "Chicago-style" steak house features an iceberg salad, we were a bit surprised. It turns out a wedge of crisp iceberg has the perfect texture and flavor to complement such a rich dressing as one made from blue cheese.

Classic Iceberg Wedges with Blue Cheese

Quick Chunky Blue Cheese Dressing (recipe follows)
2 heads iceberg lettuce

START TO FINISH: 15 MINUTES

1. Make the Quick Chunky Blue Cheese Dressing.

2. Remove and discard the core of each head of lettuce. Rinse the lettuce, drain well, and dry the outside with paper towels. Cut each head in half beginning at the core end. Cut each half into 2 wedges. You will end up with 8 lettuce wedges.

3. Place each lettuce wedge on a salad plate. Spoon about 2 tablespoons of blue cheese dressing over each wedge, or more to taste.

■ *Serves 8*

Quick Chunky Blue Cheese Dressing

Blue cheese fans will welcome an easy addition to their repertoire. The flavor actually improves with a bit of age, so feel free to get this task out of the way a couple of days before the guests arrive. Using low-fat mayonnaise and sour cream works just fine here.

> *½ cup mayonnaise*
> *½ cup sour cream*
> *1 teaspoon Worcestershire sauce*
> *½ cup (about 2 ounces) already-crumbled blue cheese*

START TO FINISH: 5 MINUTES

In a small mixing bowl, stir together the mayonnaise and sour cream. Stir in the Worcestershire sauce and blue cheese. Mash the cheese chunks against the side of the bowl to break up some of them.

■ *Makes 1¼ cups*

DO-AHEAD

The salad can be prepared through Step 2 and refrigerated, covered, for up to 4 hours.
• The blue cheese dressing can be refrigerated, covered, for up to 1 week.
• Once dressed, the salad can stand for up to 30 minutes.

Cilantro-Basil Salad with Mushrooms

Cilantro-Basil Vinaigrette (recipe follows)
8 cups medium-packed, prewashed Italian-blend
* salad greens*
1 package (8 ounces) already-sliced, fresh button
* mushrooms*

START TO FINISH: 15 MINUTES

1. Make the Cilantro-Basil Vinaigrette.

2. In a large salad bowl combine the greens and mushrooms. Just before serving, drizzle the vinaigrette over the greens and toss to coat lightly or pass the vinaigrette at the table.

■ *Serves 8*

Cilantro-Basil Vinaigrette

If you love cilantro you're going to want to make this dressing daily. We find it perfect paired with Italian blend greens and fresh button mushrooms, but it is just as lovely on any mild greens with assorted vegetables.

> *About 1 cup densely packed fresh cilantro*
> *About ⅓ cup densely packed fresh basil*
> *1 clove fresh garlic*
> *¼ cup red wine vinegar*
> *½ cup extra-virgin olive oil*
> *¼ cup vegetable oil*
> *¼ teaspoon salt*
> *⅛ teaspoon black pepper*

START TO FINISH: 10 MINUTES

1. Rinse the cilantro and basil well and shake the leaves to remove any excess water. Remove and discard the tough stems but do not

The real stars of this salad are the fresh cilantro and basil in the dressing. So we've kept things uncomplicated, using mixed Italian greens and sliced button mushrooms. The salad may be simple, but it's far from plain.

DO-AHEAD

The Cilantro-Basil Vinaigrette can be refrigerated, covered, for up to 1 week. Stir the vinaigrette before using, if necessary, to recombine.

worry about the smaller, upper stems. You should have about 1 cup of cilantro leaves and ⅓ cup of basil leaves.

2. Peel the garlic clove, drop it through the feed tube of a food processor with the machine running and finely chop. With the machine still running, drop in the cilantro and basil and finely chop, stopping the machine as necessary to scrape down the side with a rubber spatula. Add the vinegar and pulse several times.

3. With the machine running, slowly drizzle the olive and vegetable oils through the feed tube until all the oil is added. Add the salt and pepper and pulse to blend well. (Scrape down the side of the work bowl as necessary.)

4. Serve at once or refrigerate until ready to use. Let the dressing stand at room temperature for at least 15 minutes before serving, then whisk or shake vigorously to recombine.

■ *Makes about 1½ cups*

The inspiration for this salad came from one of our favorite Mediterranean restaurants, where a blue cheese dressing is served with a salad that contains sliced pears. Grapes are pretty, easier to prepare, and taste every bit as great. The salad is a treat for the eye when served on individual plates, but the ingredients can also be tossed in a big bowl. Don't dress the salad until just before serving.

Mediterranean Blue Cheese Salad

½ cup Sweet Red-Wine Vinaigrette, or more to taste (recipe follows)
½ cup walnut pieces
8 cups medium-packed, prewashed mixed salad greens with romaine lettuce
4 ripe plum tomatoes
1½ cups seedless red grapes
⅓ cup (about 1½ ounces) already-crumbled blue cheese, or more to taste

START TO FINISH: 15 MINUTES

1. Make the Sweet Red-Wine Vinaigrette.

2. Place the walnuts on a microwave-safe plate and microwave, uncovered, on high until fragrant and lightly toasted, 2 to 4 minutes, stopping once halfway through to stir.

3. Divide the lettuce evenly among 8 salad plates. Remove the walnuts from the microwave and set aside to cool. Rinse and cut the stem ends off the tomatoes, then cut them into ½-inch wedges but do not peel or seed them. Rinse the grapes.

4. Divide the grapes, tomato wedges, and toasted walnuts evenly among the salad plates. Sprinkle each with 2 teaspoons of blue cheese, or more to taste.

5. Just before serving, whisk or shake the vinaigrette to recombine and drizzle about 1 tablespoon, or more to taste, over each salad or pass the vinaigrette at the table.

■ *Serves 8*

Sweet Red-Wine Vinaigrette

Although the slight sweetness of this vinaigrette makes a nice counterpoint to sharp blue cheese, it isn't too sweet to use as an all-purpose salad dressing whenever the mood strikes. After dressing the Mediterranean Blue Cheese Salad you'll have about a cup left over to do just that.

> *⅓ cup red wine vinegar*
> *1 cup extra-virgin olive oil*
> *2 tablespoons sugar*
> *½ teaspoon salt*
> *¼ teaspoon black pepper*

START TO FINISH: 5 MINUTES

Put the vinegar, olive oil, sugar, salt, and pepper in a small bowl or 1-pint jar with a lid. Whisk or cover and shake until well combined and the sugar and salt have dissolved.

■ *Makes about 1½ cups*

DO-AHEAD

The salad can be prepared through Step 4, covered with plastic wrap, and refrigerated for up to 2 hours.

• The vinaigrette can be kept, covered, at room temperature for up to 2 weeks. Whisk or shake the vinaigrette to recombine before using.

PRECOOKED BACON? COME ON!

O ur families love bacon. And any dip or salad that has bacon in it is sure to be a crowd pleaser. But frying bacon can be a pain—you've got the grease, the smoke, the splatters, the time. Or if you cook it in the microwave, it's oily paper towels and repeat batches. For several years, we'd been eyeing the already-cooked bacon found in the meat case right alongside the regular bacon. What did it taste like? Wasn't it awfully expensive? Did it save all that much time? We finally gave in to our curiosity and tried precooked bacon out. Here's what we discovered.

First, already-cooked bacon appeared to be vastly more expensive than uncooked. But wait. We were comparing cooked weight to uncooked. For a true price comparison we looked at slices. Depending on the brand, one package (16 ounces) of premium uncooked bacon, about 18 to 20 slices, costs about the same as a package of already-cooked bacon containing 14 to 18 slices (about 3 ounces).

Second, how is was it cooked? When it comes to crispness, bacon can be a personal issue. Beverly likes hers extra-crispy. Alicia likes a little chew. The wonderful thing about heat-and-eat bacon is that you can produce both. Since it's already cooked and refrigerated, the slices are limp when they come out of the package. But after just a few minutes in the microwave, you can have perfectly cooked bacon, just the way your family orders it.

As far as the time savings is concerned, we've tested recipes three ways, frying the bacon in a skillet, cooking it in the microwave, or baking it in the oven. Then we used the precooked bacon in the same recipes. Hands down using the precooked bacon saved us enough time to shorten the recipes by as much as 20 minutes. That's the difference, for a desperate host, between getting all those toys picked up in the den or not.

As with any of our timesaving products, if you can't find precooked bacon, an equal number of slices of raw bacon can be cooked and used in the same manner. The cooked bacon can be stored in a zipper-top plastic bag in the refrigerator for up to 2 days. Recrisp it in a microwave as needed.

Could it possibly be cooked the way we like our bacon?

Marietta's Mandarin Salad

8 slices already-cooked bacon (see box opposite)
½ cup slivered or already-sliced almonds
Marietta's Marvelous Dressing (recipe follows)
8 cups medium-packed, prewashed mixed salad greens
  of your choice
1 small onion (for about ½ cup slices)
1 can (8 or 11 ounces) mandarin oranges

START TO FINISH: 15 MINUTES

1. Cover a microwave-safe plate with paper towels and place the bacon slices on top. Cover the bacon with a paper towel and microwave on high until crisp, 2 to 3 minutes.

2. Meanwhile, spread the almonds in a pan and toast in a toaster oven at 350°F just until light brown, about 5 minutes. Set the toasted almonds aside to cool.

3. Make Marietta's Marvelous Dressing.

4. Place the greens in a large salad bowl. Peel the onion and cut into thin slices. Scatter the onion on top of the greens, separating the slices into rings.

5. Drain the mandarin oranges and scatter them over the greens and onion. Crumble the bacon evenly over the salad and scatter the toasted almonds over the bacon.

6. Serve the salad with the salad dressing on the side.

■ *Serves 8*

Use bagged, prewashed lettuce, and this inspired green salad with mandarin oranges and bacon goes together in a snap. Our friend Marietta Wynands, of Raleigh, North Carolina, introduced us to the sweet-and-sour combination at a potluck dinner. It was the hit of the evening.

DO-AHEAD

The salad can be prepared through Step 4 up to 1 day ahead and refrigerated, covered. Once the mandarin oranges, bacon, and almonds have been added, the salad can stand for up to 1 hour.

Marietta's Marvelous Dressing

Anytime you're in the mood for a sweet-and-sour salad combination whip up a batch of this tangy dressing.

¼ cup honey
3 tablespoons distilled white vinegar or cider vinegar
1 teaspoon onion powder
½ teaspoon dry mustard
½ teaspoon celery seed
½ teaspoon paprika
¼ teaspoon salt
⅓ cup vegetable oil

START TO FINISH: 4 MINUTES

Place the honey, vinegar, onion powder, mustard, celery seed, paprika, and salt in a blender. Pulse to blend well. Add the oil and pulse to blend.

■ *Makes about ¾ cup*

DRESSING UP YOUR SALAD

One of the easiest ways to jazz up a simple salad is to add fruit. Fresh seedless grapes, blueberries, strawberries, raspberries, and nuts are best. But don't forget dried fruits, such as raisins, cranberries, cherries, apricots, figs, and even already-chopped dates or prunes.

Other options that require a little work, but are still delicious, are apples and pears. Most don't need to be peeled and add not only flavor but also an interesting texture to a salad. Specialty citrus—blood oranges and Clementines, for example—are exotic and beautiful flavor boosters as well.

The secret to adding fruit to your salad is to remember less is more. One or two segments of a blood orange artfully draped over the baby field greens of an individual salad or a small handful of chopped figs and cherries sprinkled over the top of crisp romaine lettuce is all you need for a memorable company salad.

Awesome Apricot Salad

Apricot Vinaigrette (recipe follows)
½ cup dried apricots
1 pint cherry tomatoes
8 cups medium-packed, prewashed romaine
  lettuce leaves
3 cups (8 ounces) broccoli coleslaw mix

We love the flavor of fresh apricots, but unfortunately their season is very short. Dried apricots are easier to find than ever and have all those contrasting sharp and sweet flavors intensely packed in every bite. With a generous sprinkling of Apricot Vinaigrette, this broccoli salad is one to treasure year-round.

START TO FINISH: 10 MINUTES

1. Make the Apricot Vinaigrette.

2. Roughly chop the dried apricots. Rinse the cherry tomatoes. Put the romaine lettuce, broccoli slaw, tomatoes, and chopped apricots in a large salad bowl and toss together.

3. Divide the salad among 8 individual bowls and pass the salad dressing at the table.

■ *Serves 8*

Apricot Vinaigrette

This unusual apricot dressing has the perfect balance of sweet and tart. To avoid masking the delicate flavor of the apricots we use white wine vinegar.

⅓ cup apricot all-fruit preserves
⅓ cup white wine vinegar or Champagne vinegar
¼ teaspoon salt
¼ teaspoon black pepper
1 cup vegetable oil

START TO FINISH: 4 MINUTES

Put the preserves in a 2-cup glass measure and microwave on high until they melt, about 15 seconds. Add the vinegar, salt, and pepper to the melted preserves and whisk until well combined. Add the oil slowly in a thin stream, whisking constantly until it is thoroughly

DO-AHEAD

The apricot salad can be refrigerated, covered, for up to 2 hours. • The vinaigrette can be refrigerated, covered, for up to 1 week.

blended. Use the dressing right away or refrigerate, covered, until ready to use. After refrigerating, allow the dressing to stand at room temperature for 10 minutes to soften and then whisk vigorously before serving.

■ *Makes about 1⅔ cups*

Carrot Salad with Fresh Pineapple

*F*resh pineapple chunks do wonders for a humble carrot-raisin salad, and so we've added them to dress up this old favorite from *Desperation Dinners!* Using already-shredded carrots cuts the work time, but if you can't find this handy item at your supermarket, grate four medium-size carrots in a food processor instead.

1 package (12 ounces) fresh pineapple chunks
 with juice
½ cup mayonnaise
3 cups (16 ounces) already-shredded carrots
½ cup raisins
½ cup walnut pieces

START TO FINISH: **8 MINUTES**

1. Drain the pineapple juice into a large serving bowl. Set the pineapple chunks aside. Add the mayonnaise to the pineapple juice and whisk well to blend.

2. Cut the pineapple chunks in half and add them to the dressing. Coarsely chop the shredded carrots and add them to the pineapple chunks. Add the raisins. Stir well until all of the carrots are covered with dressing. Stir in the walnuts.

■ *Serves 8 generously*

DO-AHEAD

*T*he carrot salad can be refrigerated, covered, for up to 6 hours. If making the salad ahead, stir in the walnuts no more than 30 minutes before serving.

Curried Confetti Coleslaw

½ cup mayonnaise
⅓ cup sour cream
2 tablespoons milk
½ teaspoon curry powder
1 large package (16 ounces) coleslaw mix
1 cup dried cranberries or other dried fruit
½ cup already-chopped walnuts
Salt and black pepper

START TO FINISH: 7 MINUTES

1. Make the salad dressing: In a large serving bowl, whisk together the mayonnaise, sour cream, milk, and curry powder.

2. Add the coleslaw mix, dried cranberries, and walnuts. Stir until the mixture is evenly coated with dressing. Season with salt and pepper to taste. Serve at once or refrigerate, covered, until ready to serve.

■ *Serves 8*

A new twist on the ever popular coleslaw, this may be the easiest salad you ever make that's fancy enough for company. Dried cranberries are sometimes sold under the brand name Craisins. If you can't find dried cranberries, substitute dried cherries, raisins, or even a mixture of dried fruit pieces. And feel free to substitute low-fat mayonnaise, sour cream, and milk as well.

DO-AHEAD

The Curried Confetti Coleslaw can be refrigerated, covered, for up to 24 hours. If making ahead, add the walnuts just before serving.

SING FOR YOUR SUPPER

From Alicia:

Karaoke is a fun evening exploit we filched from one of our friends. If you've got musicians in the family, it's always enjoyable to have live guitar or piano accompaniment. But the karaoke tapes that can be purchased from music stores are just as entertaining. Try the golden oldies tapes—they're a blast to act out as well as sing. Even small children who can't read yet can do the chorus of "It's My Party" after one time through.

I'm nuts over this refreshingly different take on coleslaw, a fact that became obvious the night I ate half a recipe all by myself and called it dinner. Super-market produce departments have finally figured out that most people don't have all day to peel and chop. If you haven't been on a sightseeing trip through the salad aisles lately, go with open eyes and an open mind. Packages of already-shredded cabbage (often called coleslaw mix) put homemade coleslaw into the realistic column for even the busiest host. So long as I've remembered to check the expiration date on the package, I've always found these bags of cabbage to be impeccably fresh.

Asian Coleslaw with Ginger Dressing

½ cup sliced almonds
Ginger Dressing (recipe follows)
1 large package (16 ounces) coleslaw mix
1 large yellow or red bell pepper (for about 1½ cups strips)
1 medium-size Kirby cucumber, or ½ hothouse
  cucumber (for about 1 cup cubes; see Note)
2 ripe plum tomatoes

START TO FINISH: 21 MINUTES

1. Spread the almonds in a pan and toast in a toaster oven at 350°F until light brown, about 5 minutes. Let cool.

2. Meanwhile, make the Ginger Dressing.

3. Put the coleslaw mix in a large serving bowl. Rinse, core, and seed the bell pepper and cut it into strips about ⅛ inch wide. Cut the bell pepper strips in half and add them to the cabbage mixture.

4. Rinse and cut off and discard the ends of the cucumber but do not peel it. Cut the cucumber into bite-size cubes and add these to the cabbage mixture.

5. Rinse and cut off and discard the stem ends of the tomatoes. Cut each tomato in half lengthwise. Do not peel but scrape out the seeds. Cut each tomato half into thin strips and add these to the cabbage mixture. Toss well to combine the vegetables.

6. Just before serving, pour the salad dressing over the slaw and toss well to coat. Sprinkle the toasted almonds on top. Serve at once.

■ *Serves 8*

Note: If you use a Kirby or hothouse (seedless English) cucumber, there's no need to peel. Other varieties should be peeled.

Ginger Dressing

While this gingery dressing is especially good with our Asian coleslaw, it works well over spring salad greens, too.

> ¼ cup peanut oil or other salad oil
> 4 teaspoons reduced-sodium soy sauce
> 5 teaspoons rice wine vinegar
> 2 teaspoons sugar
> 1 teaspoon Asian (dark) sesame oil
> 2 teaspoons bottled fresh ginger (see Note)

START TO FINISH: 8 MINUTES

Put all of the ingredients in a small bowl or 8-ounce jar with a lid. Whisk or cover and shake until the dressing is well combined and the sugar dissolves.

■ *Makes about ½ cup*

Note: Bottled fresh ginger is the perfect replacement for time-consuming fresh ginger. Called minced, chopped, crushed, or ground, depending on the brand, bottled fresh ginger is available in the produce section of larger supermarkets. Finely minced fresh ginger can be substituted.

DO-AHEAD

The toasted almonds can be stored in an airtight container at room temperature for up to 2 days.
• The salad dressing can be refrigerated, covered, for up to 2 days. Whisk or shake to recombine before using.
• The coleslaw can be prepared through Step 5 and refrigerated, covered, for up to 8 hours.

From Alicia:

Truth of the matter is that there are just about as many slaw recipes in the South as there are cooks. This one is adapted from my second cousin Louise Agner's favorite recipe, which she always brings to family gatherings. The slaw only improves as it waits in your refrigerator and will keep for a couple of weeks, although it's highly doubtful you'll have leftovers for that long. It will serve twelve, so it's perfect for larger gatherings.

Louise's Big Bowl Slaw

1 large head (about 5 pounds) cabbage
1 large yellow onion (for about 1 cup chopped)
1 cup apple cider vinegar
1 cup sugar
1 small can (5½ ounces) reduced-sodium vegetable juice, such as V8
1 teaspoon salt
1 teaspoon celery seed

START TO FINISH: 20 MINUTES, PLUS 4 HOURS UNATTENDED CHILLING TIME

1. Rinse the cabbage and remove the outer leaves. Remove and discard the core and cut the cabbage into eighths. Peel the onion and cut it into eighths. Using a food processor fitted with the steel blade attachment, process the cabbage and onion, in manageable batches, until finely chopped.

2. Put the cabbage and onion in a large container with a tight-fitting lid.

3. In a 1-quart or larger saucepan, combine the vinegar, sugar, vegetable juice, salt, and celery seed. Bring to a boil and stir until the sugar has dissolved, about 5 minutes.

4. Pour the hot vinegar mixture over the chopped cabbage mixture and toss to coat well. Cover and refrigerate until completely chilled, at least 4 hours.

 Serves 12 generously

DO-AHEAD

Louise's Big Bowl Slaw can be refrigerated, covered, for up to 2 weeks.

Unbelievable Broccoli Slaw

½ cup mayonnaise
½ cup sour cream
1 teaspoon distilled white vinegar or cider vinegar
1 teaspoon sugar
¼ teaspoon celery seed (optional)
6 cups (16 ounces) broccoli coleslaw mix
Salt and black pepper

START TO FINISH: 10 MINUTES

1. In a large serving bowl, mix together the mayonnaise, sour cream, vinegar, sugar, and celery seed, if using. Stir until well blended.

2. Add the broccoli slaw and stir until it is well coated with dressing. Season the slaw with salt and pepper to taste.

■ *Serves 8*

Even a novice cook can make Unbelievable Broccoli Slaw in 10 minutes, thanks to the convenience of broccoli coleslaw mix. Made from shredded broccoli stalks with a little carrot thrown in for color, this timesaving and mild-tasting ingredient is found in plastic bags in the supermarket produce section. It makes for a great variation on coleslaw that will have your guests scratching their heads to figure out what it's made from. And the slaw will taste every bit as good if you use reduced-fat mayonnaise and sour cream.

DO-AHEAD

The Unbelievable Broccoli Slaw can be refrigerated, covered, for up to 8 hours.

THE COLESLAW SHOW

From Beverly:

I adore my friend Phil Ward because he introduced me to my husband and because he's the only person I know who can bring drama to coleslaw. At every potluck Phil shows up with a giant cabbage, a machete-like butcher knife, a bottle of store-bought dressing, a can of roasted sunflower seeds, and a lawn-and-leaf-size black garbage bag. Loudly whacking, Phil slays his cabbage, throwing the results into the garbage bag along with everything else except the knife (okay, not the bottle or the can either). It's truly something to see—as much sideshow as side dish. After a few shakes and tosses of the bag and with a flourish worthy of a magician, Phil dumps his masterpiece into a bowl. It's always magnificent coleslaw, and it always disappears fast. Perhaps Phil is a magician after all.

From Alicia:

I'm not sure if it was the name that first intrigued me about this beautiful vegetable salad or the twist on the old boring broccoli I always struggled with. Either way, one bite and I was sold. Our thanks go to Julie Realon for sharing this new family favorite! Her beautiful side salad will serve ten with ease. If you prefer, you can make it with reduced-fat sour cream and mayonnaise.

Green-and-White Salad

10 slices already-cooked bacon (see box on page 218)
4 cups broccoli florets
4 cups cauliflower florets
2 large ribs celery (for about 1 cup diced)
1 large onion (for about 1 cup chopped)
1 small container (8 ounces) sour cream
¾ cup mayonnaise
1 teaspoon garlic powder
½ teaspoon salt

START TO FINISH: 16 MINUTES

1. Cover a microwave-safe plate with paper towels and place the bacon on top. Cover the bacon with a paper towel and microwave on high until crisp, 2 to 3 minutes. Remove from the microwave and blot any excess grease. Set aside to cool.

2. Rinse the broccoli and cauliflower florets and drain well. Break or chop the florets into bite-size pieces, if necessary. Place in a large serving bowl. Rinse and dice the celery and peel and coarsely chop the onion. Add them to the broccoli and cauliflower.

3. Make the salad dressing: Put the sour cream, mayonnaise, garlic powder, and salt in a small mixing bowl and stir to mix. Pour the salad dressing over the vegetables. Crumble the crisped bacon over the top. Toss to mix well.

■ *Serves 10*

DO-AHEAD

The Green-and-White Salad can be refrigerated, covered, for up to 24 hours.

Spinach Salad with Sweet Poppy Seed Dressing

The somewhat bitter taste of mature spinach is a perfect foil to the honey sweetness of our easy poppy seed dressing.

Poppy Seed Dressing (recipe follows)
1 medium-size red onion (for about 1 cup slices)
8 cups medium-packed, prewashed spinach leaves

START TO FINISH: 12 MINUTES

1. Make the Poppy Seed Dressing.

2. Peel and thinly slice the onion. Put the spinach in a large salad or serving bowl. Add the onion slices and toss together. Serve with the salad dressing on the side.

■ *Serves 8*

Poppy Seed Dressing

Like sweet dressings? You'll love this one; it's unbelievably simple to prepare. We've adapted the recipe from one of Raleigh's most well-known restaurants, The Angus Barn. If you order the spinach salad, you get this awesome dressing. But it's not just delicious on spinach—any type of green is enhanced by its honeyed intensity.

½ cup honey
¼ cup distilled white vinegar or white wine vinegar
1 teaspoon onion powder
½ teaspoon salt
½ teaspoon dry mustard
⅔ cup vegetable oil
1 teaspoon poppy seeds

START TO FINISH: 7 MINUTES

In a blender or food processor, combine the honey, vinegar, onion powder, salt, and mustard. With the machine running, drizzle the oil into the mixture. Add the poppy seeds and pulse to mix gently.

■ *Makes about 1½ cups*

DO-AHEAD

The spinach salad can be refrigerated, covered, for up to 4 hours. • The dressing can be refrigerated, covered, for up to 3 weeks. Stir or shake briskly before serving, if it has been refrigerated.

From Alicia:

A traditional Greek salad, *horiatiki salata,* is a flavorful combination of olives, tomatoes, onion, cucumber, sometimes capers, and always feta cheese. But the most frequent version of a Greek salad in our area always combines all the terrific flavors of the *horiatiki* with greens and potato salad. I've become so accustomed to this version, I think I'd really miss the lettuce and creamy potato salad if we left them out. If you have some capers on hand and want to throw them in too, go for it.

Greek Greens with Potato Salad

Greek Dressing (recipe follows)
8 cups medium-packed, prewashed romaine
    lettuce leaves
1 jar (6 ounces) pitted kalamata olives (see Notes)
4 ripe plum tomatoes
½ medium-size red onion (for about ½ cup slices)
2 medium Kirby cucumbers, or 1 hothouse cucumber
    (for 2 cups thin slices; see Notes)
1 pint (2 cups) creamy deli potato salad
1 package (4 ounces; about ½ cup) already-crumbled
    feta cheese, or more to taste

START TO FINISH: 13 MINUTES

1. Make the Greek Dressing.

2. Place the lettuce in a large salad or serving bowl. Drain the olives and add them to the lettuce. Rinse the tomatoes and cut into ¼-inch slices but do not peel or seed them. Peel and thinly slice the onion and add it and the tomatoes to the salad. Rinse but do not peel the cucumbers, then thinly slice and add them to the salad. Toss well.

3. To serve, drizzle the salad dressing over the salad and toss to coat. Place ¼ cup of potato salad in the center of 8 serving plates. Top each with about 1½ cups of salad. Sprinkle each salad with 1 table-spoon crumbled feta cheese, or more to taste, and serve immediately.

■ *Serves 8*

Notes: Don't forgo kalamata olives if you can't find pitted ones. It doesn't take long to pit them. Gently crush the olives a few at a time, using the flat part of a chef's knife. You'll be able to remove the pits easily. Pitted olives can be refrigerated, covered, for up to 4 days.

If you use Kirby cucumbers or a hothouse (seedless English) cucumber, there's no need to peel.

DO-AHEAD

The Greek salad can be prepared through Step 2 and refrigerated, covered, for up to 4 hours.
• The dressing can be refrigerated, covered, for up to 1 week. Whisk or shake to recombine before using.

Greek Dressing

Most Greek dressings for traditional salads are no more than oregano, olive oil, and vinegar. But we've added a touch of garlic and a hint of sugar for balance. If you are a big garlic fan, add more to suit your taste.

> *1 clove fresh garlic*
> *¼ cup red wine vinegar*
> *1 teaspoon dried oregano*
> *½ teaspoon sugar*
> *½ cup extra-virgin olive oil*

START TO FINISH: 4 MINUTES

Peel the garlic and press it through a garlic press into a small bowl or 8-ounce jar with a lid. Add the remaining ingredients. Whisk or cover and shake well to combine.

■ *Makes about ¾ cup*

DESPERATE HOLIDAYS

Nothing can strike the "Fear of Kitchen" into the heart of a Desperate Cook like the holidays. All cooks can use help with the festivities. Try these easy ways to round out a menu.

- Curried Walnuts, page 40
- Winter Spiced Pecans, page 41
- Golden Curry Dip, page 44
- Pinwheels Primavera, page 74
- Picnic Corn Relish, page 210
- Maw Maw's Pickled Cucumbers, page 211
- Carrot Salad with Fresh Pineapple, page 222
- Louise's Big Bowl Slaw, page 226
- Quick Bean Medley for a Crowd, page 254
- Oven-Roasted Green Beans with Garlic, page 263
- Cheryl's Party Potatoes, page 265
- Succotash with a Twist, page 267

TAKE IT ON THE ROAD

Does your city's entertainment lineup include outdoor concerts, plays, or fireworks displays? Is there a park with meandering grassy meadows? A shady picnic pavilion? These are some of the best reasons we know of to gather groups of friends, escape from cleaning the house, and enjoy relaxed fellowship over a simple sandwich.

The group can stretch from four to fourteen, and the host (read organizer) doesn't necessarily have to do everything. You may want to provide all of the food for a smaller group (check out our California Salad Sandwiches on page 200). But because the event is not at your house, the rules can bend.

At some of the alfresco gatherings we've attended, each family ate a picnic they'd packed at home, no coordination involved. That's okay, but in our experience, there's more harmony in shared fare. Sandwich envy is not a pretty sight.

The options can vary from each family bringing a dish, potluck style, to having the party coordinator assign specific dishes, or at least categories, such as salad, side dish, or dessert. Depending on the number of people involved, the main dish could be as stress free as a bucket of chicken.

Once the menu is settled, there's the matter of transport and picnic implements. It doesn't matter what the picnic container looks like. It's what's inside that counts. The best thing about paper shopping bags with handles is that after they're empty, you don't have to lug them home. And, as for tableware, are forks required or will fingers suffice?

Of course, we all must abide by the golden rule of picnic fare safety: Keep hot foods hot and cold foods cold. With regard to the latter, a plastic ice chest with wheels attached is worth every penny. Once it's unpacked, throw a pretty cloth or beach towel on top, and voilà, an instant buffet table. Another helpful item is an insulated picnic bag that collapses when it's empty. It's inexpensive, comes with handy shoulder straps, and actually holds a lot more food than you'd suspect from just looking at it.

If extra wheel power is required, a child's wagon does the trick. We've even been known to bring out the rolling luggage carrier normally reserved for the airport. It's great for transporting lawn chairs.

Then there's the matter of ambience. If you don't have an ice chest to turn into the buffet table, haul your goodies in a small cardboard box. Turn the box upside down, throw a cloth on top, and you'll never know that table is disposable at evening's end. To help create the proper mood, never underestimate the power of flickering candles, plastic wineglasses, some flowered paper napkins, and a pretty lawn blanket to transform a simple picnic into an elegant affair. Why not assign taking charge of decor to a member of the group who doesn't cook?

For those times when cooking ahead isn't feasible, just bring sandwich makings and assemble them on site. A small plastic cutting board, a sharp knife for slicing tomatoes, plus a knife to spread condiments is all the equipment that's generally required. If you're heading to a park where the picnic sites come complete with barbecue grills, your menu options multiply. Just about anything in our grilling chapter (see pages 150 through 187) can be thrown into a zipper-top plastic bag and flamed to perfection when you get to your destination. For those of you addicted to the ease of gas grilling, portable grills with tiny propane tanks are inexpensive and lightweight, too. We've included one as part of our basic beach equipment list for years.

Taking the show on the road does require a little forethought but not so much that the trade-off isn't worthwhile. And if you do forget something, make sure it isn't your sense of humor. Just be creative—a fork can give you tomato slices and rather artistic ones at that! (For real emergencies, there's bound to be a quick-stop shop within a 10-minute drive.) Finally, remember: If the air is fresh, the grass green, and the sky blue, all food becomes a feast.

Unless you received one as a wedding gift, forget fancy picnic hampers.

This bright salad is based on one with fresh peas that a friend sampled at a bed-and-breakfast buffet. We just couldn't wait for fresh pea season to enjoy it. With a few desperate techniques and substitutions (we've added prosciutto to the mix), we can now take pleasure in its flavors all year-round. Reduced-fat sour cream and mayonnaise work here, if you prefer them. And, if you use a Kirby or hothouse (seedless English) cucumber, you don't have to peel it.

Green Pea Salad

1 pound frozen green peas
1 medium-size Kirby cucumber, or ½ hothouse
    cucumber (for about ¾ cup chopped)
2 cloves fresh garlic
About ¼ cup densely packed fresh basil
1 medium-size red bell pepper (for about 1 cup chopped)
1 small onion (for about ½ cup chopped)
4 ounces prosciutto
⅔ cup sour cream
⅓ cup mayonnaise
¼ teaspoon black pepper, or more to taste
½ lemon

START TO FINISH: 15 MINUTES, PLUS AT LEAST 1 HOUR CHILLING TIME

1. Place the peas in a colander and run cool water over them to thaw. Set aside to drain well.

2. Rinse but do not peel the cucumber. Chop the cucumber into bite-size pieces and place it in a large serving bowl. Peel and finely mince the garlic, adding it to the cucumber. Rinse the basil well and shake the leaves to remove any excess water. Remove and discard any tough stems. You should have about ¼ cup of leaves. Finely chop the basil and add it to the cucumber. Rinse, core, then seed and finely chop the bell pepper and add it to the cucumber. Peel and finely chop the onion; add it to the cucumber. Dice the prosciutto and add it to the cucumber.

3. Add the sour cream, mayonnaise, and black pepper to the salad. Squeeze the lemon juice through a small strainer (to catch the seeds) over the salad. Stir well to mix.

4. Add the thawed peas to the salad and toss to coat and mix well. Cover and place in the refrigerator for at least 1 hour before serving.

■ *Serves 8*

DO-AHEAD

The Green Pea Salad can be refrigerated, covered, for up to 24 hours.

Cheese Tortellini Salad

2 packages (1 pound each) frozen cheese tortellini
1 pint cherry tomatoes
2 large ribs celery (for about 1 cup diced)
1 small sweet onion (for about ½ cup chopped)
1 cup frozen green peas
2 cans (2½ ounces each) sliced black olives
¾ cup bottled Italian salad dressing, or more if necessary

START TO FINISH: 25 MINUTES

1. Bring 4 quarts of water to a boil. When the water boils, add the tortellini and adjust the heat to keep the water at a slow boil. Cook the tortellini according to the directions on the package until just tender, 7 to 12 minutes (see Note).

2. Meanwhile, rinse the tomatoes, cut them in half and put in a large salad bowl. Rinse and dice the celery and add it to the salad bowl. Peel, coarsely chop the onion, and add it to the salad bowl.

3. If the frozen peas are covered with ice crystals, pour them into a colander, rinse with cold water, and drain well. Put them in the salad bowl. Drain the black olives and add them to the salad bowl.

4. When the tortellini are cooked, drain them in a colander and rinse them with cold running water for about 2 minutes to cool. Drain the tortellini well, then add to the salad bowl. Pour the dressing over the salad and toss well to mix.

■ *Serves 8 generously*

Note: You can cook the tortellini the day before you assemble the salad, but you'll need to mix them with salad dressing so they won't stick together. Place the cooked and drained pasta in a salad bowl, pour the salad dressing over it, and stir to coat. When you finish making the salad the next day, you may need to add ¼ to ½ cup more dressing to moisten the pasta.

Frozen cheese tortellini can be a wonderful secret ingredient to keep on hand in your freezer. Pull out a couple of bags, and with minimal chopping and no mixing at all, you can have a filling salad that makes a great side dish when you're serving burgers or steaks or is a welcome addition to a salad buffet.

DO-AHEAD

The completed tortellini salad can be refrigerated, covered, for up to 8 hours. Stir before serving, and if the pasta has absorbed all the salad dressing, add up to a quarter cup more.

Pretty Pasta Salad with Peas and Carrots

A delightful side salad is just what you need when you're feeding a hungry crowd, and this one, which we created to serve as many as ten generously, fits the bill. A friend of ours brought it to a Fourth of July picnic potluck and reported back that it was the only one that was gone at the end of the party. Adults and children alike love the flavor of peas and carrots tossed with the creamy pasta and bacon.

1 package (1 pound) pasta shells or other short pasta
10 slices already-cooked bacon (see box on page 218)
15 to 20 already-peeled baby carrots (for about 1 cup slices)
1 cup frozen green peas
1 cup mayonnaise (see Note)
½ teaspoon onion powder
½ teaspoon garlic powder
¼ teaspoon salt, or more to taste
⅛ teaspoon black pepper, or more to taste
Ice cubes

START TO FINISH: 20 MINUTES

1. In a large soup pot or pasta pot, bring 4 quarts of water to a boil. Add the pasta and cook according to the directions on the package, 12 to 14 minutes.

2. Meanwhile, cover a microwave-safe plate with paper towels and place the bacon on top. Cover the bacon with a paper towel and microwave on high until crisp, 2 to 3 minutes. Remove the bacon from the microwave oven and blot off any excess grease. Set the bacon aside to cool.

3. Slice the carrots about ¼ inch thick and set them aside. Put the frozen green peas in a colander and rinse with cool water to begin thawing. Let drain until the pasta is done.

4. Mix the mayonnaise with the onion powder, garlic powder, salt, and pepper in a large bowl. Taste for seasoning, adding more salt or pepper if necessary. Add the peas to the mayonnaise mixture.

5. Put the pasta in the colander to drain and throw in 2 handfuls of ice cubes. Rinse the pasta under cold running water and toss with the ice cubes until the pasta is cool, about 2 minutes. Drain well, shaking to remove as much water as possible. Remove any unmelted

DO-AHEAD

The pasta salad can be refrigerated, covered, for up to 2 days. Refrigerate the bacon separately in a zipper-top plastic bag. Recrisp the bacon in a microwave oven, if necessary, before crumbling it over the salad and stirring to mix it in.

ice cubes. Add the cooled pasta to the bowl with the mayonnaise mixture. Add the sliced carrots. Crumble the bacon over the top. Stir well to coat the pasta with the dressing.

■ *Serves 8 to 10 generously*

Note: You can use low-fat mayonnaise, if you prefer.

Red and Black Bean Salad

1 can (15 ounces) black beans
1 can (15½ ounces) light-red kidney beans
1 can (11 ounces) corn with red and green peppers,
     such as Mexicorn
3 scallions (for about ½ cup chopped, white and green parts)
3 tablespoons extra-virgin olive oil
3 tablespoons red wine vinegar
½ teaspoon garlic powder
½ teaspoon ground cumin
¼ teaspoon salt, or more to taste
¼ teaspoon black pepper, or more to taste

START TO FINISH: 20 MINUTES

1. Put the beans in a colander to drain. Put the corn on top of the beans. Rinse the vegetable mix well with cool water, then drain well. Put the beans and corn in a large storage or serving bowl.

2. Rinse and finely chop the scallions. Add the chopped scallions to the beans and corn.

3. Make the dressing: Put the olive oil in a 2-cup glass measure. Whisk in the vinegar, garlic powder, cumin, salt, and pepper. Taste for seasoning, adding more salt and pepper if necessary. Pour the dressing over the bean mixture and stir until well coated.

■ *Serves 8*

From Beverly:

If there are no canned beans in the house, I just don't feel secure. I can't tell you the number of times I've put off until the last possible moment making a dish for a potluck or figuring out what side salad I'm going to serve. Beans provide the backbone for a substantial salad, and that means only a few additional vegetables are required. The other pantry secret in this particular salad is a blend of canned corn with red and green peppers that's usually sold under the brand name Mexicorn. After you dump in the drained beans and corn, the only real work required for this colorful salad is chopping the scallions.

DO-AHEAD

The bean salad can be refrigerated, covered, for up to 2 days.

Phased and Flexible

Tangy Spinach Salad

Many spinach salads are served with a sweet-and-sour dressing, but although we love that combination, too, some menus call for something a little less on the sweet side. Our tangy rendition is a welcome addition to the spinach salad lineup.

4 large eggs
Tangy Dressing (recipe follows)
8 cups medium-packed, prewashed baby spinach (see Note)
1 small onion (for about ½ cup slices)
8 slices already-cooked bacon (see box on page 218)

PHASE 1: 15 MINUTES, PLUS 15 MINUTES UNATTENDED STANDING TIME

1. Place the eggs in a 2-quart or larger saucepan and add just enough cold water to cover them. Cover the pan, place it over high heat, and bring to a boil. When the water comes to a boil, uncover the pan and let boil for 3 minutes. Remove the pan from the heat, cover it, and let stand for 15 minutes or up to 1 hour.

2. Meanwhile, make the Tangy Dressing. *The hard-boiled eggs can be refrigerated for up to 4 days. The salad dressing can be refrigerated, covered, for up to 1 week.*

PHASE 2: 8 MINUTES

3. Put the spinach in a large serving bowl. Peel the onion and cut it into very thin slices. Separate the onion slices into rings with your fingers and scatter them over the spinach. Peel the hard-boiled eggs and cut each egg crosswise into 6 slices. Scatter the slices of egg over the spinach and onion.

4. Cover a microwave-safe plate with paper towels and place the bacon on top. Cover the bacon with a paper towel and microwave on high until crisp, 2 to 3 minutes. Remove from the microwave and blot any excess grease, then let cool. *The salad and crisped bacon can be refrigerated separately, covered, at this point for up to 4 hours.*

PHASE 3: 2 MINUTES

5. Just before serving, crumble the bacon over the salad. Whisk or shake the Tangy Dressing well to recombine the ingredients. Pour the salad dressing over the salad, toss well, and serve.

■ *Serves 8*

Note: Baby spinach is also called spinach salad. If you can't find it, look for bags of triple-washed fresh spinach. If you can't find that, buy fresh spinach and check to be sure there's no grit in it before using. If it's sandy, rinse the spinach several times and dry well. Also remove any tough stems and tear any large spinach leaves into bite-size pieces.

Tangy Dressing

Ｗith only 10 calories per tablespoon, there's a lot to love about this zesty vinaigrette. It's suitable for spinach or any other salad greens.

> *1 medium onion (for 2 teaspoons grated)*
> *⅔ cup reduced-sodium vegetable juice, such as V8*
> *¼ cup red wine vinegar*
> *2 tablespoons extra-virgin olive oil*
> *2 teaspoons Dijon mustard*
> *1 teaspoon salt*

START TO FINISH: 7 MINUTES

Peel the onion and, over a small bowl or 1-pint jar with a lid, grate enough on a handheld grater to make 2 teaspoons with juice (use the smallest holes of the grater). Set the remaining onion aside for another use. Add the rest of the ingredients and whisk or cover and shake vigorously until thoroughly blended.

■ *Makes about 1 cup*

DO-AHEAD

Ｔhe salad dressing can be refrigerated, covered, for up to 1 week. Whisk or shake to recombine before using.

Crimson beets paired with slices of hard-boiled egg and a light pink dressing make for a beautiful company salad. Choose a salad blend with radicchio in it to add a rosy hint to the salad leaves.

Russian Beet Salad

4 large eggs
Russian Dressing (recipe follows)
1 sweet onion, such as Vidalia (for about 1 cup slices)
2 cans (15 ounces each) sliced beets
8 cups medium-packed, prewashed mixed salad greens
   of your choice

PHASE 1: 9 MINUTES, PLUS 15 MINUTES UNATTENDED STANDING TIME

1. Place the eggs in a 2-quart or larger saucepan and add just enough cold water to cover them. Cover the pan, place it over high heat, and bring to a boil. When the water comes to a boil, uncover the pan and let boil for 3 minutes. Remove the pan from the heat, cover it, and let stand for 15 minutes or up to 1 hour.

2. Meanwhile make the Russian Dressing. *The hard-boiled eggs can be refrigerated for up to 4 days. The salad dressing can be refrigerated, covered, for up to 1 week.*

PHASE 2: 15 MINUTES

3. Peel the onion and cut it into very thin slices. Peel the hard-boiled eggs and cut each egg crosswise into 6 slices. Put the beets in a colander to drain.

4. Arrange 1 cup of greens on each of 8 salad plates. Place 4 to 5 beet slices over the greens on each plate. Top the beets with several slices of onion, separating the rings with your fingers. Place 3 slices of egg on each plate. Drizzle 1 to 2 tablespoons of Russian Dressing over each salad or pass the dressing at the table. *The salads can be assembled up to 4 hours ahead. Cover the plates with plastic wrap and refrigerate until ready to serve. If refrigerating, wait to drizzle the salad dressing on the salads until just before serving.*

■ *Serves 8*

Russian Dressing

Actually American in origin—as its reliance on ketchup would suggest—food lore has it that the name for this dressing comes from the fact that the earliest versions contained the famous Russian ingredient caviar. No caviar here, though; instead, our slightly sweet dressing includes a hint of horseradish to pique the palate. Since it will keep for up to a week, use any you have left over on your favorite tossed salad.

> *1 large clove fresh garlic*
> *1 cup mayonnaise (see Note)*
> *3 tablespoons ketchup*
> *1 teaspoon prepared horseradish*

START TO FINISH: 6 MINUTES

Peel the garlic. Drop the garlic clove through the feed tube of a blender or food processor with the machine running and blend on high until finely minced. Turn the blender off and add the mayonnaise, ketchup, horseradish, and ½ cup of water. Blend on high until smooth and mixed well, stopping to scrape down the sides of the blender container as necessary.

■ *Makes about 1¾ cups*

Note: You can use low-fat mayonnaise here, if you like.

DO-AHEAD

The salad dressing can be refrigerated, covered, for up to 1 week.

Denise's Vinaigrette Potatoes with Asparagus

When our good friend Denise Deen brought this salad to a potluck dinner we knew we had to have the recipe. Denise's version contained green beans, but we switched to asparagus when a springtime craving hit. This is a potato salad, but it doesn't seem like it—a welcome change from the ordinary, one diner commented after digging in.

2½ pounds small to medium-size red potatoes (see Note)
1 pound fresh asparagus
Ice cubes
3 scallions (for about ½ cup chopped, white and
    green parts)
Garlic-Dijon Vinaigrette (recipe follows)
2 tablespoons fresh parsley leaves
2 cans (2½ ounces each) sliced black olives

PHASE 1: 30 MINUTES

1. Scrub the potatoes (leave the skins on) and place them in a 4½-quart Dutch oven or soup pot. Add just enough cold water to cover the potatoes. Cover the pot and bring to a boil over high heat. Once boiling, uncover and boil the potatoes until tender, about 20 minutes.

2. Meanwhile, snap the tough ends off the asparagus where they naturally break and discard the ends. Rinse the asparagus spears and cut into 1-inch pieces. Place in a single layer in a shallow, microwave-safe bowl and microwave, uncovered, on high, just until crisp-tender, 2 to 3 minutes depending on the thickness of the pieces, stopping halfway to rotate the bowl if necessary. When done, put the asparagus in a colander to drain and throw in 2 handfuls of ice cubes. Rinse with cold running water and toss gently with the ice cubes to stop the asparagus from cooking, about 1 minute. Drain well, removing any unmelted ice cubes.

3. Rinse and finely chop the scallions.

4. Make the Garlic-Dijon Vinaigrette.

5. When the potatoes are done, put them in the colander to drain and throw in 2 handfuls of ice cubes. Rinse with cold running water and toss with the ice cubes until cool enough to handle. Drain well, removing any unmelted ice cubes, then cut the potatoes into ¼-inch

slices and place in a large serving bowl. Pour the vinaigrette over the potatoes and toss to coat. *The potato salad can be prepared to this point up to 24 hours ahead. Refrigerate the dressed potatoes, cooked asparagus, and chopped scallions, covered, separately.*

PHASE 2: 5 MINUTES

6. Rinse the parsley well and shake to remove any excess water. Mince the parsley and add it to the bowl with the potatoes. Add the cooked asparagus to the bowl. Drain the black olives and add them to the bowl. Toss well to mix. *The salad can be refrigerated, covered, at this point for up to 8 hours. Up to 30 minutes before serving, toss in the chopped scallions.*

■ *Serves 8 to 10*

Note: If your potatoes are larger than an egg, cut them in half.

Garlic-Dijon Vinaigrette

The strong garlic presence in this otherwise basic vinaigrette provides the right punch for such bland foods as potatoes.

> *4 cloves fresh garlic*
> *¼ cup red wine vinegar*
> *2 teaspoons Dijon mustard*
> *¼ teaspoon salt*
> *¼ teaspoon black pepper*
> *¾ cup extra-virgin olive oil*

START TO FINISH: 7 MINUTES

1. Peel the garlic. Drop the garlic cloves 1 at a time through the feed tube of a food processor with the machine running and finely chop.

2. Stop the machine and add the vinegar, mustard, salt, and pepper. Process to blend, about 5 seconds. With the motor running, drizzle the olive oil through the feed tube in a thin stream. Process just until well combined.

■ *Makes about 1 cup*

DO-AHEAD

The vinaigrette can be refrigerated, covered, for up to 3 days. Bring to room temperature and whisk or shake well just before serving.

Rainbow Wild Rice Salad

This colorful salad is a welcome addition to a summer salad buffet or makes a hearty and filling accompaniment to grilled chicken or pork. We prefer using converted rice, with its firmer texture, rather than long-grain rice, to augment the wild rice mix. Be sure to make the salad far enough ahead to allow it to chill before your guests arrive.

1 box (6 ounces) long-grain and wild rice with
   seasonings
½ cup converted rice
1 tablespoon vegetable oil
1 cup already-chopped pecans
1 large red bell pepper (for about 1 cup chopped)
3 scallions (for about ½ cup chopped,
   white and green parts)
½ cup frozen green peas
1 small can (2½ ounces) sliced black olives
⅓ cup extra-virgin olive oil
2 tablespoons red wine vinegar
1 tablespoon Dijon mustard

PHASE 1: 30 MINUTES MOSTLY UNATTENDED COOKING TIME, PLUS 2 HOURS CHILLING TIME

1. Place the long-grain and wild rice blend with its seasonings and the converted rice in a 2-quart or larger saucepan. Add 3⅓ cups of water, cover the pot, place it over high heat, and bring to a boil. Reduce the heat to medium-low and let simmer, covered, until the rice has absorbed most of the water, about 25 minutes. Toss the rice with the vegetable oil and refrigerate, covered, until chilled, about 2 hours. *The cooked rice can be refrigerated, covered, for up to 24 hours.*

PHASE 2: 11 MINUTES

2. Place the pecans on a microwave-safe plate and microwave, uncovered, on high, until fragrant and lightly toasted, 2 to 4 minutes, stopping once halfway through to stir. Meanwhile, put the chilled rice in a large serving bowl and fluff it with a fork to separate the grains. Rinse, core, seed, and chop the bell pepper into bite-size pieces. Add it to the rice. Rinse and mince the scallions. Add them to the rice mixture. Rinse the green peas with cool water to thaw

SANITY SAVER

Entertaining outdoors using your china? You'll save trips to the kitchen by setting a large plastic trunk (the kind kids take to camp) nearby in an inconspicuous spot and stacking all the dirty dishes in it.

slightly, drain, and add to the rice mixture. Drain the olives, add them to the rice mixture, and stir well to mix.

3. In a small bowl or jar with a lid, combine the olive oil, vinegar, and mustard. Whisk or cover and shake well to combine. Pour the dressing over the rice mixture and stir well. Serve at once or refrigerate, covered, until ready to serve. Toss in the toasted pecans just before serving. *The salad, minus the pecans, can be refrigerated, covered, for up to 24 hours.*

■ *Serves 8 generously*

SERVE UP SOME ART

From Beverly:

My prized pottery serving platter doubles as artwork, hanging in a prominent spot in the master bedroom. Alicia's favorite rainbow-colored glass fruit bowl greets guests from a table, front and center in the entrance hall.

Once I realized how beautiful—and how pricey—pottery platters were, I decided it was a shame not to put the piece to work 365 days a year. Think of it this way: If you need art to decorate your walls (or your halls), why not get a two-for-one deal? It helps justify the expense both ways. The only drawback is that every time I take my platter down from its bedroom roost to use to serve guests, I do have to give it a quick wash to banish the dust.

Many pottery plates, platters, and pitchers, whether hand-crafted in your own city or imported from Italy, Portugal, or Mexico, are just too beautiful to hide in the closet. Frequently these pieces come already fitted in back with a hole for slipping in a wire for hanging. Or you can buy inexpensive stands that are designed especially for putting plates on display.

Saving up enough spare cash to invest in my party platter took several months, but it was well worth it. Every time I serve whatever I've cooked on this platter, my efforts look elegant—even if dinner is just London broil and baked potatoes.

CHAPTER SEVEN

Super Simple

We've found the oven to be so forgiving, now we nearly always bake our vegetables for company meals.

When your main dish is easy and straightforward, say a savory meat loaf or a juicy grilled burger, it's not always a simple matter to figure out what to serve alongside it. A time-saving meal can quickly grow time-consuming if the side dishes are too complex or if you're trying to choose from an A-to-Z list of go-with vegetables. That's why we've come to rely on a fail-proof arsenal of effortless sides.

We figured out many entertaining moons ago that steaming vegetables—as simple as it might sound—really isn't so simple at all. It's a last minute task, and there's not enough margin for error when you stand stoveside waiting for a pot to boil, then watch nervously for broccoli or asparagus spears to reach the perfect state of crisp-tenderness, especially if guests are waiting in the dining room.

Using our oven method, you can prepare your vegetables and refrigerate the whole dish up to 24 hours ahead. Then, just preheat the oven at your convenience and, when it's hot, bake the vegetables straight from the refrigerator for the specified time—anywhere from 15 minutes for broccoli and asparagus to half an hour or so for corn. In the event that you need an extra few minutes before removing that broccoli or corn from the oven, you won't end up with a soggy mess since the oven cooks more gradually than steaming does.

Often we rely on potatoes, and in this chapter you'll find two of our favorite Southern-style potato casseroles to serve with

Sides

your favorite meats. One is made from commercially prepared refrigerated mashed potatoes that we dress up with cream cheese and sour cream and the other is laced with cheese and made speedy by using frozen hash brown potatoes. Using thin-skinned red potatoes in our Smashed Potatoes with Horseradish provides the pleasure of homemade mashed potatoes without the headache of peeling. The hint of horseradish is a signature addition that gives a delicious party feel to an old favorite. Our baked potato recipe is actually more method than recipe—an utterly perfect method that we've borrowed from the best steak house chefs who have relied on it for decades. For those times when the baked potato needs to be a bit dressed up, try adding a dollop of our Blue Cheese Butter instead of sour cream.

When it comes time to grill burgers and hot dogs, our hands-down choice for a quick side dish is beans. They're versatile, inexpensive, and tailor-made for preparing in advance. Wow your guests with our exotic Cuban Black Beans, Beverly's childhood favorite Best Baked Beans, or our colorful Quick Bean Medley for a Crowd. For something truly innovative, try our Succotash with a Twist, which dresses up the traditional Southern mix of lima beans and corn with a south of the border touch of Mexican tomatoes and black beans.

With our tried-and-true, timesaving simple sides you'll find your side dish dilemma is solved.

fast and fabulous

Red Rice

2 tablespoons butter
3 cups converted rice
2 cans (14½ ounces each) low-fat chicken broth
1 jar (16 ounces) medium-hot salsa
½ teaspoon ground cumin

START TO FINISH: 30 MINUTES

1. Melt the butter in a 3-quart or larger saucepan over medium heat. Add the rice and stir constantly until the rice is slightly browned, about 2 minutes.

2. Add the chicken broth, salsa, cumin, and 2 cups water. Stir well. Raise the heat to high and bring the mixture to a boil.

3. Cover and reduce the heat to medium-low. Let the rice steam for 20 minutes. Fluff with a fork before serving.

◼ *Serves 8 generously*

Quick Spanish-style rice goes with just about everything, but we enjoy it most with Enchanting Chicken Enchiladas (see page 114) and Big Beefy Burritos (see page 140). Using medium-hot salsa gives this rice a bit of fire. You can punch it up a bit more with hot salsa or calm it down with mild, in which case it will be kid friendly.

DO-AHEAD

The cooked rice can be refrigerated, covered, for up to 24 hours. Reheat in the microwave oven on high, stirring frequently, until hot and steamy, 3 to 5 minutes.

Smashed Potatoes with Horseradish

3 pounds red potatoes
4 tablespoons (½ stick) butter
½ cup half-and-half
2 tablespoons prepared horseradish, or more to taste
½ teaspoon salt
¼ teaspoon black pepper, or more to taste

START TO FINISH: 30 MINUTES

1. Bring 2½ quarts of water to a boil in a 4½-quart Dutch oven or soup pot over high heat. Meanwhile, scrub the potatoes. Leaving the peels on, slice each potato into quarters. Cut each quarter in half.

2. When the water boils, carefully add the potatoes to the pot. Cover the pot and let return to a boil. Uncover the pot, reduce the heat to medium-high, and continue to cook at a moderate boil until the potatoes are tender, 12 to 15 minutes.

3. Drain the potatoes and return them to the pot. Cut the butter into 4 pieces and add to the pot. Add the half-and-half. Use a potato masher to "smash" the potatoes until all of the large lumps disappear (small lumps are fine).

4. Add the horseradish, salt, and pepper and stir to thoroughly mix. Taste for seasoning, adding more horseradish or pepper if necessary.

■ *Serves 8*

POTATO MASHERS

What's the difference between desperate smashed potatoes and no smashed potatoes at all? At my house that would be a very simple, age-old tool called a potato masher. Made with a sturdy handle of plastic or wood connected to a thick wavy wire or circular cutout grid, a potato masher is very effective. Just give a few assertive jabs to the cooked potatoes, right in the pot, and the job is done.

It's amazing how liberating it is not to have to peel potatoes. Even the most upscale restaurants are leaving the peels on these days, and we like the way they add color and texture to our "smashed" spuds. A hint of horseradish adds an even more delightful note. This is the perfect accompaniment for any hearty meat dish like Great-Grandma's Beef Stew (see page 132).

DO-AHEAD

Once cool, the mashed potatoes can be refrigerated, covered, for up to 24 hours. To reheat refrigerated potatoes, place them in a microwave-safe bowl, cover with microwave-safe plastic wrap, and cut a small vent in the center. Microwave on high for 3 minutes, then stir well. Continue to microwave on high until hot and steamy, 2 to 3 minutes more.

OUR IDEA OF DECORATIONS

Decorations can take over your life. Especially if you're like us and never moved beyond the novice level in craft class. But unless it's really your thing to make elaborate centerpieces and develop themes for your gatherings, take a hint from the Desperate Duo and keep it simple.

Don't go overboard. It should be the food that stands out.

• **Candles** are easy, fast, and very festive. Small mirror tiles can be purchased from glass and mirror replacement stores for a fraction of the cost of purchasing them at craft stores. Ask the store to round the edges so they're safe and then "plant" a candle garden in the center of your table. A few drips of hot wax from a lit candle on the tile will allow the candle to stick without toppling over. Use the same or different candle colors and vary the heights for the most dramatic effect.

• **Flowers,** either from your yard or a small bunch purchased at the market, can be separated into several simple yet elegant bouquets. Wire-edge ribbon is striking when tied around the plainest of vases (it even dresses up a Mason jar). Other vases, such as those made of pottery or clay, are perfectly appropiate and will spotlight any small grouping of flowers nicely.

We love to buy several "specialty" flowers such as gerbera daisies, orchids, or oversize sunflowers and let them shine in individual vases. Group the vases together or with a candle or two, or place them throughout the house all by themselves.

• **Christmas lights**—tiny white or colored ones woven through deck rails, or a silk ficus tree in a corner, say fun, and as simple as these decorations are, they set a festive mood.

Perfect Baked Potatoes

8 large (14 to 16 ounces each) baking potatoes
Blue Cheese Butter (recipe follows), plain butter,
or sour cream, for serving

START TO FINISH: 5 MINUTES, PLUS 1 HOUR UNATTENDED BAKING TIME

1. Preheat the oven to 450°F.

2. Scrub the potatoes and prick each twice with a fork. Bake, uncovered, directly on the rack in the middle of the oven for 1 hour.

3. Using oven mitts or long tongs, carefully remove the potatoes from the oven. Serve at once with the topping of your choice.

■ *Serves 8*

Blue Cheese Butter

If a Perfect Baked Potato is great plain, just imagine what happens when you give it a dollop of this gourmet butter. It's a magic five-minute mix that lets your guests know you're thrilled they've decided to visit.

3 tablespoons already-crumbled blue cheese
8 tablespoons (1 stick) butter at room temperature

START TO FINISH: 5 MINUTES, PLUS 1 HOUR UNATTENDED CHILLING TIME

1. Place the blue cheese in the bowl of a food processor fitted with a steel blade. Cut the butter into 4 pieces and add them to the bowl of the food processor. Process to mix well, stopping once to scrape down the side of the processor bowl with a rubber spatula. Place in a ¾-cup ramekin or other serving dish.

2. Cover the butter and place in the refrigerator for at least 1 hour but preferably 1 day.

■ *Makes about ½ cup*

We'd never been able to bake a potato just right—they were either half done or the skins were soggy. Our goal was to duplicate the potatoes at our favorite steak house, with the skin a little crunchy and the middle moist and fluffy. After consulting with a friend who owns several restaurants, we discovered that "real" baked potatoes need to cook at a very high temperature, without aluminum foil or fat, for an hour. After our first try and the astounded look on our husbands' faces, we knew we'd hit the jackpot. These potatoes are wonderful plain, with butter or sour cream, or with Blue Cheese Butter. And, of course, with a serving of Amazing Steaks (see page 152) sharing the plate.

DO-AHEAD

The Blue Cheese Butter can be refrigerated, covered, for up to 3 days.

Phased and Flexible

Dressed-Up Asparagus

2 pounds fresh asparagus
4 tablespoons olive oil
Salt and black pepper
1 tablespoon balsamic vinegar
1 teaspoon Dijon mustard

When you want something a bit different for your asparagus, try our worry-free version straight from the oven. Tossing the spears in a light mixture of balsamic vinegar, olive oil, and mustard adds interest without overpowering the springtime flavor. (Choose pencil-thin asparagus, if possible, to avoid any urge you may have to peel them.) Serve the asparagus with Perfect Party Pork (see page 175) or Vacation Fish Boats (see page 182).

SANITY SAVER

Nervous about entertaining? Practice on people you trust, friends who are so familiar, or so laid-back, there's no way you'll be intimidated.

PHASE 1: 5 MINUTES

1. Snap the tough ends off the asparagus where they naturally break and discard the ends. Rinse the asparagus spears and drain well. Place the spears in a 13 × 9-inch glass baking dish. Drizzle with 1 tablespoon of the olive oil and toss to coat the spears. Season lightly with salt and pepper. Cover the baking dish snugly with aluminum foil. *The seasoned asparagus can be refrigerated in the covered baking dish for up to 24 hours.*

PHASE 2: 16 MINUTES

2. Preheat the oven to 450°F.

3. Bake the asparagus, covered, until crisp-tender, about 15 minutes.

4. Meanwhile, whisk the remaining 3 tablespoons olive oil together with the vinegar and mustard in a small bowl.

5. Remove the aluminum foil from the asparagus and pour the oil mixture over the spears. Toss gently to coat well. Serve immediately.

■ *Serves 8*

Best Baked Beans

Cooking oil spray
3 cans (16 ounces each) baked beans (see Note)
1 large onion (for about 1 cup chopped)
¼ cup ketchup
2 tablespoons firmly packed light brown sugar
2 tablespoons yellow prepared mustard
2 teaspoons Worcestershire sauce
½ teaspoon garlic powder

PHASE 1: 7 MINUTES

1. Spray a 13 × 9-inch baking dish or 3-quart casserole with cooking oil spray. Put all of the beans with their liquid into the baking dish. Peel and coarsely chop the onion and add it to the beans.

2. Add the ketchup, brown sugar, mustard, Worcestershire sauce, and garlic powder. Stir gently, but thoroughly, until the ingredients are mixed well. *The bean mixture can be refrigerated, covered, for up to 24 hours.*

PHASE 2: 30 MINUTES UNATTENDED BAKING TIME

3. Preheat the oven to 350°F.

4. Remove the cover and place the baking dish on the middle rack of the oven. Bake the beans until bubbly and the onion is tender, about 30 minutes. (Any leftovers store well, covered, in the refrigerator for several days and are best reheated in a microwave oven.)

■ *Serves 8 generously*

Note: For a vegetarian dish, choose vegetarian baked beans (made without pork) and omit the Worcestershire sauce.

From Beverly:

Jerry Cashwell of Elizabethtown, North Carolina, hasn't crossed my path in nearly thirty years, but every time I crave baked beans, this lovely lady—my mom's dear pal when I was just a kid—comes springing to mind. There she is at the backyard cookout, and again at the beach picnic, always bearing a steaming casserole of beans with just the right hint of brown sugar toned down by a squirt of good-old yellow mustard. Hot dogs, burgers, and grilled chicken all tasted better with Best Baked Beans alongside.

This recipe is so simple (7 minutes to mix, then a half-hour bake), I learned to make it even before hitting puberty. When I headed for my first college apartment, I carefully copied it on an index card and stuck it in my suitcase. The card is almost brown now, splattered with bean juice, with notes scribbled from various experiments over the years. But I always come back to Jerry's original version. What can you expect, when the only real work is peeling an onion!

This is deck food—a great twist on traditional baked beans for casual cookouts. Throw together a colorful array of beans and suddenly, plain-old food becomes party food. The beans will feed as many as twelve, but leftovers reheat nicely in the microwave and the flavors actually improve the second time around.

Quick Bean Medley for a Crowd

Cooking oil spray
1 can (15 ounces) chickpeas (garbanzo beans)
1 can (15 ounces) pinto beans
1 can (15½ ounces) red kidney beans
1 can (15 ounces) navy beans
1 large onion (for about 1 cup chopped)
1 medium-size green bell pepper (for about 1 cup chopped)
3 tablespoons honey
2 tablespoons Dijon mustard
2 teaspoons olive oil
2 teaspoons bottled minced garlic

PHASE 1: 11 MINUTES

1. Spray a 13 × 9-inch baking dish or 3-quart casserole with cooking oil spray. Open all of the cans of beans but drain only the chickpeas. Add the pinto beans, kidney beans, and navy beans with their liquid to the baking dish. Add the drained chickpeas to the other beans.

2. Peel and dice the onion and add it to the beans. Rinse, core, seed, and coarsely chop the bell pepper and add it to the bean mixture. Add the honey, mustard, olive oil, and garlic. Stir gently but thoroughly until all the ingredients are mixed. *The bean mixture can be refrigerated, covered, at this point for up to 24 hours.*

PHASE 2: 30 TO 35 MINUTES UNATTENDED BAKING TIME

3. Preheat the oven to 350°F.

4. Bake the beans, uncovered, until bubbly and the onion and bell pepper are tender, 30 to 35 minutes. Serve at once or let rest until ready to serve, for up to 20 minutes. (Leftovers store well, covered, in the refrigerator, for several days.)

■ *Serves 12*

Cuban Black Beans

2 teaspoons olive oil

2 large onions (for about 2 cups chopped)

1 large green bell pepper (for about 1½ cups chopped)

1½ tablespoons bottled minced garlic

2 teaspoons ground cumin

1 teaspoon dried oregano

½ teaspoon black pepper

3 cans (15 ounces each) black beans

2 bay leaves

1 tablespoon Worcestershire sauce

Fresh cilantro, for garnish (optional)

2 tablespoons balsamic vinegar

6 cups hot cooked rice (optional; from 2 cups uncooked
  converted rice; see page 120 for cooking instructions)

PHASE 1: 20 MINUTES

1. Heat the olive oil in a 12-inch nonstick skillet over medium heat. Peel and coarsely chop the onions, adding them to the skillet as you chop. Cook the onions, stirring from time to time. Meanwhile, rinse, core, and seed the bell pepper. Coarsely chop the bell pepper, adding it to the skillet as you chop. Add the garlic, cumin, oregano, and black pepper. Raise the heat to medium-high. Cook, stirring from time to time, until the onions are soft, about 5 minutes.

2. While the vegetables cook, rinse and drain 1 can of black beans. Add the drained black beans, plus the remaining 2 cans with their liquid. Bring to a boil and reduce the heat to medium-low. Add the bay leaves and Worcestershire sauce. Stir well to mix.

3. Let the beans simmer for 10 minutes to blend the flavors, stirring from time to time. Remove and discard the bay leaves. *The bean mixture can be refrigerated, covered, at this point for up to 24 hours.*

In every Cuban restaurant in Miami's Little Havana you'll find a kettle of savory black beans simmering. When served over hot steamed rice, this staple is a meal in itself. A pot of spicy beans can be made several days ahead and reheated to dress up pork or a platter of grilled sausages.

MONEY SAVER

Think ethnic to spice up the ordinary. Cuban Black Beans (at left) or Red Rice (see page 248), for example, are inexpensive yet for many feel exotic. They're filling, too.

PHASE 2: 7 TO 10 MINUTES

4. Return the bean mixture to the skillet and heat over medium-high heat, stirring frequently, until heated through, 7 to 10 minutes. If using the cilantro, rinse well and shake the leaves to remove any excess water. Remove and discard the tough stems but do not worry about the smaller, upper stems. Chop the cilantro up to 2 hours before serving and refrigerate, covered. Add the vinegar just before serving. Serve the bean mixture in bowls, garnished with a sprinkle of cilantro, if desired. Serve over rice, if desired. *The beans can remain on the heat at a very slow simmer for up to 2 hours before serving.*

■ *Serves 8*

From Beverly:

I have whipped up this classic Southern broccoli casserole for more than two decades, and it has served as everything from my "funeral food" to a casserole to share with new neighbors. Over the years, the recipe has changed to reflect the times. The original, from the Junior League of Charlotte, North Carolina, called for a whole stick of butter and a cup of mayonnaise. While my version is still something of a splurge, albeit a worthwhile one, with only a tiny bit of butter, the reduced-fat mayonnaise and virtually fat-free soup trim off quite a few calories. The casserole tastes great served with Mom's Original Meat Loaf (see page 106).

Southern Broccoli Casserole

2 tablespoons butter or margarine
1 box (10 ounces) frozen chopped broccoli
1 medium-size onion (for about ¾ cup chopped)
2 large eggs
1 can (10¾ ounces) low-fat cream of mushroom soup
1 cup already-shredded sharp Cheddar cheese
1 cup already-shredded Swiss cheese (see Notes)
½ cup low-fat mayonnaise
1 bag (16 ounces) frozen broccoli cuts (see Notes)
Cooking oil spray
1 cup bread crumbs or cracker crumbs

PHASE 1: 17 MINUTES

1. Place the butter in a 1-cup or larger glass measure, cover with a paper towel, and microwave on high until melted, 30 to 45 seconds. Remove the butter from the microwave.

2. Place the chopped broccoli in a colander and rinse with warm running water until the frozen block breaks apart. Set aside to drain. Peel and coarsely chop the onion.

3. Break the eggs into a large mixing bowl and lightly beat. Add the melted butter, chopped onion, mushroom soup, Cheddar and Swiss cheeses, and mayonnaise. Stir well. Press the chopped broccoli with the back of a spoon to remove as much water as possible. Add the chopped broccoli to the egg mixture.

4. Place the frozen broccoli cuts in the colander and rinse with warm running water for about 1 minute to partially thaw and remove any ice crystals. Drain well, pressing with the back of a spoon to remove as much water as possible, and add the broccoli cuts to the broccoli mixture. Stir well until all the broccoli is coated with sauce. *The broccoli mixture can be refrigerated, covered, for up to 8 hours or frozen for up to a month in a 13 × 9-inch baking dish sprayed with cooking oil spray. Let thaw in the refrigerator overnight.*

PHASE 2: 3 MINUTES, PLUS 45 MINUTES MOSTLY UNATTENDED BAKING TIME

5. Preheat the oven to 350°F.

6. Spray a 13 × 9-inch baking dish with cooking oil spray, if you have not already done so. Put the broccoli mixture in the baking dish and smooth with the back of a spoon to even it out.

7. Place the baking dish on the middle rack of the oven and bake, uncovered, until the top begins to brown and the edges bubble, about 35 minutes.

8. Remove from the oven and sprinkle the bread crumbs evenly on top. Continue to bake, uncovered, until the crumbs brown, about 10 minutes more.

■ *Serves 8 generously*

Notes: If you can't find shredded Swiss cheese and don't want to grate your own, substitute an additional cup of Cheddar.

Broccoli cuts (pieces smaller than florets but not quite as fine as chopped) add texture to the chopped broccoli, which serves as a necessary binder. If you can't find frozen cuts, substitute florets or spears and chop them into bite-size chunks.

Finding a no-fail approach to perfect broccoli is the best thing that has happened to our company dinners in a long time. No more worrying about oversteaming on the stove top. Now our broccoli is perfectly crisp-tender every time and matches beautifully with Pork Chops with Fruit Sauces (see page 156) or Chicken with Mustard Glazes (see page 160).

Oven-Steamed Broccoli

10 cups (about 20 ounces) fresh broccoli florets
1 lemon
4 tablespoons (½ stick) butter
Salt and black pepper

PHASE 1: 5 MINUTES

1. Cut any large broccoli florets into bite-size pieces. Rinse the broccoli well, drain, and place in a 13 × 9-inch baking dish. *The rinsed broccoli can be refrigerated, covered, for up to 24 hours.*

PHASE 2: 15 MINUTES MOSTLY UNATTENDED BAKING TIME

2. Preheat the oven to 450°F.

3. Cut the lemon in half and squeeze the juice through a small strainer (to catch the seeds) into a 2-cup or larger glass measure. Add the butter, cover with a paper towel, and microwave on high until the butter is melted, about 1 minute. Stir well to mix and drizzle over the broccoli in the baking dish. Season with a generous sprinkling of salt and pepper. Cover tightly with aluminum foil. Bake for 10 to 12 minutes for crisp-tender broccoli or longer to desired doneness. Carefully uncover and serve immediately.

■ *Serves 8*

DEALING WITH GARLIC

There's nothing like the ease of scooping already-minced garlic right out of a jar—most of the time. Bottled minced garlic is our favorite Desperation Prescription for speeding the way for most of our soups, stews, and casseroles. However, there are times when only the sharp bite of fresh will do—namely when the garlic remains raw or is a main ingredient.

Dealing with a fresh garlic clove is a lot easier if you have the right equipment. To peel it yourself, there are three choices—a microwave, a chef's knife, or a small rubber tube called a garlic peeler, sold at kitchen equipment shops for less than $10.

One of our favorite quick tricks is to stick a clove of garlic in the microwave and blast it, on high, for 3 to 5 seconds. The number of seconds depends on your microwave's wattage, so you might have to experiment a couple of times to nail the time exactly. Once micro-waved, the papery garlic peel slips right off the clove.

The next method takes a bit more practice, but once you get the hang of it, you'll be addicted. Place a chef's knife flat over a garlic clove with the sharp edge pointed away from you and give the blade a firm whack with the heel of your hand. The garlic peel will split and fall right off. The trick is in mastering how hard to whack. Hit too hard and you'll smash the clove, but it will still be fine for most recipes. A chef's knife is best for this task because of its wide stable surface, but in a pinch, a metal spatula will work okay.

If you're into gadgets, garlic peeling tubes are pretty amazing, too. Stick the clove inside, use the heel of your hand to roll it on the counter, and the peel disappears. (Actually, it stays inside the tube, which you'll need to rinse afterward.) The biggest advantage of the peeler over the knife is that it's easier to control the pressure and not mistakenly smash cloves.

Finally, if none of these tactics appeal to you, there's good news on the horizon. Specialty foods markets are already beginning to sell plastic containers that hold about twenty-five already-peeled garlic cloves, so it shouldn't be long before regular supermarkets follow suit. The already-peeled cloves don't cost significantly more, but the main drawback is that you'll waste garlic if you don't use them before the expiration date, about two weeks from purchase.

We can't imagine cooking without garlic, but how do you get rid of those pesky peels?

Before we hit upon the roasting method, we rarely served corn for a crowd. Now it's a favorite menu star. The oven becomes your best friend when a pan of corn can be prepared in advance and disappears to roast only to reemerge ready for the table. No more waiting for a huge caldron to come to a boil; no more struggling to get scorching corn buttered. Pair the ears with a flavored butter and the ordinary seems fancy for sure. Serve the corn alongside Citrus Shrimp Kebabs (see page 180) and a bowl of the ripest summer tomatoes, cut into wedges.

Can-Do Corn on the Cob

8 ears yellow corn
8 teaspoons Cilantro-Garlic Butter, Roasted Garlic
Butter (recipes follow), or plain butter

PHASE 1: 15 MINUTES

1. Shuck the corn and remove the silk. Place each ear on a 12-inch square of aluminum foil. Smear a teaspoon of butter over each ear and then roll the ear up in the foil, twisting the ends to seal. *The wrapped corn can be refrigerated for up to 24 hours.*

PHASE 2: 30 TO 40 MINUTES UNATTENDED BAKING TIME

2. Preheat the oven to 450°F.

3. Place all of the wrapped ears of corn on a baking sheet that has a rim all the way around, such as a jelly roll pan. Roast the corn until tender, 30 to 40 minutes. Serve at once or turn off the oven and leave the corn inside until ready to serve, for up to 1 hour.

■ *Serves 8*

Cilantro-Garlic Butter

Hints of cilantro and garlic liven up corn on the cob or any steamed vegetables. A little goes a long way.

1 large clove fresh garlic
About ¼ cup densely packed fresh cilantro
8 tablespoons (1 stick) butter at room temperature

START TO FINISH: 5 MINUTES, PLUS 1 HOUR UNATTENDED CHILLING TIME

1. Peel the garlic, drop it through the feed tube of a food processor with the machine running and finely chop. Rinse the cilantro well

DO-AHEAD

The Cilantro-Garlic Butter can be refrigerated, covered, for up to 3 days.

and shake the leaves to remove any excess water. Remove and discard the tough lower stems but do not worry about the smaller, upper stems. You should have about ¼ cup of leaves. Drop the cilantro through the feed tube of the food processor with the machine running and finely chop. Scrape down the side of the processor bowl with a rubber spatula.

2. Cut the butter into 4 pieces and add them to the bowl of the food processor. Process to mix well, stopping once to scrape down the side of the processor bowl. Place in a ¾-cup ramekin or other serving dish.

3. Cover the butter and place in the refrigerator for at least 1 hour but preferably 1 day.

■ *Makes about ½ cup*

Roasted Garlic Butter

Having a stash of roasted garlic on hand makes quick work of an herb butter that works well on Oven-Steamed Broccoli (see page 258) or any simply prepared vegetables. It's also delicious spread on French bread.

3 cloves roasted garlic (see page 262)
8 tablespoons (1 stick) butter at room temperature

START TO FINISH: 5 MINUTES, PLUS 1 HOUR UNATTENDED CHILLING TIME

1. Peel the garlic cloves and place them in the bowl of a food processor fitted with a steel blade. Cut the butter into 4 pieces and add them to the bowl of the food processor. Process to mix well, stopping once to scrape down the side of the processor bowl with a rubber spatula. Place in a ½-cup ramekin or other serving dish.

2. Cover the butter and place in the refrigerator for at least 1 hour but preferably 1 day.

■ *Makes about ½ cup*

DO-AHEAD

The Roasted Garlic Butter can be refrigerated, covered, for up to 3 days.

ROASTED GARLIC

Roasted garlic is the mystery ingredient in several recipes in this book. The good news is just how easy it is to make. In fact it's just as easy to roast ten or more heads of garlic as it is to roast one, and so this recipe calls for ten heads. If you decide to roast more or less, adjust the amount of oil accordingly. Make sure you use enough oil to seep down into the cloves, but be careful not to drown them. The timing here yields a firm roasted clove, ideal for mincing by hand or in a food processor. If you prefer a softer clove, roast it 10 minutes or so longer. Cooked that way, the garlic is good spread on crackers, *crostini,* or baguettes.

10 heads garlic
Cooking oil spray
¼ cup extra-virgin olive oil

START TO FINISH: ABOUT 30 MINUTES

1. Preheat the oven to 375°F.

2. Lay a head of garlic on its side, and holding it steady, use a sharp knife to cut off the top ¼ to ½ inch of each clove. Repeat with the remaining heads.

3. Spray the inside of a small baking dish (one large enough that each head of garlic can stand without being crowded, but not too large) with cooking oil spray. Place the garlic in the dish, cut side up, and drizzle with the olive oil.

4. Bake, uncovered, until the garlic is soft but not mushy, 15 to 25 minutes. Poke a clove in each of the heads with a wooden toothpick to determine if the garlic is done. The toothpick should slide in easily with no resistance. Remove the garlic from the oven and let cool. Refrigerate in the peel or squeeze each head to extract the cloves. *Roasted garlic will keep in the peel in a plastic container with a lid or in a zipper-top plastic bag in the refrigerator for up to 3 weeks.*

■ *Makes 10 heads of garlic*

The mellow flavor of roasted garlic provides an undertone that may fool even the most developed palate.

Oven-Roasted Green Beans with Garlic

Cooking oil spray
2 pounds fresh green beans
1 large onion (for about 1 cup slices)
8 cloves fresh garlic
2 tablespoons olive oil
Salt and black pepper
2 tablespoons balsamic vinegar

PHASE 1: 20 MINUTES

1. Spray a 13 × 9-inch or larger baking pan with cooking oil spray. Rinse and drain the green beans and trim off and discard the stem ends. Place the beans in the baking pan.

2. Peel the onion and cut it into slices ¼ inch wide. Separate the rings and scatter them over the green beans. Peel the garlic, cut the cloves in half, and scatter them over the onions.

3. Drizzle the olive oil over the vegetables. Sprinkle lightly with salt and pepper. *The pan of beans can be refrigerated, covered, at this point for up to 24 hours.*

PHASE 2: 30 MINUTES MOSTLY UNATTENDED BAKING TIME

4. Preheat the oven to 400°F.

5. Bake the vegetables, uncovered, for about 30 minutes, opening the oven after 10 minutes and again after 20 minutes to stir briefly. After 20 minutes, taste a bean and cook until crisp-tender, about 10 minutes more (or longer if a softer bean is desired). Remove from the oven and transfer to a serving bowl. Drizzle with the vinegar and stir well. Serve at once or let cool to room temperature before serving. *The cooked green beans will keep for up to 1 hour at room temperature.*

■ *Serves 8*

Our original version of this recipe, on a computer printout from our friend Felicia Gressette, is so stained with vinegar we can barely read it. Beverly makes these green beans almost once a week since they are her daughter's "most favorite vegetable in the world." Serve them piping hot with everything from Portobello Mushroom "Steak" Sandwiches (see page 184) to Vacation Fish Boats (see page 182), or add them to a summer buffet at room temperature. Either way, the combination of green beans and garlic is addictive.

SPACE SAVER

If you are running out of room, borrow space in a neighbor's refrigerator a few days before your gathering. Then you can return the favor sometime.

If your guest list includes young children and you aren't sure what they might like to eat, think of this recipe as an insurance policy. Children like nothing better than the simple pleasure of butter and cheese on noodles. Our kids—and a lot of other kids we know—practically lived on "cheesy noodles" in their earlier years. We like to serve them with meat loaf or beef tips, but even if we've already got the menu planned and noodles don't seem to fit it, we'll often make them as an extra side dish to ensure that all of the tykes at the table are happy. The noodles are easy to throw together (if you want to prepare them from start to finish, simply dot the hot noodles with the butter and sprinkle with the Parmesan immediately after draining and adding the olive oil). You might find that even adults appreciate the comfort of unadorned buttery noodles.

Simple Butter and Cheese Noodles

1 package (12 ounces) egg noodles
1 tablespoon olive oil
3 tablespoons butter
½ cup already-grated Parmesan cheese

PHASE 1: 10 MINUTES

1. Bring 4 quarts of water to a boil in a large soup pot or pasta pot. Add the noodles and cook according to the directions on the package, 10 to 12 minutes. Drain the noodles in a colander, then drizzle the olive oil over them. Toss gently and let cool to room temperature. *The cooked noodles can be stored in a zipper-top bag for up to 2 days.*

PHASE 2: 7 MINUTES

2. Place the noodles in a large microwave-safe bowl. Slice the butter into 3 pieces and place on the cold noodles. Cover the bowl with a paper towel and microwave on high until the noodles are heated through, about 5½ minutes.

3. Sprinkle the Parmesan cheese over the hot noodles and toss to mix. Serve immediately.

■ *Serves 8 generously*

Cheryl's Party Potatoes

3 packages (1 pound, 4 ounces each) already-prepared
   mashed potatoes
1 package (8 ounces) cream cheese
1 small container (8 ounces) sour cream
4 tablespoons (½ stick) butter
1 tablespoon bottled minced garlic
2 teaspoons freeze-dried chives
½ teaspoon salt, or more to taste
¼ teaspoon black pepper, or more to taste
Cooking oil spray
1½ cups already-shredded sharp Cheddar cheese

PHASE 1: 12 MINUTES

1. Microwave the potatoes, in their packages, on high until just
warm, about 5 minutes.

2. Meanwhile, cut the cream cheese into 4 pieces. Cream together
the sour cream, butter, and the pieces of cream cheese in the large
bowl of an electric mixer. Add the garlic, chives, salt, and pepper.
Add the warm potatoes. Mix on medium speed until smooth, about
1 to 2 minutes, scraping down the side of the bowl frequently. Taste
for seasoning, adding more salt and pepper if necessary.

3. Spray a 13 × 9-inch glass baking dish or 3-quart casserole with
cooking oil spray and spread the potatoes evenly in the dish. Top
evenly with the Cheddar cheese. *The potatoes can be refrigerated,
covered, at this point for up to 24 hours.*

PHASE 2: 30 MINUTES UNATTENDED BAKING TIME

4. Preheat the oven to 350°F.

5. Bake the potatoes, uncovered, until the cheese is melted and lightly
browned, about 30 minutes.

■ *Serves 8 to 10*

From Alicia:

My sister-in-law, Cheryl
Ross, is famous in our
family for her party potatoes.
Cheryl will painstakingly peel
and boil bags of potatoes to
make this delicious creamy
potato casserole. Our family
gatherings are never small
either, usually numbering at
least twelve to fifteen people,
depending on who's in town.

We've downsized her
recipe and plugged in
refrigerated mashed potatoes
instead of starting with raw.
This simple substitution
skips the most laborious step
and yet you still end up with
rich, creamy potatoes you'll
be pleased to serve your
guests. And if you want
to use low-fat sour cream
and Neufchatel in place of
cream cheese, you'll still get
delicious results.

The simple potato
casserole is easy to assemble
ahead and then bake right
before serving or bake and
transport to another location
for a potluck or buffet meal.
Light and fluffy in texture,
these potatoes are very filling
and will go a long way
toward feeding your hungry
crowd. We particularly like
them with Italian Meat Loaf
(see page 108).

Hash brown casserole has always been one of our favorite standbys. Homey and comforting, it was just right for a hungry crowd. Then one day we did a little math on the fat content and, oh my word! What were we serving our guests? So, we did a little tinkering with the recipe. Now with a few substitutions of reduced-fat products, we can still serve this versatile side—without all the fat.

Old-Fashioned Hash Brown Casserole

Cooking oil spray
1 package (2 pounds) Southern-style (cubed) frozen
* hash brown potatoes*
2 cans (10¾ ounces each) low-fat cream of mushroom
* soup*
½ cup low-fat sour cream
1 teaspoon onion powder
2 cups already finely shredded sharp Cheddar cheese

PHASE 1: 10 MINUTES

1. Spray a 13 × 9-inch glass baking dish or 3-quart casserole with cooking oil spray. Place the potatoes in the bottom of the dish, separating any large chunks that are stuck together. Open both cans of mushroom soup and dollop spoonfuls evenly over the potatoes. Repeat with the sour cream. Sprinkle the onion powder evenly over the potatoes. Sprinkle 1 cup of the Cheddar cheese over all, then stir gently but thoroughly to mix. Smooth out the potato mixture to fill the baking dish.

2. Sprinkle the remaining Cheddar cheese evenly over the top of the potato mixture. *The casserole can be refrigerated, covered, at this point for up to 24 hours.*

PHASE 2: 50 MINUTES UNATTENDED BAKING TIME

3. Preheat the oven to 350°F.

4. Uncover the potatoes and place the baking dish on the middle rack of the oven. Bake until the potatoes are bubbly along the edges and the cheese starts to brown lightly, about 50 minutes.

■ *Serves 8*

Succotash with a Twist

Cooking oil spray
1 box (10 ounces) frozen baby lima beans
1 large onion (for about 1 cup chopped)
1 large red bell pepper (for about 1 cup chopped)
1 can (14½ ounces) Mexican-style stewed tomatoes
   (see page 51) or diced tomatoes seasoned with jalapeño
   or chile peppers
2 teaspoons bottled minced garlic
2 cups frozen yellow corn kernels
1 can (15 ounces) black beans
¾ cup already-shredded sharp Cheddar cheese

PHASE 1: 12 MINUTES

1. Spray a 13 × 9-inch glass baking dish or 3-quart glass casserole with cooking oil spray. Place the lima beans in the dish, cover with microwave-safe plastic wrap, and cut a 1-inch slit in the center as a vent. Microwave on high for 5 minutes to thaw.

2. Meanwhile, peel and coarsely chop the onion. Rinse, core, seed, and coarsely chop the bell pepper. Add the onion, bell pepper, tomatoes with their juice, garlic, and corn to the thawed lima beans. Rinse and drain the black beans; add them to the lima beans. Stir to mix well. *The succotash can be refrigerated, covered with aluminum foil, at this point for up to 24 hours.*

PHASE 2: ABOUT 1 HOUR MOSTLY UNATTENDED BAKING TIME

3. Preheat the oven to 375°F.

4. Bake the succotash, covered with aluminum foil, until bubbly and the vegetables are tender, 55 minutes to 1 hour. Remove the dish from the oven, sprinkle the Cheddar cheese on top, and bake, uncovered, just until the cheese melts, about 5 minutes. Serve at once or let the succotash rest, for up to 30 minutes.

■ *Serves 8*

O ne of our friends was pretty frank about his affection for our take on an old Southern side dish. "This was so good it made me forget that I don't like lima beans," he said. Another friend who's fond of spicy foods added a can of chopped green chiles when he made the succotash. A hefty dash of Tabasco sauce would add a kick, too. London Broil with Molasses Marinade (see page 168) or Carolina Crock-Pot Barbecue (see page 143) benefit from a side of this vegetable combo.

CHAPTER EIGHT

Everybody's

If you've all but given up on finding a time to get your busy friends and family together, think brunch.

Brunch is too good—and too easy—to serve only to overnight guests and relatives visiting from out of town. Whether it's a Saturday morning at ten or right after a Sunday morning run, the flexible melding of breakfast and lunch can let you take time you didn't think you had and turn it into priceless memories with people you treasure.

Morning gatherings are especially appealing when young children and young-at-heart grandparents are included. As the day kicks off everybody's energetic, anticipation runs high, and moods are apt to be congenial. Brunch settings can range from as casual as sitting on the deck with trays to a dining room buffet, if you're game for a more formal gathering. In either case—or in the wide expanse of possibilities in between—one of the very best things about brunch is that the food being served is easy on the host.

Both of us love those breakfast casseroles that get assembled the night before and then, after the alarm goes off the next morning, go directly into the oven to appear steaming and fragrant the moment guests arrive. We've included our favorites—wait until you taste the traditional Mother's Brunch Casserole, loaded with ham and cheese, and also a spicier Southwestern combination with rice, for those of you who like an adventure in the morning. Quiches are always a welcome choice, and we've come up with the perfect recipes. Look for Three-Cheese Broccoli Quiches and the Swiss cheese and

Brunch

mushroom quiches, which are packed with meaty portobellos. Try one of our surprising takes on familiar egg dishes: an omelet with a zippy Italian salsa or eggs Benedict and French toast casseroles. Yes, every one of these can be prepared ahead and baked the morning you plan to entertain.

Rounding out a brunch menu can be tricky, but we've kept it very simple. Plenty of ready-to-serve suggestions appear on pages 284 and 291. Or whip up our delicate coffee cake based, of course, on a cake mix. Then there are Fastest Fruit Salad, Brown Sugar Bacon, and Overnight Cheese Grits—all are easy to prepare and sure to please.

Maybe your guests are out-of-towners bunking out in the spare bedroom or perhaps you're hosting another family after a crack-of-dawn soccer game. Armed with a collection of no-fail recipes that practically make themselves, you'll find you look forward to brunch as much as we do.

fast and fabulous

Fastest Fruit Salad

From Alicia:

Y ou won't believe how far ahead this delicious fruit salad can be made. I didn't believe it, either, until the time the leftovers got pushed to the back of my refrigerator and I only found them five days later. Granted five days is too long to wait to serve company, but three days is a godsend for a Desperate Do-aheader. You'll find this adaptable salad is perfect for dinner as well.

1 can (15¼ ounces) pineapple tidbits, packed in juice (see Note)
1 can (15 ounces) mandarin orange segments
2 medium Granny Smith apples (for about 3 cups chopped)
2 medium Red Delicious apples (for about 3 cups chopped)
2 kiwi fruit

START TO FINISH: 7 MINUTES

1. Put the pineapple tidbits with their juice in a large serving bowl. Drain the mandarin oranges and add them to the pineapple.

2. Rinse but do not peel the apples. Core them and cut into bite-size pieces, adding these to the bowl as you work. Stir the fruit occasionally to coat the apples with the juices; this will prevent them from discoloring.

3. Peel and slice the kiwis, adding them to the bowl as you slice. Stir the fruit to mix.

■ *Serves 8 generously*

Note: If you can't find pineapple tidbits, you can use pineapple chunks instead.

DO-AHEAD

T he fruit salad can be refrigerated, covered, for up to 3 days.

BRING ON THE BAGELS

From Beverly:

Until I married into a family that knows how to treat a bagel right, I'm not sure I had even tasted one. But, from my very first gathering with the Gyllenhaal clan in eastern Pennsylvania, it was clear that brunch was about to take on a whole new dimension.

The first person up in the morning went out to get the paper, then kept on going to the bakery, not permitted to return without giant sacks of still-steaming bagels. Those left at home would fry some bacon, slice ripe tomatoes, and bring out the cream cheese to soften. Sometimes we would luck out and have lox with thin slivers of Bermuda onion and buttery ripe avocado slices.

So now, the neighborhood bagel shop saves my neck on a regular basis. Family room crawling with cousins? Meeting friends for a quick bite at the park? How many kids on the cul-de-sac are munching at the house today? I've never met anyone who doesn't appreciate a good, fresh bagel. And since shops abound with assorted bagels and cream cheese spreads in every conceivable flavor, it's practically effortless to put together a bagel smorgasbord. There's nothing like a still-warm bagel, but if you don't have anyone willing to go in search of bagels first thing in the morning, buy yours a day or so ahead and freeze them. Just allow a couple of extra minutes for thawing.

Even supermarkets are getting into the act with frozen bagels and flavored cream cheeses. Still, if you have a few minutes, it's easy to make your own flavored spreads. Just mix soft cream cheese with all-fruit jams, or with sliced olives and scallions, or with shrimp with a little horseradish and ketchup. Peanut butter and hummus make tasty toppings, too. Alicia and I have experimented a lot and found that most of our appetizer spreads also make wonderful bagel toppings. For starters, try Smoked Oyster Spread (see page 57), Old English Cheese Spread (see page 61), Black Bean "Hummus" (see page 47), or Riviera Tuna Spread (see page 56).

Bagels are a strictly assemble-your-own food, which naturally makes things much easier on the host—after a bagel brunch, nobody mentions food again for hours.

When I was growing up in a one-stoplight town in eastern North Carolina, bagels may as well have been a foreign food.

Phased and Flexible

Night-Before Mexican Breakfast Casserole

Think breakfast enchiladas. Instead of chicken or beef, our tortillas wrap around a savory mix of scrambled eggs and bell peppers, and we top everything with taco sauce and cheese. Feel free to use reduced-fat sour cream and milk if you wish. The combination of red and green bell peppers makes for a colorful casserole, and the night-before assembly makes for a happy morning for the host, especially if the company is the sleepover kind.

2 teaspoons olive oil
1 large onion (for about 1 cup chopped)
1 large red bell pepper (for about 1 cup chopped)
1 medium-size green bell pepper (for about 1 cup chopped)
1 teaspoon bottled minced garlic
About ⅓ cup densely packed fresh cilantro or parsley
9 large eggs
¼ cup milk
½ cup sour cream
Cooking oil spray
8 small flour tortillas (6½ to 7 inches)
1 jar (16 ounces) mild taco sauce
1½ to 2 cups already-shredded Mexican cheese blend,
*   such as Monterey Jack and Cheddar*

PHASE 1: 10 MINUTES

1. Place 1 teaspoon of the olive oil in a 12-inch nonstick skillet and heat over medium heat. Peel and coarsely chop the onion, adding it to the skillet as you chop. Stir from time to time. Rinse, core, seed, and coarsely chop the bell peppers, adding them to the skillet as you chop. Continue to stir from time to time. After all of the bell pepper is added, add the garlic, and continue to cook, stirring frequently, for 1 minute. *The cooked vegetables can be refrigerated, covered, for up to 24 hours.*

PHASE 2: 20 MINUTES

2. Rinse the cilantro well and shake the leaves to remove any excess water. Remove and discard the tough stems but do not worry about the smaller, upper stems. You should have about ⅓ cup of leaves. Finely mince the cilantro and set aside.

3. Heat the remaining 1 teaspoon olive oil in a 12-inch nonstick skillet over medium heat. Break the eggs into a medium-size mixing bowl, add the milk, and whisk until light and frothy. Add the egg mixture to the skillet and cook, stirring frequently, until medium-scrambled (not runny but still moist).

4. Remove the skillet from the heat. Drain off any liquid that might have escaped from the cooked vegetables. Add the vegetables, sour cream, and cilantro to the scrambled eggs. Stir gently to blend well.

5. Spray a 13 × 9-inch glass or ceramic baking dish with cooking oil spray. If the tortillas are stiff, place them on a paper towel and microwave, uncovered, on high, just until pliable, about 30 seconds. Spoon a generous ½ cup of the egg mixture in the middle of each tortilla and roll up lengthwise, enchilada-style (with both ends open). Place the filled tortillas, seam side down, side by side in the prepared baking dish in 2 rows of 4 (one end of each will meet another one in the middle of the dish). *The filled tortillas can be refrigerated, covered with aluminum foil, at this point for up to 24 hours.*

PHASE 3: ABOUT 30 MINUTES MOSTLY UNATTENDED BAKING TIME

6. Preheat the oven to 375°F.

7. Pour the taco sauce evenly on top of the filled tortillas. Spread it with the back of a spoon if necessary.

8. Bake the casserole, covered with aluminum foil, until hot and bubbly, about 25 minutes. Remove the dish from the oven, uncover it, and sprinkle the cheese evenly over the top, using enough to cover well. Return the casserole to the oven and bake, uncovered, just until the cheese melts, 3 to 5 minutes longer. Serve at once or let stand for up to 10 minutes.

■ *Serves 8*

MONEY SAVER

*S*erving wine, beer, and other alcoholic beverages can add exponentially to the party tab. Since few guests tend to imbibe early in the day, consider hosting a brunch when the budget is tight.

I adore plain ol' hash browns, and no one does them better than the short-order cooks at my favorite roadside breakfast joint. But when company comes to call, the last thing you want to be is a short-order cook. Hash browns rise to a whole new level with the addition of cream cheese and eggs. Rich and hearty, this casserole isn't a side dish, it's the main course. Perfect for the vegetarians at your table, it goes together in a mere 17 minutes. Like all of our breakfast casseroles, it waits patiently in the refrigerator until you are ready to bake and serve. Because the work is done the night before, the only evidence your guests will have that brunch is on its way will be the amazing aromas wafting out of your kitchen.

If you prefer, substitute Neufchatel cheese and low-fat milk for the cream cheese and whole milk.

Company Breakfast Casserole

1 tablespoon butter
1 large onion (for about 1 cup chopped)
1 large green bell pepper (for about 1½ cups chopped)
Cooking oil spray
8 large eggs
½ cup milk
1½ teaspoons salt
¼ teaspoon black pepper
2 small packages (3 ounces each) cream cheese
1 package (1 pound, 4 ounces) refrigerated shredded hash
   brown potatoes, such as the Simply Potatoes brand
1½ cups already finely shredded sharp Cheddar cheese

PHASE 1: 17 MINUTES

1. Melt the butter in a 12-inch nonstick skillet over medium heat. Peel and coarsely chop the onion, adding it to the skillet as you chop. Rinse, core, seed, and dice the bell pepper and add it to the skillet. Raise the heat to medium-high and cook, stirring occasionally, until the onion is soft, about 4 minutes.

2. Meanwhile, spray a 13 × 9-inch glass or ceramic baking dish with cooking oil spray. Break the eggs into a blender. Add the milk, salt, and black pepper. Cut the cream cheese into 1-inch chunks and add these to the blender. Blend on medium-high until the eggs are foamy and the cream cheese is thoroughly incorporated, about 30 seconds.

3. When the vegetables are done, scatter them evenly in the prepared baking dish. Scatter the potatoes evenly over the vegetables. Pour the egg mixture over the potatoes.

4. Cover the baking dish with plastic wrap and refrigerate until ready to bake. *The casserole can be refrigerated, covered, at this point, for up to 12 hours.*

PHASE 2: 40 MINUTES MOSTLY UNATTENDED BAKING TIME, PLUS 5 TO 10 MINUTES RESTING TIME

5. Preheat the oven to 350°F.

6. Bake the egg mixture, uncovered, 35 minutes, or until almost set. Remove the dish from the oven and sprinkle the Cheddar cheese evenly over the top. Bake the casserole just until the cheese is melted and the eggs are set, about 5 minutes longer. Let the casserole rest for 5 to 10 minutes before cutting it into squares and serving.

■ *Serves 8*

Southwestern Brunch Casserole

1 can (14½ ounces) fat-free chicken broth
2 cups converted rice
6 large eggs
⅔ cup milk
2 teaspoons ground cumin
1 teaspoon salt
1 teaspoon black pepper
2 jars (4 ounces each) diced or sliced pimientos
3 cups already-shredded Mexican cheese blend, such as Monterey Jack and Cheddar
2 cans (4 ounces each) diced green chiles
Cooking oil spray

PHASE 1: 30 MINUTES

1. Bring the chicken broth and 2 cups of water to a boil in a medium-size saucepan over high heat. Add the rice, cover, reduce the heat to low, and simmer until the rice has absorbed the liquid, about 20 minutes (see Note). *The cooked rice can be refrigerated, covered, at this point for up to 24 hours.*

C redit for the original version of this recipe goes to the USA Rice Council, the folks responsible for promoting you know what. Then our friend Felicia Gressette adapted it for *The Miami Herald* while she was food editor there. Our rendition is slightly different still, but the result remains a yummy bake that's easy to assemble. Rice is far from bland when mixed with eggs, a Mexican cheese blend, cumin, and green chiles. Although this rice bake is a star at brunch, it also makes a good side dish with simple grilled or roasted meat.

PHASE 2: 10 MINUTES

2. Break the eggs into a large mixing bowl and whisk well. Whisk in the milk, cumin, salt, and pepper. Drain the pimientos and add them to the egg mixture. Add the cooked rice (slightly warm or cold), 2 cups of the cheese, and the chiles with their juice. Stir to mix well.

3. Spray a 13 × 9-inch glass or ceramic baking dish with cooking oil spray. Spread the rice mixture evenly in the dish. *The casserole can be refrigerated, covered, at this point for up to 12 hours.*

PHASE 3: ABOUT 45 MINUTES MOSTLY UNATTENDED BAKING TIME

4. Preheat the oven to 375°F.

5. Bake the casserole, uncovered, until the eggs are almost set, 35 to 40 minutes. Remove the dish from the oven and sprinkle the remaining 1 cup cheese evenly over the top. Bake just until the cheese melts, 3 to 5 minutes. The casserole may stand for up to 10 minutes before being cut into squares and served.

■ *Serves 8*

Note: If you are proceeding directly from Phase 1 to Phase 2, you will need to let the cooked rice cool by refrigerating it for 15 minutes before beginning Step 2.

TIME SAVER

If you own a cotton or linen tablecloth and hate to iron it, many dry cleaners offer iron-and-starch service. We suggest washing it yourself, however, especially if you need to treat any stubborn spots.

THE FAIL-PROOF BREAKFAST CASSEROLE

From Alicia:

O kay. I'll admit it. I'm not a morning person. It takes me a good hour to really wake up and be able to function properly. Let alone cook. So what happens when I'm truly desperate for a breakfast or brunch entrée to feed a crowd? I fall back on the known, the predictable, and the no fail. For me, that means the handy and hearty breakfast casserole.

Breakfast casseroles, or *stratas,* are simply layers of bread, cheese, vegetables, and often meat combined with a creamy egg custard. I've been enjoying their flexibility for years. Before that, I struggled with breakfast and brunch entrées that weren't filling enough and required so much time in the kitchen, I had little energy left to spend with my guests. But the one-dish breakfast casserole is simple and satisfying. And, the best thing about it is you can assemble one the night before. When the only thing in my kitchen that's sharp in the morning is my knife, that's a good thing.

Together Beverly and I have put several twists on the traditional casserole, from a crunchy cereal topping on our Mother's Brunch Casserole (see page 286) to a Mexican-inspired casserole with a zesty taco sauce and flour tortillas. We've even substituted potatoes for the bread in the Hot Sausage and Hash Brown Casserole with sautéed onions and roasted garlic (see page 280) and worked up a delicious casserole version of eggs Benedict (see page 282). For something completely different, our Overnight French Toast Casserole (see page 288) is amazingly rich and satisfying and the perfect way to serve French toast to a crowd.

With the work done preparty, all you have to do in the morning is heat the oven and bake the casserole while the coffee's brewing. Even a morning-challenged individual like me can handle that.

Expecting a pack of people around your table? Turn to a breakfast casserole.

Just about everyone loves omelets, but making them for a crowd can be cumbersome and time-consuming. Not so with our baked version. It's mostly assembled the night before. The next morning, all you have to do is beat some egg whites and stir them in right before you pop it in the oven. The result is an omelet that is elegant in its simplicity and so light it practically melts in your mouth. Served with a spoonful of our Italian Salsa, you've got a brunch dish that will wake up everybody's taste buds.

Baked Omelet with Italian Salsa

Italian Salsa (recipe follows)
12 large eggs
¼ cup all-purpose flour
¼ cup half-and-half
¾ cup already-grated Parmesan cheese
¾ cup already-shredded sharp Cheddar cheese
Cooking oil spray

PHASE 1: 15 MINUTES

1. Make the Italian Salsa (see Note).

2. Separate the eggs, placing the whites in a large mixing bowl and the yolks in a small mixing bowl. Cover and refrigerate the whites until ready to use.

3. Add the flour to the bowl with the egg yolks and whisk until smooth. Add the half-and-half and whisk until well combined. Stir in the Parmesan and Cheddar cheese. Refrigerate until ready to use. *The salsa, egg yolk and cheese mixture, and egg whites can each be refrigerated separately, covered, for up to 24 hours.*

PHASE 2: 7 MINUTES, PLUS 25 TO 30 MINUTES UNATTENDED BAKING TIME

4. Preheat the oven to 350°F.

5. Spray a 13 × 9-inch glass or ceramic baking dish with cooking oil spray, making sure to spray the sides well.

6. Using an electric mixer, beat the reserved egg whites until stiff peaks form, about 2 minutes. Using a rubber spatula, add about a fourth of the whites to the reserved yolk-and-cheese mixture and stir to make the mixture less dense. Add the yolk mixture to the bowl with the remaining whites and gently stir until no large white streaks remain but do not overmix.

7. Pour the egg mixture into the prepared dish. Bake until the omelet is puffed and golden and the center doesn't move when the dish is shaken, 25 to 30 minutes.

8. Meanwhile, if the salsa is refrigerated, microwave it, uncovered, on high just until it comes to room temperature, 1½ to 2 minutes. Cut the omelet into squares and serve, spooning Italian Salsa on top.

■ *Serves 8*

Note: If you prefer, you can make the salsa while the omelet is baking.

Italian Salsa

The fresh flavors of garlic and parsley transform an ordinary can of stewed tomatoes into a treat. You won't believe it. Try this salsa with grilled fish, too.

> *2 cloves garlic (see Note)*
> *About ⅓ cup densely packed fresh parsley*
> *1 can (14½ ounces) Italian-style stewed tomatoes*
> *½ lemon*

START TO FINISH: 5 MINUTES

1. Peel the garlic. Rinse the parsley well and shake the leaves to remove any excess water. Remove and discard the tough stems but do not worry about the smaller, upper stems. You should have about ⅓ cup leaves.

2. Drop the garlic cloves 1 at a time through the feed tube of a food processor with the machine running and finely chop. Drop the parsley through the feed tube of the food processor with the machine running and mince finely. Drop in the tomatoes with their juice. Stop the machine and squeeze the juice from the lemon half through a strainer (to catch the seeds) directly into the tomato mixture. Pulse the motor 3 times just until the tomatoes reach a salsa consistency (still a little chunky). Serve at once or refrigerate, covered, until ready to serve. Let return to room temperature before serving.

■ *Makes about 1¾ cups*

Note: Fans of powerful salsa can add 2 or 3 more garlic cloves.

DO-AHEAD

The Italian Salsa can be refrigerated, covered, for up to 24 hours.

My family's nickname for this casserole is "Scattered, Smothered, and Covered." Scattered hash brown potatoes are smothered with onions, roasted garlic, and spicy hot pork sausage, then covered with cheese. Everything bakes up bubbly in a creamy egg mixture that will serve as many as twelve. If that doesn't tempt you then maybe the fact that this casserole goes together in just 20 minutes will tempt the Desperate Cook in you. As long as you have your stash of already-roasted garlic in the fridge, you can throw this together after you tuck the kids in bed the night before your brunch. Then all that needs to happen the next morning is a quick preheat and bake. Brunch anyone?

Hot Sausage and Hash Brown Casserole

1 teaspoon olive oil

2 large onions (for about 2 cups slices)

1 pound hot breakfast-style bulk sausage

Cooking oil spray

1 package (1 pound, 4 ounces) refrigerated shredded
   hash brown potatoes, such as the Simply Potatoes brand

½ teaspoon salt

¼ teaspoon black pepper

3 cups already-shredded sharp Cheddar cheese

1 head already-roasted garlic (for about ¼ cup cloves;
   see recipe page 262)

1 tablespoon balsamic vinegar

8 large eggs

3 cups milk

PHASE 1: 20 MINUTES

1. Heat the olive oil in an extra-deep, 12-inch nonstick skillet over medium heat. Peel and slice each onion in half. Placing the onion cut side down on the cutting board, cut the onion halves into crescent shaped slices about ¼ inch wide, adding them to the skillet as you work. Add the sausage to the skillet, breaking it up with a wooden spoon. Cook, stirring occasionally, until the onions are brown around the edges and the sausage is browned, 6 to 8 minutes.

2. Meanwhile, spray a 13 × 9-inch glass or ceramic baking dish with cooking oil spray and then spread the hash browns evenly in it. Top with the salt, pepper, and 1 cup of Cheddar cheese. Peel and chop the roasted garlic and sprinkle it evenly over the potatoes. When the onions and sausage are done, drain off any grease and then add the balsamic vinegar to them and stir well. Spread the onions and sausage over the potatoes and garlic.

3. Break the eggs into a medium-size mixing bowl, add the milk, and whisk together. Pour the egg mixture over the ingredients in the baking dish. Sprinkle the remaining 2 cups of cheese evenly over the top of the cassserole. *The casserole can be refrigerated, covered, at this point for up to 12 hours.*

PHASE 2: 45 MINUTES UNATTENDED BAKING TIME AND 10 MINUTES RESTING TIME

4. Preheat the oven to 350°F.

5. Bake the casserole, uncovered, until the center is firm and the top begins to brown, about 45 minutes. Let the casserole rest for 10 minutes before cutting it into squares and serving.

■ *Serves 10 to 12*

DISHING IT OUT

When it comes time to serve a breakfast casserole, the easiest thing to do is to use a metal spatula to cut it into squares in the baking dish and to transfer them to your guests' plates. An attractive baking dish will fit right in at the table. Lasagnas can also be cut into squares for serving, and meat loaves are easily sliced in the pan. We even do the same thing with cakes. (Certainly if you have the time and inclination, you can place the squares on a pretty serving platter, but we never seem to get around to it, and our guests have never once complained.)

Looking for eggs Benedict—without the last-minute struggle? This casserole tastes exactly like the classic egg dish. Just assemble the English muffins, Canadian bacon, and eggs like a *strata,* refrigerate them overnight, and then all you have to do in the morning is pop the casserole in the oven and microwave our easy hollandaise sauce to pour on top. Okay, the runny egg yolks are missing, but no one seems to notice.

Eggs Benedict Casserole

6 English muffins
2 packages (10 to 12 ounces total) Canadian bacon
8 large eggs
2 cups milk
1 teaspoon onion powder
Cooking oil spray
Hollandaise in Minutes (recipe follows)

PHASE 1: 9 MINUTES, PLUS 8 HOURS REFRIGERATION TIME

1. Cut the English muffins into bite-size cubes. Cut the Canadian bacon into bite-size pieces.

2. Break the eggs into a medium-size mixing bowl and whisk well. Whisk in the milk and onion powder.

3. Spray a 13 × 9-inch glass or ceramic baking dish with cooking oil spray. Scatter half of the Canadian bacon pieces evenly over the bottom of the dish, then scatter the English muffin cubes evenly over the Canadian bacon. Top with the remaining Canadian bacon, scattering it evenly over the muffin cubes. Pour the egg mixture over the casserole. Refrigerate for at least 8 hours. *The casserole can be refrigerated, covered with aluminum foil, at this point for up to 24 hours.*

PHASE 2: 10 MINUTES

4. Make the Hollandaise in Minutes. *The sauce can be refrigerated at this point in a covered container for up to 24 hours or held for up to 4 hours in a thermos.*

PHASE 3: 60 MINUTES OF MOSTLY UNATTENDED BAKING TIME AND 5 TO 10 MINUTES RESTING TIME

5. Preheat the oven to 375°F.

6. Bake the casserole, covered with aluminum foil, for 40 minutes. Remove from the oven, remove the aluminum foil, return the casserole to the oven, and continue to bake until the eggs are set and the Canadian bacon on top begins to crisp, about 20 minutes more. Let the casserole rest for 5 to 10 minutes before cutting it into squares. Pour warm hollandaise sauce on top just before serving (you'll find directions for rewarming in the Do-Ahead box below).

■ *Serves 8*

Hollandaise in Minutes

This sauce is a real bargain where time and energy are concerned. Standing at the stove to make a traditional hollandaise sauce is nerve-racking, what with the constant stirring and fears that it will curdle. Not so with our microwave version. We've been making it for years without a single bead of perspiration. You simply won't believe how easy it is. The sauce is also great served over Oven-Steamed Broccoli (see page 258) or with steamed asparagus.

> *8 tablespoons (1 stick) butter*
> *4 large eggs*
> *½ cup heavy (whipping) cream*
> *2 tablespoons fresh lemon juice*
> *1 teaspoon Dijon mustard*

START TO FINISH: 10 MINUTES

1. Place the butter in a 2-cup or larger glass measure, cover with a paper towel, and microwave on high until melted, about 1 minute.

2. Separate the eggs, placing the yolks in a small bowl and setting the whites aside for another use. Beat the yolks well with a whisk or fork, then add them to the melted butter and stir well.

3. Add the cream and lemon juice to the egg mixture and stir well. Microwave the mixture, uncovered, on high until just slightly thick, 1 to 2 minutes, stopping every 20 seconds to stir with a fork.

4. Remove the sauce from the microwave oven, stir in the mustard, and serve.

■ *Makes about 1½ cups*

DO-AHEAD

The sauce can be kept warm in a thermos for up to 4 hours or allowed to cool to room temperature and refrigerated in a covered microwave-safe container for up to 24 hours.
• To warm refrigerated sauce, cover it with microwave-safe plastic wrap and cut a small vent in the center. Microwave on 50 percent power until heated through, 3 to 4 minutes, stopping halfway through to stir. Do not allow the sauce to boil.

ALMOST-INSTANT BREAKFAST FIX-UPS

Rounding out the first meal of the day won't take hours if you look for things to serve that do the work for you.

Whether your company brunch is a bagel with all of the trimmings (see page 271) or a bowl of cereal, it's easy to include some trouble-free extras to make the menu more festive. Here are some of our favorites that require minimal preparation. For other suggestions, see "Giving Breakfast an International Flavor" on page 291.

• **Yogurt:** The flavor options are practically endless. Set individual containers in a big bowl filled with ice or ladle out a single flavor in a pretty serving bowl. You could even offer yogurt in tubes to the youngsters—they'll get a thrill out of squirting it directly into their mouths (the tubes are sold under the brand name Go-Gurt). What will they think of next?

• **Cereals:** Offer several varieties with different textures. Shredded wheat anyone? When choices abound, suddenly cereal becomes a buffet.

• **Granola:** If your supermarket stocks granolas in bulk bins, buy several kinds and set them out to sprinkle over cereal, oatmeal, or yogurt.

• **Oatmeal:** Put out the instant oatmeal packets if you like, but you'll get raves with the real thing. You'll find microwave directions are on the boxes of both old-fashioned and quick oatmeal. Making a serving takes just 3 minutes. You don't even have to boil water, and your lucky guests can zap bowls for themselves at their leisure.

• **Honey:** Just a drizzle of orange-blossom or some other "boutique" or locally produced honey will do wonders for that simple bowl of oatmeal. So will maple syrup or brown sugar.

• **Doughnuts:** Microwave a Krispy Kreme for 10 seconds and you've got it hot now. (It's best to do this one at a time, on high, uncovered, and eat it right away. Overmicrowaving will toughen an airy doughnut beyond recognition.) This technique works equally well for all types of doughnuts.

• **Muffins and breakfast breads:** Set out an assortment, plug in the toaster, and jazz them up by offering a selection of your favorite gourmet jellies and jams.

• **Precooked bacon:** Want the aroma and decadence of bacon without the ordeal? Look for packages of already-cooked bacon. All you need to do is pop the slices in the microwave for a quick crisping and you'll have instant gratification (see page 218 for more information).

• **Fresh fruit:** Red and green seedless grapes are always popular and you don't have to peel them. But why peel anything? A large bowl of whole fruits, such as apples, oranges, plums, and bananas makes a ready-made centerpiece in addition to providing a nutritious side dish. Strawberries (with the caps still attached) or blueberries and raspberries are low-maintenance options when they're in season.

• **Dried fruit:** An attractive bowl filled with raisins is nice, but add some dried cranberries and apricots and you've got eye appeal as well as a welcome addition to cereal or yogurt. Throw in a few walnuts or pecans and folks are sure to nibble the mix right out of the dish. Think of it as a brunch appetizer.

• **Fresh orange juice:** Many supermarkets sell fresh-squeezed orange juice and a glassful is always a treat. If you happen to have a juicer, set it out with a bowl of oranges cut in half so guests can take a turn at squeezing their own.

• **Specialty juices:** Cartons of tempting juice combinations abound in the refrigerated section of the supermarket alongside plain orange juice. Offerings include everything from pineapple-orange-strawberry to strawberry-banana-kiwi. The idea must be to put smoothie flavors in a carton. Combination juices lack the consistency of a smoothie, of course, but they are a bit thicker than plain orange or apple juice. Kids tend to drink them straight up, but most adults we know prefer the juice diluted with a shot of seltzer or club soda for a refreshing wake-me-up.

Mother's Brunch Casserole

We first encountered this casserole several years ago at a Mother's Day brunch at St. Mark's preschool in Raleigh, North Carolina. It reminds us of what we think of as a traditional *strata,* a layered egg dish, here including a generous serving of ham and cheese. With its buttery corn flakes on top, even the three-year-old children at the brunch ate every crumb.

8 slices white loaf bread
1 pound thinly sliced Virginia baked or other
  good-quality deli ham
6 large eggs
2 cups milk
½ teaspoon onion salt
½ teaspoon dry mustard
Cooking oil spray
3 cups (12 ounces) already-shredded sharp Cheddar cheese
4 tablespoons (½ stick) butter
3 cups cornflakes

PHASE 1: 18 MINUTES, PLUS 8 HOURS REFRIGERATION TIME

1. Cut the bread and ham into bite-size pieces.

2. Break the eggs into a medium-size mixing bowl and whisk well. Whisk in the milk, onion salt, and mustard.

3. Spray a 13 × 9-inch glass or ceramic baking dish with cooking oil spray. Scatter the pieces of bread evenly in the dish. Scatter the ham pieces and the cheese evenly over the bread. Pour the egg mixture over the ham and cheese. Refrigerate for at least 8 hours. *The casserole can be refrigerated, covered, at this point for up to 24 hours.*

PHASE 2: 5 MINUTES, PLUS 45 MINUTES UNATTENDED BAKING TIME AND 5 TO 10 MINUTES RESTING TIME

4. Preheat the oven to 375°F.

5. Place the butter in a 2-cup or larger glass measure, cover with a paper towel, and microwave on high until melted, about 45 seconds.

6. Place the cornflakes in a large freezer-weight, zipper-top plastic bag and crush the cornflakes using your hands or a rolling pin. Add half the melted butter to the bag and shake vigorously. Add the

TIME SAVER

Once you've decided on a scrumptious and affordable menu, be sure to take notes. You are likely to want to repeat all or some portion of this menu down the road.

remaining butter and continue to shake until most of the cereal is coated. Sprinkle the cornflakes evenly over the casserole.

7. Bake the casserole, uncovered, until lightly browned on top and the eggs are set, about 45 minutes. Let the casserole rest for 5 to 10 minutes before cutting it into squares and serving.

■ *Serves 8*

SCHOOL'S IN! MOM'S SPECIAL BRUNCH

From Alicia:

Summer's over and school's in session. On the one hand I always hate to see summer go, but on the other hand, it's a reason to celebrate. It's time to invite your friends to a midweek brunch. Nothing fancy and nothing that will stress you out, but something special, befitting a gathering that doesn't include the kids. Most of our friends can't spare more than a morning and it's a blast to start the day together.

Like all of our overnight casseroles, Mother's Brunch Casserole (opposite) is easy to throw together the night before, then pop it into the oven after you've gotten the kids off to school. When your guests arrive, the kitchen will be filled with fantastic aromas.

The Fastest Fruit Salad (see page 270) can be whipped up even a few days ahead. Our only warning is to make sure the kids don't know about it or you'll have none left over for your guests.

Round out your menu with Cinnamon-Swirl Sour Cream Coffee Cake (see page 296), or for a no-fuss alternative, purchase frozen mini croissants. Ten minutes in a hot oven and they're ready. Fruity Tea Punch (see page 29) is especially nice for the noncoffee drinkers in your crowd.

Treat yourself to the fun of a school's in special brunch. Make it an annual affair to kick off the school year with flair.

When you wake up to luscious French toast without spending a single minute slaving over the stove, you'll think you're still dreaming. And dreamy it is. Golden brown on top, with just the right crunch, yet moist in the middle, with a cinnamon kick, this version of the traditional recipe is sure to redefine what French toast should be about.

Overnight French Toast Casserole

Cooking Oil Spray
1 large loaf (1 pound) Italian-style or French-style
*   bread (for about 16 cups cubes)*
6 large eggs
1½ cups half-and-half
1½ cups orange juice
2 teaspoons ground cinnamon
6 tablespoons (¾ stick) butter
¾ cup (3 ounces) already-chopped pecans or walnuts
Maple syrup, for serving

PHASE 1: 10 MINUTES

1. Spray a 13 × 9-inch glass or ceramic baking dish with cooking oil spray. Cut the bread into bite-size cubes. Place 1 cup of the cubes in an airtight container and set aside until just before baking. Place the remaining cubes in the baking dish.

2. Break the eggs into a large bowl and whisk well. Whisk in the half-and-half, orange juice, and cinnamon until well combined. Pour the egg mixture over the bread cubes in the baking dish. Press the bread cubes down into the egg mixture. Refrigerate the egg mixture for at least 8 hours. *The casserole can be refrigerated, covered, at this point for up to 24 hours.*

PHASE 2: 5 MINUTES, PLUS 35 MINUTES UNATTENDED BAKING TIME AND 5 TO 10 MINUTES RESTING TIME

3. Preheat the oven to 375°F.

4. Place the butter in a 2-cup or larger glass measure, cover with a paper towel, and microwave on high until melted, about 45 seconds. Put the nuts in the container with the reserved bread cubes. Drizzle the melted butter over the bread mixture and stir until the bread cubes and nuts are mixed and coated with butter. Uncover the casserole

and press down the bread cubes already in it to remoisten. Sprinkle the mixture of buttered bread cubes and nuts evenly over the top.

5. Bake the casserole, uncovered, until lightly browned on top, about 35 minutes. Let rest for 5 to 10 minutes before cutting it into squares and serving. Pass maple syrup at the table to drizzle on top.

■ *Serves 8*

Three-Cheese Broccoli Quiches

1 box (10 ounces) frozen chopped broccoli
1 package (15 ounces; 2 crusts) refrigerated pie crusts,
    such as Pillsbury (see Notes)
1 large onion (for about 1 cup chopped)
1 cup already-shredded Swiss cheese (see Notes)
1 cup already-shredded sharp Cheddar cheese
½ cup already-grated Parmesan cheese
6 large eggs
1 tablespoon all-purpose flour
1⅔ cups half-and-half
2 tablespoons Dijon mustard
1 tablespoon Worcestershire sauce
2 teaspoons dried Italian-style seasoning
¼ teaspoon garlic powder
¼ teaspoon onion powder
¼ teaspoon black pepper

PHASE 1: 23 MINUTES

1. Place the frozen broccoli in a colander. Run warm water over it just until the block loosens into very small pieces (the broccoli may still be partially frozen). Drain well, pressing with your hand or the back of a spoon to remove excess water. Set aside to finish draining.

From Beverly:

Once I froze my quiches a month ahead to serve at a baby shower and they tasted as fresh as the day they were made. If the work can be done weeks in advance and nobody knows the difference, sounds like a great Desperate Entertaining solution to me! Emphasizing a trio of cheeses, our broccoli quiches will turn any brunch into a special occasion.

2. Place 1 crust in each of 2 deep-dish 8-inch pie pans, following the directions on the package. Peel and coarsely chop the onion. Place half of the chopped onion in each of the pie crusts. Scatter half of the drained broccoli in each pie pan. Evenly scatter half the Swiss, Cheddar, and Parmesan cheeses over the broccoli in each pie pan.

3. Break the eggs into a medium-size mixing bowl and whisk until light and foamy. Add the flour and whisk vigorously to blend well (all of the flour lumps may not disappear). Add the half-and-half, mustard, Worcestershire sauce, and all remaining spices. Whisk to blend well. Using a ladle or ½-cup measure, spoon half of the egg mixture over each pie crust. *The quiches can be refrigerated, covered, at this point for up to 24 hours.*

PHASE 2: **45 TO 55 MINUTES UNATTENDED BAKING TIME AND 15 MINUTES RESTING TIME**

4. Preheat the oven to 350°F.

5. Bake the quiches, uncovered, until set and lightly browned, 45 to 55 minutes. If serving at once, let the quiches rest for 15 minutes before slicing. *Once cool, the quiches can be covered with aluminum foil and refrigerated for up to 2 days or frozen for up to 1 month. Thaw in the refrigerator overnight, if necessary, and reheat, uncovered, in a 325°F oven until heated through, about 20 minutes.*

■ *Serves 8*

Notes: Really desperate? Although we prefer the texture of refrigerated pie crutsts, frozen deep-dish pie shells may be substituted.

If you can't find shredded Swiss cheese and don't want to grate your own, substitute one more cup of Cheddar cheese.

GIVING BREAKFAST AN INTERNATIONAL FLAVOR

From Beverly:

The first radish I spied on a breakfast buffet did seem a bit odd. Maybe it was the exotic atmosphere at the ancient hotel in Tel Aviv, but after one bite I was hooked. Ditto with the smoked fish, slabs of cheese, bowls of olives, and baskets of crusty breads. What a way to start the day.

Then in Switzerland, Austria, and Germany, I might well have mistaken the first meal of the day for the last had it not been for the bowls brimming with yogurt. In town after town, bountiful trays of salami and other sliced deli meats and cheeses greeted travelers as early as sunrise. I grew addicted to the various hearty mixes of nuts and grains in the guise of granola, or muesli, which the locals usually proceeded to eat topped with a dollop of yogurt. Dishes of dried fruits to sprinkle on top would often be standard.

This same array of meats and cheeses, supplemented with breads ranging from hard rolls to croissants to black breads studded with raisins greeted me in Italy and many parts of Spain. One morning on a trek to Scotland our bed-and-breakfast host presented a plate of plump sausages, sliced tomatoes, and baked beans.

Sampling these unusual breakfast foods has made me inclined to experiment early in the day, especially when I have guests. The deli trays of Germany coupled with granola and yogurt are easy to fix the night before and set out the next morning for guests to eat at their leisure. Here are some tips:

- Buy thinly sliced salami, ham, and cheeses from the deli.
- Put together an array of breads that includes varieties of texture and taste. Croissants, fruit breads, hard rolls, and hearty wheat bread are our favorites.
- Granola and plain and fruit-flavored yogurts look great when set out in glass bowls.
- We sometimes add one kind of cereal to the mix that isn't sweet (for adults) and one kind that is (for kids).
- Offer a bowl of apples, tangerines, grapes, and bananas and let guests help themselves.

In Beijing I got my fill of steamed buns and soda pop (yes, for breakfast). The French, however, dished out first-rate coffee and a lonely croissant.

Here's another do-way-ahead-and-freeze quiche that seems far too elegant to be so easy. The piquant flavor of roasted red pepper plays off the combination of mushrooms and Swiss cheese to put an *aahh* in every bite. At least that was the satisfied response of our friends, who then begged for a sneak-preview copy of this recipe.

Swiss and Mushroom Quiches

1 tablespoon olive oil

1 package (8 ounces) already-sliced, fresh button mushrooms

1 package (6 ounces) already-sliced, fresh portobello mushrooms

1 package (15 ounces; 2 crusts) refrigerated pie crusts, such as Pillsbury (see Notes)

1 large onion (for 1 cup chopped)

1 jar (12 ounces) roasted red peppers

2 cups already-shredded Swiss cheese (see Notes)

6 large eggs

1 tablespoon all-purpose flour

1⅔ cups half-and-half

1 tablespoon Worcestershire sauce

1 teaspoon dried basil

¼ teaspoon black pepper

PHASE 1: 25 MINUTES

1. Heat the olive oil in a 12-inch nonstick skillet over medium-high heat. Coarsely chop all of the mushrooms and add them to the skillet. Cook, stirring from time to time, until the mushrooms release their liquid, about 7 minutes.

2. While the mushrooms cook, place 1 crust in each of 2 deep-dish 8-inch pie pans, following the directions on the package.

3. Peel and coarsely chop the onion. Place half of the chopped onion in each pie crust. Drain the red peppers and coarsely chop. Sprinkle half of the red peppers over the onion in each pie pan. Using a slotted spoon to drain as much liquid as possible, spoon half of the cooked mushrooms evenly over the peppers in each crust. Evenly scatter half of the Swiss cheese over the vegetables in each crust.

4. Break the eggs into a medium-size mixing bowl and whisk until light and foamy. Add the flour and whisk vigorously to blend well (all of the flour lumps may not disappear). Add the half-and-half, Worcestershire sauce, basil, and black pepper. Whisk to blend well. Using a ladle or ½-cup measure, spoon half of the egg mixture over each pie crust. *The quiches can be refrigerated, covered, at this point for up to 24 hours.*

PHASE 2: 45 TO 55 MINUTES UNATTENDED BAKING TIME AND 15 MINUTES RESTING TIME

5. Preheat the oven to 350°F.

6. Bake the quiches, uncovered, until set and lightly browned, 45 to 55 minutes. If serving at once, let the quiches rest for 15 minutes before slicing. *Once cool, the quiches can be covered with aluminum foil and refrigerated for up to 2 days or frozen for up to 1 month. Thaw in the refrigerator overnight, if necessary, and reheat, uncovered, in a 325°F oven until heated through, about 20 minutes.*

■ *Serves 8*

Notes: Really desperate? Although we prefer the texture of refrigerated pie crusts, frozen deep-dish pie shells may be substituted.

If you can't find already-shredded Swiss cheese, it just takes a couple of minutes to shred your own. You'll need about 8 ounces.

SPACE SAVER

If you have a small table and are trying to squeeze everybody around it, use a tablecloth instead of place mats. It's easier to be comfortably cozy if you don't have the defined space place mats create.

It used to be that only Southerners served grits, but now that restaurants all over the country are serving polenta, a close first-cousin, we figure everybody should get with the program. We think no-fuss, creamy Southern grits are dynamite. Neufchatel cheese works as a low-fat substitute, but don't use low-fat Cheddar.

Overnight Cheese Grits

½ teaspoon salt
1 cup quick (not instant) grits
1 small package (3 ounces) cream cheese
2 cups (8 ounces) already-shredded sharp Cheddar cheese
1 teaspoon garlic powder
Cooking oil spray

PHASE 1: 15 MINUTES MOSTLY UNATTENDED COOKING TIME

1. Pour 4 cups of water into a 2½-quart or larger saucepan, preferably nonstick, and add the salt. Place the saucepan over high heat, cover, and bring to a boil. Stir in the grits, reduce the heat to low, cover, and let simmer until tender, 6 to 7 minutes. Stir from time to time.

2. While the grits cook, cut the cream cheese into 4 pieces. Remove the grits from the heat and stir in the cream cheese, Cheddar cheese, and garlic powder. Stir until the cheeses melt and blend in.

3. Spray an 8-inch-square baking dish with cooking oil spray. Put the grits mixture in the baking dish and spread them evenly. *The grits can be refrigerated, covered, at this point for up to 24 hours.*

PHASE 2: 45 TO 50 MINUTES UNATTENDED BAKING TIME

4. Preheat the oven to 375°F.

5. Bake the grits, uncovered, until heated through, 45 to 50 minutes. Serve the grits at once or let stand until ready to serve, for up to 30 minutes.

■ *Serves 8*

Brown Sugar Bacon

Cooking oil spray
⅓ cup firmly packed light or dark brown sugar
1 teaspoon dry mustard
8 slices bacon (see Note)

PHASE 1: 11 MINUTES

1. Spray a broiler pan with cooking oil spray.

2. Put the brown sugar and mustard in a small bowl and stir. Spread out a piece of waxed paper. Place a slice of bacon on the waxed paper. Sprinkle 1 teaspoon of brown sugar mixture evenly over one side of the bacon. Press the sugar mixture into the bacon with your fingers. Turn the slice over and repeat with 1 teaspoon of the brown sugar mixture on the second side. Place the sugared bacon slice on the broiler pan. Repeat the process with the remaining bacon slices (you may have a small amount of the sugar mixture left over). *The sugared bacon can be refrigerated, uncovered on the broiler pan, at this point for up to 1 hour.*

PHASE 2: 25 MINUTES UNATTENDED BAKING TIME

3. Preheat the oven to 350°F.

4. Place the bacon on the broiler pan on the middle rack of the oven and bake until crisp, about 25 minutes. Drain briefly on paper towels to absorb any excess fat and then transfer to a serving dish. Serve at once. *If using for bacon bits, the cooked bacon can be refrigerated in a zipper-top plastic bag for up to 2 days and then diced or it can be diced and frozen for up to 1 month.*

■ *Makes 8 slices of bacon*

Note: You can substitute turkey bacon for regular bacon. It doesn't have much fat for the sugar mixture to adhere to, so sprinkle it over only one side of the bacon after placing it on the broiler pan.

"This is a real treat—something you'd expect to have at a bed-and-breakfast," says our friend Marietta Wynands, who served this bacon at a birthday brunch. Not only does it make a good breakfast side dish, it's wonderful chopped and sprinkled over a spinach salad. We've also served the bacon bits in a plain-old tossed salad to make it not so plain after all.

Cinnamon-Swirl Sour Cream Coffee Cake

From Beverly:

In one form or another, this recipe has been in my family for nearly thirty years. My grandmother Flonnie Hood shared it with my mother, who used it to help teach me to bake. Now my own daughter, Grey, is breaking the eggs. Who would believe this yummy coffee cake starts out with a cake mix? You may never buy supermarket coffee cake again. The surprise brown sugar and cinnamon filling makes it even more special. It will feed twelve to sixteen people, and if you bake it in a glass baking pan, you can serve it right from the pan.

4 large eggs
½ cup vegetable oil
¼ cup granulated sugar
1 small container (8 ounces) sour cream (see Note)
1 package (1 pound, 2¼ ounces) yellow cake mix
⅔ cup firmly packed light brown sugar
1 tablespoon cinnamon
Cooking oil spray
⅓ cup all-purpose flour
3 tablespoons cold butter

PHASE 1: 20 MINUTES

1. Break the eggs into a large mixing bowl. Using an electric mixer, beat the eggs at medium speed for 1 minute. Add the vegetable oil, granulated sugar, sour cream, and cake mix. Beat on medium speed until blended, about 2 minutes.

2. Stir together ⅓ cup of the brown sugar with 2 teaspoons of the cinnamon in a small mixing bowl. Spray a 13 × 9-inch glass or metal baking pan with cooking oil spray.

3. Pour roughly half of the cake batter into the baking dish and, using a knife or spatula, spread it evenly. Sprinkle the cinnamon-sugar mixture over the batter. Pour the remaining cake batter over the cinnamon-sugar and spread it out evenly. Be sure the batter meets the sides of the dish. Don't worry if a little of the cinnamon-sugar mixture comes out on top.

4. Make a topping by putting the remaining ⅓ cup brown sugar, the remaining 1 teaspoon cinnamon, and the flour in the same mixing bowl used for the cinnamon-sugar mixture. Stir to blend. Cut the butter into small pieces and add it to the brown sugar mixture. Using a pastry blender or 2 knives, cut the butter into the brown sugar mixture until the butter is the size of small peas. Sprinkle the topping evenly over the cake batter. *The unbaked coffee cake can be refrigerated, covered, for up to 24 hours.*

PHASE 2: 45 MINUTES TO 55 MINUTES UNATTENDED BAKING TIME AND 10 TO 15 MINUTES COOLING TIME

5. Preheat the oven to 325°F if you are using a glass baking pan or to 350°F if you are using a metal baking pan.

6. Bake the coffee cake until a toothpick inserted in the middle comes out clean, 45 to 55 minutes. Let cool 10 to 15 minutes, then serve. *The baked coffee cake can be frozen for up to 1 month. Let it thaw for 4 to 6 hours, uncovered, on a counter top.*

■ *Serves 12 to 16*

Note: You can use low-fat sour cream here, if you like.

CHAPTER NINE

Decadent

The Desperate Dessert Philosophy? If you're going to eat it, dessert simply must be worth the calories.

Dessert needs to be fun and it needs to be indulgent, but it doesn't need to do-in the host. Those of you who love spending all day baking towering cakes that will be the pride of your dinner party, well, you know who you are. For you, dessert is not a challenge. The rest of us need to pick our battles . . . uh, recipes . . . carefully.

When the host is producing the entire meal, before-dinner nibbles and dessert included, something has to give. That something is likely to be the all-day cake. The easiest option is to find a really good bakery and buy a knockout dessert. If the flavor sends guests into ecstasy, they won't care who spent 24 hours baking. The second solution is to rely on a trusted list of recipes that are practically effortless but that taste like you labored all day. These are the recipes you'll find here.

We start with the Fast-and-Fabulous, Almost-Instant Sauce Solution. When we say sauce, we don't mean a headache-causing, stir-forever-or-it-might-curdle one. We mean sauce "magic," as in mix, microwave (or swirl in a skillet), and presto, before your eyes a luscious topping appears: fudge, brandied butterscotch, strawberry-pineapple, or red-wine glaze. Pour these over ice cream, banana slices, or canned pears and guests will swoon. For the sauce-based dessert we call Flexible Fruit Fondue you dip in some whole strawberries, canned pineapple chunks, store-bought pound cake pieces, and apple slices.

In keeping with the ice cream and sauce theme, we've taken a cue from the restaurant world and one of America's best-loved

Desserts

delights, the brownie sundae. Our variations on this theme—rocky road, triple chocolate, and peanut butter fudge brownies each piled high with ice cream—are most definitely well worth leaving room for. The brownies are based on a very good friend we trust you know well—the brownie mix. A close cousin to the brownie mix, the cake mix, can be transformed into an old family treasure simply by adding the right flavor boosters. When guests *ooh* and *aah* over your red velvet cake or chocolate/caramel cake, just tell them Grandma made it.

Grandma does get credit for at least one of our favorite dessert masterpieces, the most incredible pecan pie you can imagine. Pie? In case you're shocked by our sudden veer toward what sounds difficult, relax. Remember the old saying "easy as pie?" It's true. All you have to do is whip up a simple filling. Thanks to refrigerated pie crusts from the supermarket, nobody will ever guess you didn't make your crust from scratch. If you can't bring yourself to think of pie crust at all, think variations on the pie theme, as in vanilla cream custard, peach cobbler, blueberry crisp, or apple brown betty. They're virtually no fail, even when you're under the guests-are-coming gun. You may be forced to pinch yourself as you pull these steaming desserts out of your very own oven.

Whether you sauce 'em, slice 'em, or simply serve 'em, our Desperate Decadent Desserts do everything but tap dance. They save your sanity. They preserve your pride. They produce satisfied smiles. We leave the dancing for joy up to you.

fast and fabulous

Old-Fashioned Fudge Sauce

We have been known to forget about the ice cream altogether and just go straight to the fudge sauce. The rich flavor takes us back to our childhoods and those special times at an old-fashioned ice cream parlor. Our friend Denise Deen, who tried this recipe, declared it the best fudge sauce on the planet, guaranteed.

3 squares (1 ounce each) unsweetened baking chocolate
4 tablespoons (½ stick) butter
½ cup evaporated milk
1 cup sugar
1 teaspoon pure vanilla extract
2 pinches salt
Ice cream, for serving

START TO FINISH: 10 MINUTES

1. Put the chocolate, butter, and evaporated milk in a 4-cup glass measure. Microwave, uncovered, on high until the chocolate and butter are nearly melted, about 2 minutes, stopping once halfway through to stir. Remove from the microwave oven and stir until the chocolate and butter finish melting.

2. Stir in the sugar. Microwave 1 minute, uncovered, on high. Remove and stir well with a wire whisk. If the sauce is grainy, microwave just until the sugar melts, 30 seconds to 1 minute more. Do not overcook. Whisk to stir well.

3. Whisk in the vanilla extract and salt and let the mixture cool a little. Serve warm or at room temperature over ice cream.

■ *Makes about 2 cups*

DO-AHEAD

The fudge sauce can be refrigerated, covered, for up to 2 weeks. Reheat in the microwave oven, uncovered, on high until warmed through, about 1 minute.

Brandied Butterscotch Sauce

8 tablespoons (1 stick) butter
1 cup lightly packed light brown sugar
½ cup heavy (whipping) cream
2 tablespoons light corn syrup
1 tablespoon brandy
Ice cream, for serving

START TO FINISH: 10 MINUTES

1. Cut the butter into 4 pieces and place in a 4-cup glass measure. Add the brown sugar, cream, and corn syrup. Stir to mix. Cover with microwave-safe plastic wrap and cut a small vent in the center. Microwave on high until the mixture boils, about 3½ minutes. Uncover and stir well.

2. Stir in the brandy and let the mixture cool to a warm temperature. Serve warm or at room temperature over ice cream.

■ *Makes about 1⅔ cups*

Just a drop of brandy takes a butterscotch sauce that's a kid's delight and makes it sophisticated enough for the young at heart. With an elegant sauce this simple, you'll be tempted to open your own ice cream parlor.

DO-AHEAD

The butterscotch sauce can be refrigerated, covered, for up to 1 week. Reheat in the microwave oven, uncovered, on high until warmed through, about 1 minute.

THE ICE CREAM SUNDAE SOCIAL

What do you like on your ice cream? Customizing is not only fun, it's guest friendly and smart.

When it's hot and muggy outside, the easiest and most refreshing party to throw is one that involves ice cream. It requires so little work, you'll want to invite the whole block.

Here's what to do: Find a good spot to set up the "parlor." Provide several flavors of ice cream and toppers—hot and cold, wet and dry—and let each person assemble his or her own sundae. If little Betsy likes plain vanilla ice cream, so be it. If Fred likes everything that will fit in the bowl—go for it big guy! No matter which way your guests like their sundaes, it's no stress for you.

Already-prepared butterscotch, chocolate, and assorted other ice cream sauces fill entire supermarket shelves. These are okay in a pinch, but in about 10 minutes (we promise) you can throw together one of our recipes for a rich homemade sauce that will be the star of the day. The desperate bonus is that each sauce will keep a week or more.

Ice cream parties are well suited to potluck. We've outlined what you'll need to have on hand to satisfy as many as thirty ice cream lovers. Have each family bring its favorite ice cream topper to share. You might be surprised by what people come up with, but whatever it is, everyone is guaranteed to have plenty of fun!

Ice Cream and Go-Withs

- 2 to 3 gallons of ice cream in a variety of flavors (count on 8 servings per half-gallon)
- Old-Fashioned Fudge Sauce, page 300
- Brandied Butterscotch Sauce, page 301
- Strawberry-Pineapple Sundae Sauce, page 304
- Ready-made butter cookies
- Plenty of ice water—those 5-gallon coolers with the push-button spouts work great!

Favorite Toppings

- Chopped nuts
- Cherries—any kind
- Whipped cream from an aerosol can
- Crushed peppermint candies
- Crushed pineapple
- Canned mandarin oranges
- Fruit preserves
- Crushed toffee bars
- Chocolate chips
- Colored candy sprinkles
- Crushed cookies
- Gummy bears and gummy worms

The Equipment You'll Need

- One long table or two card tables covered with a decorative plastic tablecloth
- Lawn chairs and picnic blankets for sitting on
- Plastic spoons, bowls, and cups
- Napkins and paper towels
- Wet wipes (unscented are best) for a final cleanup of hands (and sticky little faces)
- Approximately four ice cream scoops and volunteers to do the scooping

If you have extra freezer space and are serving only one or two flavors of ice cream, you can prescoop the ice cream into bowls. Place the filled bowls on a cookie sheet or tray, drape plastic wrap on top of them to cover, and place everything in the freezer. Filling bowls in advance makes for faster service, and you avoid long lines at the beginning of the table. The do-ahead scooping can be accomplished up to 4 hours before party time.

As lovely to look at as it is to eat, this strawberry-pineapple sauce is made almost entirely from pantry ingredients, so you can whip it up any time you like in 10 minutes flat.

Strawberry-Pineapple Sundae Sauce

1 lemon
1 jar (10 ounces) fruit-sweetened
*   strawberry preserves*
¼ cup firmly packed light brown sugar
1 can (8 ounces) crushed pineapple
*   packed in juice*
Ice creeam, for serving

START TO FINISH: 10 MINUTES

1. Zest the lemon (see Note). Reserve the rest of the lemon for another use. Put the zest and the preserves and brown sugar in a medium-size microwave-safe bowl. Add the crushed pineapple with its juice to the preserves mixture. Stir to mix well.

2. Microwave, uncovered, on high until the preserves are melted and the mixture is warm throughout, about 2 minutes. Remove from the microwave oven and stir until the brown sugar is dissolved. Serve warm or at room temperature.

■ *Makes about 2 cups*

Note: The zest of the lemon is the yellow part of the rind only. Do not grate the bitter, white pith underneath. A lemon zester, available at kitchen and department stores, makes quick work of removing the zest. If you don't have a zester, the smallest side of a handheld grater will work just fine.

DO-AHEAD

The strawberry-pineapple sauce can be refrigerated, covered, for up to 2 weeks. Reheat in the microwave oven, uncovered, on high until warmed through, about 1 minute. Stir and serve.

Easy Elegant Pears with Red Wine Glaze

4 cans (15 ounces each) pear halves packed in
  fruit juice
2 cups sugar
1 cup dry red wine
1 lemon
Ground cinnamon, for serving

START TO FINISH: 15 MINUTES

1. Drain the juice from the pears and discard or reserve for another use. Put 2 pear halves cored side up, in each of 8 serving dishes.

2. Combine the sugar and wine in a medium-size saucepan. Cut the lemon in half and squeeze the juice through a small strainer (to catch the seeds) directly into the pan. Place the pan over high heat and, stirring frequently, bring the mixture to a boil, 4 to 5 minutes.

3. Reduce the heat to medium-high and let the mixture boil, stirring constantly, until it thickens slightly, 4 to 6 minutes. Remove the pan from the heat. To serve, drizzle some glaze evenly over each pear, letting the glaze pool in the cored centers of the fruit. Dust the pears very lightly with ground cinnamon.

■ *Serves 8*

Poaching pears in red wine usually starts with peeling and coring fresh pears and simmering the fruit in the wine for nearly an hour, which turns it a garnet color. But guess what? Color aside, the texture and flavor of poached pears are pretty much the same as plain old pears right out of a can. And with canned pears, you don't have to peel anything, plus the ingredients can be kept on hand in your pantry for any time you need an impromptu dessert.

We get brilliant color, too, by making a speedy wine syrup to drizzle on top. Since the wine supplies the essential flavor, be sure to choose a dry red, such as a cabernet sauvignon, that's of a quality you'd be happy to drink. Since the recipe calls for only a cup, the rest will be available for sipping. This Very Desperate Dessert is so elegant, who knows, you could even be inspired to light some candles.

Pour our quick microwave caramel sauce over pears and the words *canned fruit* take on a whole new meaning. This dessert is so fast and fabulous that inviting friends over after the theater or a movie may become second nature.

Pears with Cinnamon-Caramel Sauce

8 tablespoons (1 stick) butter
1 cup lightly packed light brown sugar
½ cup heavy (whipping) cream
2 tablespoons light corn syrup
½ teaspoon ground cinnamon
4 cans (15 ounces each) pear halves packed in
    fruit juice
Cinnamon sticks and fresh mint leaves,
    for garnish (optional)

START TO FINISH: 15 MINUTES

1. Cut the butter into 4 pieces and place in a 4-cup glass measure. Add the brown sugar, cream, corn syrup, and cinnamon. Cover with microwave-safe plastic wrap and cut a small vent in the center. Microwave on high until the mixture boils, about 3½ minutes.

2. Meanwhile, drain the pears and discard the juice or reserve it for another use. Place the pears, cored side up, in a microwave-safe dish, such as a deep-dish glass pie plate.

3. Remove the sauce from the microwave oven. Microwave the pears, uncovered, on high until warmed through, about 2 minutes. While the pears are warming, uncover the sauce and stir well. To serve, put 2 pear halves in each of 8 serving dishes, keeping the cored side up, and drizzle some sauce evenly over each pear, letting the sauce pool in the cored centers of the fruit. Garnish with cinnamon sticks and/or mint leaves, if desired.

■ *Serves 8*

SANITY SAVER

Say "Yes!" when guests ask if they can help. Enlisting the aid of your company to get dinner on the table while it's still hot is smart and saves you from anxiety. Suggest doing anything from pouring the wine to lighting the candles. Guests would much rather feel helpful than eat with a stressed-out host.

Tropical Bananas

4 ripe bananas
2 tablespoons butter
⅓ cup firmly packed light brown sugar
¼ cup orange juice
¼ cup light or dark rum
⅛ teaspoon ground allspice or cinnamon
¼ cup raisins
½ gallon premium vanilla ice cream, for serving

START TO FINISH: 15 MINUTES

1. Peel the bananas and cut them in half crosswise. Slice each half lengthwise. (You will have 16 pieces.)

2. Melt the butter in a 10-inch or larger skillet over medium-high heat. Add the brown sugar, orange juice, rum, and allspice and stir to mix well. Cook until the mixture begins to boil, 2 to 3 minutes. Reduce the heat to medium and cook, stirring constantly, until the sauce begins to thicken, about 2 minutes. Add the banana pieces and the raisins and cook, stirring constantly but gently, so as not to break up the bananas, until the bananas are heated through, 1½ to 2 minutes.

3. Serve the warm bananas at once over scoops of ice cream.

■ *Serves 8*

Bananas with Caribbean accents of rum, allspice, raisins, and orange juice put us in a vacation frame of mind. In other words, they are happy flavors that make a festive end to a party meal. Add vanilla ice cream and you've got a gourmet dessert in minutes. All of these ingredients are easy to keep on hand—we stock bananas and vanilla ice cream even in the most desperate of times.

DESPERATE WAYS TO DECORATE THAT DESSERT

We all know the old saying about how people eat first with their eyes, but you don't have to pretend you're dressing your cakes for the prom.

Part of leading the Desperate Life is about making wise choices with limited resources. When it comes to garnishing our desserts, we're frequently forced to choose between the wrappings and what's in the package. We can only hope our guests aren't the type who'd prefer to play with the box. However, this doesn't mean we don't want our sweets to look appetizing. But our goal is to get guests to salivate, not to head off in search of their cameras. Here are some of our favorite fast and easy ways to dress up those desserts.

• **Squirt-can whipped cream:** Forget pastry bags. Pretty darn good whipped cream comes in aerosol cans, and their decorator tips are just like the ones used in bakeries. A quick squirt will make rosettes as pretty as you please for dressing up a cake, pie, or mousse.

• **Perfect berries:** Strawberries with their green caps, blueberries, and raspberries just need to be rinsed, drained, and scattered to get that "Wow!" No peeling. That's the *real* wow! Arrange a few berries in the center of our Lemon Chess Pie (see page 331) or Heirloom Fudge Pies (see page 326) or around Lemon Cake Sandwiches with Strawberry Purée (see page 312).

• **Edible flowers:** If you happen to have a source for pansies, flowering mint, or other edible blossoms grown without pesticides, these natural adornments are beyond compare.

• **Paper doilies:** Cover up an ugly plate with a doily. When frills fit the bill, these are cheap and easy to come by at the supermarket or in the craft section of a discount store.

• **Toasted nuts:** Sprinkled on top of cakes and pies a few toasted nuts add eye appeal. Ditto toasted coconut.

Flexible Fruit Fondue

½ small (10¾ ounces) frozen all-butter pound cake,
    such as Sara Lee
16 whole fresh strawberries (about 1 pound)
1 can (20 ounces) pineapple chunks packed in juice
    (for about 2¼ cups)
2 tart, firm red apples. such as Fuji or Gala
1 container (16 ounces) milk chocolate frosting, such as
    Duncan Hines
2 tablespoons liqueur of your choice (see Note)
Toothpicks, bamboo skewers, or fondue forks,
    for serving

START TO FINISH: 15 MINUTES

1. Cut the pound cake into 4 slices, each 1-inch thick. Cut each slice
into 8 bite-size chunks. Place the cake pieces on a serving platter.
Rinse and drain the strawberries but don't remove the caps. Arrange
them on the platter with the cake. Drain the pineapple chunks over
a medium-size mixing bowl and reserve the juice in the bowl. Place
the pineapple chunks on the platter.

2. Rinse but do not peel the apples and cut them into quarters.
Core and cut each apple piece into 4 bite-size chunks. Put the apple
chunks in the bowl with the pineapple juice and toss to coat; this
will prevent them from discoloring. Remove the apple pieces from
the bowl with a slotted spoon and place them on the platter.

3. Just before serving, put the frosting in a microwave-safe bowl.
Microwave, covered with a paper towel, on high, stirring and testing
at 30-second intervals, until the frosting is very warm but not hot,
45 seconds to 1½ minutes. Remove the frosting from the oven and
stir in the liqueur.

4. To serve, spoon a little chocolate sauce into each of 8 individual
serving bowls and invite your guests to spear cake and fruit from the

Devised around a
container of chocolate
frosting from the super-
market, this adaptable dessert
can be ready when you are.
A shot of liqueur adds
sophistication—use any
flavor that suits your fancy.
Strawberries are available
practically year-round, but if
you don't have any, you can
just slice more cake. Ditto
with the apples.

DO-AHEAD

The fruit and cake
platter can be
assembled up to 2 hours
ahead. Cover the platter
with plastic wrap and
refrigerate it until ready
to serve.

platter with toothpicks, bamboo skewers, or fondue forks and dip them into the chocolate sauce, fondue style. Replenish the chocolate sauce as necessary.

■ *Serves 8*

Note: Chocolate lends itself to many flavor combinations. Select a liqueur for the fondue based on the flavor match that appeals to you. Triple sec or Grand Marnier will give the taste of orange, kirsch that of cherry. Amaretto will contribute an almond flavor, while Frangelico adds a hint of hazelnut. Feel free to experiment with liqueurs based on any flavor you like with chocolate. For that matter, you could use brandy or bourbon. If you want a nonalcoholic version of the fondue, substitute almond or vanilla extract, but reduce the amount to 1 teaspoon.

THE ELEGANT TRIFLE BOWL

Nothing makes a fancier centerpiece than a handsome trifle, with its layers of fruit, pudding, and cake. A trifle dish is a large (sixteen cup), straight-sided clear glass bowl on a pedestal. Showing off the beautiful layers of the dessert and rising above everything else, a trifle dish really makes a statement.

The good news is how perfect a trifle is for Desperate Entertaining. Our recipe (opposite) is all make-ahead and sits waiting until dessert time is near.

As for the actual serving dish, that's good news, too. We've seen trifle dishes for less than $20 in most mart-type and discount kitchen stores. So it's an inexpensive and easy, yet elegant, way to add to your Desperate Equipment arsenal.

Strawberry Shortcake Trifle

*1 family-size (16 ounces) frozen all-butter pound cake,
    such as Sara Lee*
¼ cup cream sherry
2 pounds (about 2 quarts) fresh, ripe strawberries
¼ cup sugar
*1 package (3.4 ounces) instant French vanilla pudding,
    such as Jell-O brand (use the amount of milk
    specified on the package)*
2 cups whipped topping, such as Cool Whip, defrosted

START TO FINISH: 20 MINUTES, PLUS 4 HOURS CHILLING TIME

1. Slice the cake into 1-inch slices and then cut each slice into 1-inch cubes. Place the cubes in the bottom of a trifle bowl or glass bowl with a 16-cup capacity. Drizzle the sherry over the cake.

2. Rinse and drain the strawberries. Set aside about 2 cups of the smallest berries for garnish. Cap the remaining strawberries, put them in a food processor, and process until puréed, about 30 seconds. Add the sugar and process to mix. Pour the puréed strawberries over the cake cubes.

3. In a medium-size mixing bowl, prepare the pudding according to the directions on the package and pour it over the puréed strawberries.

4. Spoon the whipped topping over the pudding and spread to seal the edges. Garnish with the reserved strawberries. Cover and refrigerate for at least 4 hours.

5. To serve, spoon the trifle into small sherbet bowls or dessert cups.

■ *Serves 8 to 12*

When those beautiful berries are in abundance, strawberry shortcake is one of our favorite summertime desserts. But serving shortcake to a crowd can be tricky—there's the last minute assembly that holds up the show every time. So we've combined the flavors of shortcake with a traditional trifle. Trifles have long been stunning desserts for company and are perfect for the Desperate Host because they are best when prepared ahead so the flavors mingle. Serve the trifle at the table so your guests can appreciate its impressive appearance before everyone digs in.

DO-AHEAD

The trifle can be refrigerated, covered, for up to 12 hours.

Lemon Cake Sandwiches with Strawberry Purée

Here's a dressy dessert that can either be made in 15 minutes start to finish or else phased so that the lion's share of the work can be completed up to 4 hours before you serve it. The impressive confection is so easy that if you can put together peanut butter sandwiches, you can zip through it. Sandwiches, yes, but so much more! Look for lemon curd in the supermarket jelly aisle or with imported or gourmet foods.

1 family-size (16 ounces) frozen all-butter pound cake, such as Sara Lee
1 jar (11¼ ounces) lemon curd
1 pound fresh strawberries (about 4 cups)
Whipped cream from an aerosol can, for garnish
Fresh berries, such as raspberries or more strawberries, for garnish (optional)

START TO FINISH: 15 MINUTES

1. Cut a ¼ inch-thick slice off each end of the pound cake and discard or reserve for another use. Cut the remaining cake into 16 equal pieces, slicing it the way you would a loaf of bread. Spread about 3 tablespoons lemon curd on 8 slices of cake and top each with a second slice of cake, making 8 sandwiches.

2. Rinse, drain, and cap the strawberries. Purée them in a food processor, 10 to 12 seconds on the high speed, stopping once to scrape down the side.

3. To serve, place each cake sandwich on a serving plate. Spoon about 3 tablespoons of strawberry purée over each sandwich. Garnish the sandwiches with decorative squirts of whipped cream and whole berries, if using, and serve.

■ *Serves 8*

Superquick Cobbler

4 tablespoons (½ stick) butter
1 cup self-rising flour (see Note)
1 cup sugar
1 large egg
1 cup milk
3 bags (16 ounces each) frozen peaches
½ gallon premium vanilla ice cream, for serving

START TO FINISH: 10 MINUTES, PLUS 1 HOUR UNATTENDED BAKING TIME AND 5 MINUTES FOR TOPPING WITH ICE CREAM

1. Preheat the oven to 350°F.

2. Cut the butter into 4 pieces and place in a 13 × 9-inch glass baking dish. Put the baking dish in the oven while it preheats to melt the butter.

3. Meanwhile, in a medium-size mixing bowl, mix together the flour, sugar, egg, and milk. Carefully remove the baking dish from the oven and pour the batter over the melted butter. Do not stir. Add the frozen peaches to the batter, arranging them evenly throughout the dish.

4. Bake, uncovered, until the crust browns, about 1 hour. To serve, spoon the cobbler into individual serving bowls and top each with ice cream.

■ *Serves 8*

Note: Using self-rising flour makes even quicker work of the cobbler, since you don't have to add baking powder and salt. If you don't keep self-rising flour in your pantry, you can substitute a cup of all-purpose flour mixed with 1½ teaspoons baking powder and ½ teaspoon salt.

From Alicia:

If you are lucky to have enough fresh peaches during peach season to freeeze your own, you can enjoy this delight with the fruits of your own labor. But if you're like me, rest at ease that there are 1-pound bags of frozen sliced peaches in your grocer's freezer ready to make a cobbler your guests will remember for a long time. And no one will know you didn't use fresh peaches!

This cobbler can be put together in just 10 minutes before your guests arrive, then bakes without worry for an hour, filling your home with a welcoming aroma, indeed. The cobbler should be through baking just as you're finishing up with dinner, or it can easily wait a while.

DO-AHEAD

The cobbler can be baked up to 4 hours ahead and let stand, uncovered, at room temperature. Rewarm before serving, if necessary, in a 325°F oven for 10 to 15 minutes.

Phased and Flexible

Apple Brown Betty

8 tablespoons (1 stick) butter
1 cup graham cracker crumbs
½ cup plain dry bread crumbs
½ cup pecan pieces
½ cup firmly packed light brown sugar
1 tablespoon apple pie spice
4 large (about 2½ pounds total) Granny Smith apples
2 lemons
Cooking oil spray
Premium vanilla ice cream, for serving (optional)

Betties date back to Colonial times, but there's nothing outdated about this simple way to turn apples into a rich and satisfying dessert for guests. Mixing already-crushed graham cracker crumbs with bread crumbs makes a crisp, flavorful, and easy topping. Apple pie spice, one of our favorite desperate spice blends, makes it even easier. The "hardest" part of making this dessert is peeling and slicing the four apples.

PHASE 1: 20 MINUTES

1. Put the butter in a microwave-safe bowl, cover with a paper towel, and microwave on high until melted, about 45 seconds.

2. Combine the graham cracker crumbs, bread crumbs, pecans, brown sugar, and apple pie spice in a medium-size mixing bowl. Toss to mix well. Add the melted butter to the mixture and stir to mix well.

3. Peel, core, and slice the apples into wedges. Place the apple slices in a bowl. Cut the lemons in half and holding the halves over the apples, squeeze the lemon juice through a strainer to catch the seeds. Toss the apples to coat well.

4. Spray a 10 × 8-inch or 2-quart glass baking dish with cooking oil spray. Spread about one third of the crumb mixture in the bottom of the dish. Place half of the apple wedges on top. Top these with one third of the crumb mixture, the remaining apple wedges, and any remaining lemon juice in the bowl. Top with the remaining crumb mixture. *The baking dish can be covered with aluminum foil and refrigerated at this point for up to 4 hours.*

PHASE 2: ABOUT 70 MINUTES MOSTLY UNATTENDED BAKING TIME

5. Preheat the oven to 375°F.

6. Bake the betty covered with aluminum foil until the apples are almost tender, about 50 minutes.

7. Uncover the baking dish for even browning and bake until the betty is completely browned on top, about 15 minutes more. (It may be necessary to cover the baking dish with aluminum foil to prevent overbrowning.) Serve hot or warm, topped with vanilla ice cream, if desired. *The betty can stand at room temperature, uncovered, for up to 4 hours. Rewarm in a 325°F oven, about 10 minutes.*

■ *Serves 8*

MONEY SAVER

Think of entertaining as a gift you give to your friends and family, and plan the expense into the household budget along with gifts for birthdays and holidays.

Berkshires Blueberry Crisp

From Beverly:

The August family reunion in the Berkshire mountains of Massachusetts wouldn't be the same without blueberry crisp. The tradition started when the local farm markets were teeming with plump berries, but back in the lake cabin kitchen, baking provisions were scarce. Just a few common ingredients can produce a homey dessert that's sure to make everyone's eyes light up. When they're available, I've often substituted a pound of peaches in place of a pound of blueberries. One thing you can't substitute: Be sure to use quick-cooking oats (uncooked), not old-fashioned oats or instant oatmeal.

3 pints (2 pounds) fresh or frozen blueberries
Cooking oil spray
2 teaspoons pure almond extract
¾ cup all-purpose flour
¾ cup firmly packed light or dark brown sugar
⅔ cup quick-cooking oats
2 teaspoons ground cinnamon
6 tablespoons (¾ stick) cold butter
½ gallon premium vanilla ice cream, for serving

PHASE 1: 15 MINUTES

1. Put the blueberries in a colander and rinse under cold running water. Pick off any stems and remove any debris. Shake the colander to remove excess water. Set aside to drain.

2. Spray a 13 × 9-inch glass baking dish with cooking oil spray. Put the drained blueberries in the dish. Drizzle the almond extract evenly over the blueberries. Toss gently to mix. Shake the dish to distribute the berries evenly.

3. Put the flour, brown sugar, oats, and cinnamon in a medium-size mixing bowl. Stir well to combine. Cut the cold butter into 6 even pieces and then cut these pieces in half. Add the pieces of butter to the bowl. Using a pastry blender or 2 knives, cut the butter into the flour mixture until it forms pieces that look like peas. Sprinkle the flour mixture evenly over the berries. *The baking dish can be covered and refrigerated at this point for up to 4 hours.*

PHASE 2: ABOUT 30 MINUTES UNATTENDED BAKING TIME

4. Preheat the oven to 375°F.

5. Bake the crisp, uncovered, until it bubbles and the topping begins to brown, 30 to 35 minutes (see Note). *The crisp can stand at room* *temperature, uncovered, for up to 4 hours at this point or the crisp can be refrigerated, covered, for up to 12 hours.*

PHASE 3: 10 TO 30 MINUTES UNATTENDED WARMING TIME, PLUS 5 MINUTES SERVING TIME

6. Preheat the oven to 325°F.

7. Bake the crisp, uncovered, until it is very warm throughout, about 10 minutes if the crisp is at room temperature or 20 to 30 minutes if it has been refrigerated. Serve the crisp topped with vanilla ice cream.

■ *Serves 8*

Note: If you want to serve the crisp at this point, let it cool for at least 10 minutes.

THE PEPPERMINT PARABLE

From Beverly:

Every time my entertaining agenda goes unexpectedly haywire and I can't seem to get it all done, I recall one of the most desperate and most creative desserts I ever witnessed. At a neighborhood cookout, I watched a friend take a punch bowl and fill it nearly to the brim with scoops of pink peppermint ice cream. Then she whacked a bag of peppermints on the counter and sprinkled the candy pieces over the bowl. Next came an array of colorful candles. In less than five minutes the desperate hostess had produced her daughter's birthday cake to the sheer delight of the guests—young and old alike.

This "cook" is a dedicated mother of two and a fine minister and theologian who more often than not teaches by example. But that night my friend spoke some sage words in the kitchen just as she lit the candles on her masterpiece:

"You know," she said, "life just doesn't need to be so difficult."

From Alicia:

Nothing satisfies like a brownie stuffed with nuts, chocolate chips, and mini marshmallows. Thanks to a purchased brownie mix, these are ready for the oven in just 5 minutes. My kids beg for this quick and easy favorite weekly. Add a scoop of vanilla ice cream and a squirt of chocolate sauce and enjoy. You can serve as many as twelve at one time.

Rocky Road Brownie Sundaes

Cooking oil spray
1 package (1 pound, 3½ ounces) fudge brownie
   mix (use the number of eggs and amount of
   vegetable oil and water specified on the package
   for a 13 × 9-inch pan)
1 cup already-chopped pecans or walnuts
1 cup semisweet chocolate chips
1 cup mini marshmallows
½ gallon premium vanilla ice cream
Bottled chocolate syrup
Whipped cream from an aerosol can, for serving
   (optional)
Maraschino cherries, for serving (optional)

**PHASE 1: 5 MINUTES, PLUS 30 MINUTES UNATTENDED
BAKING TIME AND 15 MINUTES COOLING TIME**

1. Preheat the oven to 325°F or to the temperature specified on the brownie mix package.

2. Spray a 13 × 9-inch glass baking dish with cooking oil spray (see Note). Prepare the brownie mix following the directions on the package. Stir the nuts, chocolate chips, and marshmallows into the brownie batter. Spread the batter evenly in the prepared baking dish.

3. Place the baking dish on the middle rack of the oven and bake the brownies according to the directions on the package or until a toothpick inserted into the center of the pan comes out clean, about 30 minutes.

4. Remove the brownies from the oven and let cool on a wire rack for 15 minutes, then cut into 12 roughly 3-inch squares. *The brownies can be stored in an airtight container for up to 2 days or frozen for up to 1 month.*

PHASE 2: 5 MINUTES

5. To serve, place a brownie on the center of each of 12 dessert plates. Top with a generous scoop of ice cream and drizzle chocolate sauce over it. Top with whipped cream and a cherry, if desired.

■ *Serves 12*

Note: If you are using a metal baking dish, increase the oven temperature to 350°F or the temperature specified on the package.

Triple Chocolate Fudge Brownie Sundaes

Cooking oil spray
1 package (1 pound, 3½ ounces) fudge brownie mix (use the number of eggs and amount of vegetable oil and water specified on the package for a 13 × 9-inch pan)
1 cup semisweet chocolate chips
1 cup white chocolate chips
½ gallon premium chocolate ice cream
Butterscotch ice cream topping or Brandied Butterscotch Sauce (see page 301)
Whipped cream from an aerosol can, for serving (optional)
Maraschino cherries, for serving (optional)

PHASE 1: 5 MINUTES, PLUS 30 MINUTES UNATTENDED BAKING TIME AND 15 MINUTES COOLING TIME

1. Preheat the oven to 325°F or to the temperature specified on the brownie mix package.

2. Spray a 13 × 9-inch glass baking dish with cooking oil spray (see Note). Prepare the brownie mix following the directions on the package. Stir in the semisweet and white chocolate chips. Spread the batter evenly in the prepared baking dish.

From Beverly:

I need my chocolate fix on a regular basis, and most of my friends do, too. So serving up these chock-full-of-chocolate brownies, slathered with chocolate ice cream and a little butterscotch sauce for contrast, is a fitting end to any meal so far as I'm concerned. Disguising a box of brownie mix so deftly is a true triumph. It will make enough brownies for a dozen sundaes.

3. Place the baking dish on the middle rack of the oven and bake according to the directions on the package or until a toothpick inserted in the center comes out clean, about 30 minutes.

4. Remove the brownies from the oven and let cool on a wire rack for 15 minutes, then cut into 12 roughly 3-inch squares. *The brownies can by stored in an airtight container for up to 2 days or frozen for up to 1 month.*

PHASE 2: 5 MINUTES

5. To serve, place a brownie on the center of each of 12 dessert plates. Top with a generous scoop of ice cream and drizzle butterscotch sauce over it. Top with whipped cream and a cherry, if desired.

■ *Serves 12*

Note: If you are using a metal baking dish, increase the oven temperature to 350°F or the temperature specified on the package.

Who would have thought that a simple swirl of peanut butter could transform a plain-old brownie mix? Add a scoop of ice cream, drizzle chocolate syrup on top, and you've got a dessert sensation. The pan of brownies makes enough to fix twelve sundaes, but come the next day, we assure you nobody will complain about the leftovers.

Peanut Butter Fudge Brownie Sundaes

Cooking oil spray
1 package (1 pound, 3½ ounces) fudge brownie mix (use the number of eggs and amount of vegetable oil and water specified on the package for a 13 × 9-inch pan)
¾ cup smooth peanut butter
½ cup already-chopped, unsalted or lightly salted roasted peanuts
½ gallon premium vanilla, chocolate, or peanut butter ice cream (see Notes)
Chocolate syrup or Old-Fashioned Fudge Sauce (see recipe page 300)
Whipped cream from an aerosol can, for serving (optional)
Maraschino cherries, for serving (optional)

**PHASE 1: 7 MINUTES, PLUS 30 MINUTES UNATTENDED
BAKING TIME AND 15 MINUTES COOLING TIME**

1. Preheat the oven to 325°F or to the temperature specified on the brownie mix package.

2. Spray a 13 × 9-inch glass baking dish with cooking oil spray (see Notes). Prepare the brownie mix following the directions on the package. Place the peanut butter in a microwave-safe bowl and microwave, uncovered, on high just until soft and easy to pour, about 30 seconds. Pour the peanut butter over the brownie batter in an S shape. Using a knife, swirl the peanut butter evenly through the batter, then spread out the batter evenly in the prepared baking dish. Sprinkle the peanuts evenly over the top of the batter.

3. Place the baking dish on the middle rack of the oven and bake according to the directions on the package or until the brownies start to pull away from the sides, about 30 minutes. (Because of the peanut butter, you can't test for doneness using the standard "toothpick comes out clean" test.)

4. Remove the brownies from the oven and let cool on a wire rack for 15 minutes, then cut into 12 roughly 3-inch squares. *The brownies can be stored in an airtight container for up to 2 days or frozen for up to 1 month.*

PHASE 2: 5 MINUTES

5. To serve, place a brownie on the center of each of 12 dessert plates. Top with a generous scoop of ice cream and drizzle chocolate syrup over it. Top with whipped cream and a cherry, if desired.

■ *Serves 12*

Notes: Some vanilla and chocolate ice creams have peanut butter swirled in. These combinations would work well, too.

   If you are using a metal baking dish, increase the oven temperature to 350°F or the temperature specified on the package.

SANITY SAVER

I f at all possible, issue invitations while speaking to someone over the telephone or in person. This strategy can take a bit more time on the front end, but the payoff is well worth your investment. The most obvious advantage is that you'll get a pretty good idea on the spot whether or not your guests can come.

My friend Martie Leming researched red velvet cake on the Internet and then tried dozens of versions before coming up with this, the perfect recipe. The German chocolate cake mix makes it a snap to put together what used to be a complicated cake. You'll have a cake large enough for twelve, and you can serve it right out of the baking dish. The only note of warning is this: Beware the tablespoon of red food coloring. The first time I made the cake, I added it while the beaters were moving and ended up with red spatters all over the kitchen as it flew out of the bowl.

SPACE SAVER

Storage idea! Plastic under-the-bed boxes are great for holding extra entertaining equipment.

Martie's Red Velvet Cake

1 package (18¼ ounces) German chocolate
  cake mix
2 large eggs
1 cup low-fat buttermilk
¼ cup vegetable oil
1 tablespoon cider vinegar
1 tablespoon red food coloring
Butter and flour for lining the baking dish
Cream Cheese Frosting (see Note;
  recipe follows)
½ cup already-chopped pecans, for garnish
  (optional)

PHASE 1: 8 MINUTES

1. Make the Cream Cheese Frosting. *The frosting can be refrigerated, covered, for up to 3 days.*

PHASE 2: 10 MINUTES PREPARATION, PLUS 30 MINUTES UNATTENDED BAKING TIME AND 30 MINUTES COOLING TIME

2. Preheat the oven to 350°F.

3. Put the cake mix in the large bowl of an electric mixer. Add the eggs, buttermilk, oil, vinegar, and ½ cup water and beat for 1 minute at low speed to begin to combine. Turn off the mixer and add the food coloring. Beat 2 minutes at high speed. Grease and lightly flour a 13 × 9-inch glass baking dish. Pour the batter into the prepared pan.

4. Place the baking dish on the middle rack of the oven and bake until a toothpick inserted in the center comes out clean, about 30 minutes. Remove the cake from the oven and let cool for at least 30 minutes. *The cake can be stored, covered, at room temperature for up to 24 hours.*

5. Frost the cooled cake with the Cream Cheese Frosting. Garnish by sprinkling with chopped pecans, if desired. *The frosted cake can be refrigerated, covered, for up to 3 days.*

■ *Serves 12*

Note: When you're starved for time, frost the cake using a 12-ounce container of ready-made cream cheese frosting.

Cream Cheese Frosting

Oh so rich, with a slight bite from the cream cheese, this frosting is soft enough at room temperature to spread with ease. We've paired it with Martie's Red Velvet Cake, but almost any cake would be the better for it. Because the frosting is made in the food processor, you don't have to wait for the cream cheese to come to room temperature before mixing it in.

> *4 tablespoons (½ stick) butter*
> *1½ cups confectioners' sugar*
> *2 small packages (3 ounces each) cream cheese*
> *1 teaspoon pure vanilla extract*

START TO FINISH: **8 MINUTES**

1. Put the butter in a small microwave-safe bowl and microwave, uncovered, at 50 percent power for 45 seconds to 1 minute to soften it slightly.

2. Put the confectioners' sugar in the bowl of a food processor and process for 1 minute to sift.

3. Cut each piece of cream cheese in half and add to the confectioners' sugar. Add the softened butter and the vanilla extract. Process until smooth, about 30 seconds, stopping as necessary to scrape down the side of the bowl.

■ *Makes 1⅓ cups*

DO-AHEAD

The frosting can be refrigerated, covered, for up to 3 days. Let return to room temperature before using.

Craving chocolate? We know when we do nothing else will satisfy those yearnings. But we have several family members who don't share our desire for the delectable chocolate alone. So what's a good compromise? Chocolate Caramel Cake! Rich chocolaty cake with ooey-gooey caramel drizzled throughout, topped off with yummy whipped cream . . . Craving cake yet?

SANITY SAVER

Inviting toddlers but you don't have any? Even if you do, drop by the video store for a kid's movie or two, invest in some inexpensive crayons and coloring books, and be sure to stock up on fruit juice and plain crackers. Clear away the crystal coffee table knickknacks before your underage guests arrive.

Chocolate Caramel Cake

Cooking oil spray
1 package (18¼ ounces) dark chocolate or devil's food
*   cake mix (use the number of eggs and amount of*
*   vegetable oil and water specified on the package for a*
*   13 × 9-inch pan)*
1 jar (12 ounces) caramel ice cream sauce
4 Heath or Skor candy bars (see Note)
1 container (12 ounces) whipped topping, such as
*   Cool Whip, thawed*

**PHASE 1: 9 MINUTES, PLUS 30 MINUTES UNATTENDED
BAKING TIME AND 45 MINUTES TO 1 HOUR COOLING TIME**

1. Preheat the oven to 325°F or to the temperature specified on the the cake mix package.

2. Spray a 13 × 9-inch glass baking dish with cooking oil spray. Prepare the cake mix following the directions on the package. Spread the batter evenly in the prepared baking dish. Place the baking dish on the middle rack of the oven and bake according to the directions on the package or until a toothpick inserted in the center comes out clean, about 30 minutes.

3. When the cake is done, remove it from the oven. With a wooden pick, such as a chop stick or narrow spoon handle, poke holes in the cake over the entire surface. Pour the caramel sauce over the cake, filling the holes. Set the cake in its baking dish on a wire rack to cool for 45 minutes to 1 hour. *The cake can be refrigerated, covered, at this point for up to 8 hours.*

PHASE 2: 7 MINUTES

4. Using a sturdy chef's knife, chop the candy bars.

5. When cake has cooled completely, spread half of the candy bar pieces over it. Frost the cake with the whipped topping, spreading it to the sides of the baking dish. Sprinkle the rest of the candy bar pieces evenly over the cake.

6. Cover the frosted cake with plastic wrap. If the baking dish is not deep enough to keep the plastic wrap from sticking to the whipped cream, insert several wooden toothpicks into the cake and then cover, letting the plastic wrap seal the edges but rest on top of the toothpicks. Refrigerate until ready to serve.

7. To serve, run warm water over a very sharp knife, dry it, and slice the cake into 8 to 10 pieces at the table. *The frosted cake can be refrigerated, covered, for up to 24 hours.*

■ *Serves 8 to 10*

Note: Heath or Skor (chocolate-covered toffee bars) are not always available on the candy aisle in the grocery. To find them check the checkout stands or drug store candy shelves.

THE DESPERATE DISH

Our take on serving desperately is that if you bake in attractive dishes you can go from oven to table without wasting steps. Think of the last time you tried to flip a cake out of its baking pan. Need we say more? It's much easier and faster to serve an attractive cake if all you have to do is spread a layer of frosting over it while it's still in the dish. Plus, you'll never have to worry about the missing chunk that stuck to the cake pan when you tried to turn it out!

For other foods like vegetables and casseroles, serving straight from a baking pan means fewer bowls to wash, and you aren't likely to burn yourself transferring steaming hot food from one container to another. Most of our cakes, brownies, lasagnas, and casseroles call for a glass baking dish that measures 13 by 9 inches. We tend to use the oblong Pyrex-brand baking dishes because they're inexpensive. However, if you have a similar shallow, oblong decorative 3-quart ceramic dish (such as one made by Corning Ware), it will work well also. For larger casseroles such as the Baked Party Paella (see page 116), choose the slightly larger 15 by 10-inch glass Pyrex dish.

For decades, this rich concoction has satisfied friends of all ages at parties, church suppers, and informal dinners. With only 20 minutes of actual work, it's just as easy to make two fudge pies as it is one, and since they freeze beautifully, that's what we usually do.

The pies are heavenly served slightly warm, and if we don't have one fresh from the oven, we just stick one in a 300°F oven about 10 minutes before serving. Whipped cream makes an elegant garnish (don't let the pie get hot or it will melt the whipped cream), but if you don't have time to whip your own, buy real whipped cream in an aerosol can or use vanilla ice cream.

Heirloom Fudge Pies

6 squares (1 ounce each) unsweetened baking chocolate
1½ cups (3 sticks) butter
3¾ cups sugar
¾ cup milk
1½ teaspoons pure vanilla extract
6 large eggs
1 package (15 ounces; 2 crusts) refrigerated pie crusts,
    such as Pillsbury (see Note)
Whipped cream from an aerosol can or premium
    vanilla ice cream, for garnish (optional)

**PHASE 1: 20 MINUTES, PLUS 40 MINUTES UNATTENDED
BAKING TIME**

1. Preheat the oven to 350°F.

2. Place the chocolate and butter in a 2-quart microwave-safe bowl, cover with a paper towel, and microwave, uncovered, on high just until the chocolate and butter are almost melted, about 2 minutes. Remove from the microwave and stir until the chocolate and butter finish melting, about 1 minute.

3. Add the sugar, milk, and vanilla extract to the melted chocolate and butter. Whisk the eggs lightly in a bowl and add them to the chocolate mixture. Whisk until well combined.

4. Place each pie crust in an 8-inch glass pie pan, following the directions on the package, and crimp the edges in a decorative fashion. Pour half the chocolate mixture into each pie crust.

5. Place the pies on the middle rack of the oven and bake just until the pie filling is set, about 40 minutes.

PHASE 2: ABOUT 30 MINUTES COOLING TIME

6. Remove the pies from the oven and let them cool on a wire rack for at least 30 minutes.

7. Garnish the pies with whipped cream or vanilla ice cream, if desired, and serve. *The pies can be stored, covered, at room temperature for up to 24 hours or frozen for up to 1 month. Take them out to thaw at room temperature the morning of the day you plan to serve them.*

■ *Makes 2 pies, 8 servings each*

Note: Look for these pie crusts in the refrigerated section of the supermarket. They will fit in 8-inch pie pans and are slightly larger than frozen crusts. If you prefer to use frozen crusts, use extra-deep ones. Or, if you're forced to use regular-size frozen crusts, don't overfill them. You'll have some pie filling left over.

EASY, EQUITABLE SLICING

From Beverly:

Math and spatial relationships are not my strong suits. I can't tell you the number of pies I struggled over, trying to eyeball the slices to cut them exactly the same size. Then one day I saw Alicia cut a pie into perfectly even slices so effortlessly, my jaw dropped. She used the "clock" method. Obvious as it was, I hadn't thought of it!

In case you've been challenged in the cutting department, too, here's Alicia's easiest way ever to get eight exact portions of pie:

1. Think of the pie as a clock. Cut it in half, slicing from noon to 6 o'clock.

2. Cut it in half again from 9 o'clock to 3 o'clock.

3. You now have four slices. Cut each in half, one at a time, with a gentle sawing motion rather than a knife-dragging motion. You now have eight equitable servings.

Here's an extra tip. Since the first piece of pie almost never comes out beautifully, consider it a sacrificial slice. Slide it onto a plate and quickly set it aside. That's the host's portion. Once you have some room to maneuver the spatula, the remaining servings will generally look great for your guests.

From Beverly:

From Beverly:

Why it took me years to perfect this simple recipe may be a testament to my ineptitude, but I prefer to think it was because I'm so picky when it comes to pecan pie. Of all of my recipes in all of my years, this is my absolute favorite. Even my mother, one of the world's best bakers, asked for the recipe. The original version came from my father's mother, Zeta Fetzer Mills, and one of her secrets was the odd configuration of baking temperatures—the initial blast of high heat toasts the pecans. My contribution is the unusual combination of sweeteners (it's not too sweet) and the timing for beating the eggs (it makes for a lighter pie).

This recipe makes two pies (it's just as easy as making one), and they freeze beautifully for up to a month. When I make the pies ahead, I like to refresh the crust by warming it slightly before serving. A dollop of whipped cream makes a heavenly garnish.

Granny Zeta's Pecan Pies

6 large eggs
6 tablespoons (¾ stick) butter
1 cup firmly packed light brown sugar
½ cup granulated sugar
1 cup light corn syrup
2 teaspoons pure vanilla extract
¼ teaspoon salt
1 package (15 ounces; 2 crusts) refrigerated pie crusts,
   such as Pillsbury (see Notes)
2 cups already-chopped pecans
Whipped cream from an aerosol can or premium
   vanilla ice cream, for garnish (optional)

PHASE 1: 20 MINUTES, PLUS 32 MINUTES MOSTLY UNATTENDED BAKING TIME

1. Preheat the oven to 400°F.

2. Break the eggs into the small bowl of an electric mixer (see Notes). Beat the eggs at medium-high speed until very frothy, about 2 minutes. Meanwhile, put the butter in a small microwave-safe bowl, cover with a paper towel, and microwave on high until melted, about 1½ minutes. (If your mixer's large bowl is glass, you can melt the butter right in that bowl in the microwave.)

3. Put the melted butter, brown sugar, and granulated sugar in the large bowl of an electric mixer. Mix at medium speed until well combined, about 2 minutes. Meanwhile, measure out the corn syrup. Add the beaten eggs and the corn syrup, vanilla extract, and salt to the sugar mixture. Increase the speed to medium-high and beat for 3 minutes.

4. Place each crust in an 8-inch glass pie pan, following the directions on the package, and crimp the edges in a decorative fashion. Pour half the pie filling into each crust (it won't look like enough filling, but it will rise to fill the shell during baking). Sprinkle 1 cup of chopped pecans over the filling of each pie.

5. Place the pies on the middle rack of the oven and bake for 12 minutes. Lower the heat to 325°F and continue to bake until the filling is set (no longer moves when you jiggle the pie), about 20 minutes more.

PHASE 2: ABOUT 30 MINUTES COOLING TIME

6. Remove the pies from the oven and let them cool on a wire rack for at least 30 minutes.

7. Garnish the pies with whipped cream or vanilla ice cream, if desired, and serve. *The pies can be refrigerated, covered, for up to 24 hours or frozen for up to 1 month. Take them out to thaw at room temperature the morning of the day you plan to serve them.*

■ *Makes 2 pies, 8 servings each*

Notes: Look for these pie crusts in the refrigerated section of the supermarket (near the refrigerated cookie dough, not with the frozen foods). They will fit in 8-inch pie pans and are slightly larger than frozen crusts. If you prefer to use frozen crusts, use extra-deep ones. Or, if you're forced to use regular-size frozen crusts, don't overfill them. You'll have some pie filling left over.

If you have a stand mixer, use it for this recipe. If you don't, you may find it will take you a couple more minutes to make the pies.

Pucker power is what really gauges a good Key lime pie. Tart and tangy, this one passes the test. Then there's the texture. It must be thick, rich, and creamy. We adapted our recipe from the Green River Coffee Company, in Wilson, North Carolina, where owner Paul Little describes this pie as "embarrassingly easy." But that's just what a Desperate Cook needs, a dessert that's easy to make yet looks and tastes like it's not.

True Key lime juice is the secret to the success of the pie. Don't be tempted to substitute regular lime juice. Key limes (named after the Florida Keys) are golf-ball-size limes with a color more yellow than green. Their flavor is a bit brighter than a regular lime, hence the zesty kick at the first bite. Check the section of the supermarket where drink mixes are located for Key lime juice if it's not carried in the fruit juice section, or try a specialty food store.

Sunset Key Lime Pies

16 large eggs
4 cans (14 ounces each) sweetened condensed milk
2 cups (16 ounces) Key lime juice
2 large (9 ounces each) prepared graham cracker crumb crusts
Whipped cream from an aerosol can, for garnish (optional)

PHASE 1: 20 MINUTES, PLUS ABOUT 25 MINUTES BAKING TIME AND 1 HOUR COOLING TIME

1. Preheat the oven to 350°F.

2. Separate the eggs, reserving the whites for another use. Place the yolks in the large bowl of an electric mixer and beat at medium speed until thoroughly blended and pale yellow, about 3 minutes. Add the condensed milk and Key lime juice. Mix at medium speed until well combined. Let rest for 5 minutes.

3. Divide the batter equally between the 2 pie crusts. Place the pies on the middle rack of the oven and bake until the outside edge is set but the center is custardlike, 20 to 25 minutes. Remove the pies from the oven and let them cool on a wire rack to room temperature, about 1 hour.

PHASE 2: MINIMUM 1 HOUR REFRIGERATION TIME

4. Refrigerate the pies for at least 1 hour before serving. Garnish the pies with whipped cream, if desired. *The pies can be refrigerated, covered, for up to 24 hours or they can be frozen for up to 1 month. Place them in the refrigerator at least 12 hours and up to 24 hours before serving to thaw.*

■ *Makes 2 pies, 8 servings each*

Lemon Chess Pie

1 refrigerated pie crust, such as Pillsbury (see Notes)
1⅓ cups sugar
2 teaspoons plain white cornmeal (optional; see Notes)
2 teaspoons all-purpose flour
3 large eggs
3 tablespoons butter
2 small lemons
3 tablespoons milk

PHASE 1: 15 MINUTES, PLUS 40 MINUTES UNATTENDED BAKING TIME

1. Preheat the oven to 325°F.

2. Place the pie crust in an 8-inch glass pie plate, following the directions on the package, and crimp the edges in a decorative fashion.

3. Combine the sugar, cornmeal, if using, and flour in the large bowl of an electric mixer (see Notes). With the mixer running on low, add the eggs one at a time. Mix at medium speed until the egg mixture is pale yellow and slightly foamy and the sugar is dissolved, about 4 minutes.

4. Meanwhile, place the butter in a small microwave-safe bowl, cover with a paper towel, and microwave on high until melted, about 30 seconds. Cut the lemons in half and squeeze the juice through a small strainer (to catch the seeds) into a measuring cup until you have ¼ cup of juice. Add the lemon juice, melted butter, and milk to the egg mixture and continue to mix until well blended.

5. Pour the batter into the pie crust. Carefully place the pie on the middle rack of the oven and bake until the pie filling is light brown on top and the crust begins to brown, about 40 minutes. When done, the center of the pie will have a custardlike texture and will still jiggle.

From Alicia:

Lemon Chess is a classic Southern pie. It's a great ending to just about any meal that begs for a finish that's both sweet and tart. I even make this pie to give as a birthday present for friends and family alike. I first encountered the terrific old-fashioned favorite at Robert's Grocery in Wilmington, North Carolina, and I've worked and reworked its much larger recipe to make one perfect pie.

To ensure a creamy filling, blend the eggs and sugar mixture until the eggs are light and slightly foamy and the sugar is dissolved. Insufficient blending will cause the pie to have a gritty texture. Two small lemons should provide the quarter of a cup of juice needed.

Unfortunately, freezing changes the creamy custard texture, but if you need more than one pie, the recipe can be doubled.

PHASE 2: 1 HOUR COOLING TIME

6. Remove the pie from the oven and place it on a wire rack to cool to room temperature. *The pie can be refrigerated, covered, for up to 2 days.*

■ *Serves 8*

Notes: Look for these pie crusts in the refrigerated section of the supermarket (near the refrigerated cookie dough, not with the frozen foods). They will fit in 8-inch pie pans and are slightly larger than frozen crusts. If you prefer to use frozen crusts, use extra-deep ones. Or, if you're forced to use regular-size frozen crusts, don't overfill them. You'll have some pie filling left over.

For those of you accustomed to making lemon chess pies, you may wonder why the cornmeal is an optional ingredient here. Cornmeal does give the pie a different texture from that of a lemon custard pie. So, if you can easily find plain white cornmeal, then by all means use it. If not, use an additional teaspoon of flour instead.

If you have a stand mixer, use it for this recipe. If you don't, you may find it will take you a couple more minutes to make the pie.

From Alicia:

I love the creamy smooth custard crème brûlée. But I never thought I'd be able to turn out the same super-smooth texture. Then I tried this recipe. Adapted from the Wicked Smile restaurant in Raleigh, North Carolina, the secret to the custard is a simple water bath. I've substituted fresh berries for the burnt sugar topping. You don't need fancy equipment to make this easy recipe, and your guests will love you for trying it.

Individual Crème Custards with Berries

3 cups heavy (whipping) cream
1½ teaspoons pure vanilla extract
6 large eggs
¾ cup sugar
1 pint fresh berries, such as raspberries or blackberries

PHASE 1: 25 MINUTES, PLUS 45 MINUTES UNATTENDED BAKING TIME AND 2 HOURS COOLING TIME

1. Preheat the oven to 325°F.

2. Place the cream in a heavy 3-quart or larger saucepan and heat over medium heat until it just starts to steam, about 5 minutes. Remove from the heat and stir in the vanilla extract. Let cool for 5 minutes.

3. Separate the eggs, reserving the whites for another use. Place the yolks and sugar in a large bowl and whisk together. When the cream has cooled for 5 minutes, transfer half of it to a glass measure with a pouring spout. Add this to the egg mixture, pouring in a thin, slow drizzle and whisking constantly. Pour the egg-and-cream mixture into the cream remaining in the saucepan. Stir to mix.

4. Divide the egg-and-cream mixture among eight 5- or 6-ounce ramekins or custard cups. Place the ramekins in a 13 × 9-inch glass or ceramic baking dish and fill the baking dish with water until it rises a third of the way up the sides of the ramekins. Place the baking dish on the middle rack of the oven and bake until the custards are just set in the center and are firm yet still jiggly, with a pudding-like consistency, about 45 minutes. Carefully remove the baking dish from the oven. Remove the ramekins from the water. Let the custards cool to room temperature, then refrigerate them, covered, for at least 2 hours. *The baked custards can be refrigerated, covered, for up to 24 hours.*

PHASE 2: 5 MINUTES

5. Rinse the berries in a colander and drain well. Top each custard with several berries and serve.

■ *Serves 8*

THE PARTY'S OVER

Getting the guests out the door while everyone is still having fun is a crucial aspect of being a competent host.

A word about getting your guests to go home: Congratulations! You've done such a great job hosting that now your guests can't bear to see the evening end. Nobody likes to be a party pooper—especially a host—but all good gatherings must, at some point, cease. It's better that guests leave wanting a little more than to have their parting image of the evening be a wilted host trying to corral crying children.

This lesson didn't come easily to us. We are both blessed with sociable husbands who would love nothing more than for life to be a nonstop celebration. "Just one more song." "Have another beer." "You don't need to leave now." How many times we've heard those words, and in fact our spouses' approach to weekend fun worked fine until our children came along. Young kids wake up at the same time every morning (6:30 most likely) no matter what time you put them to bed. And, there's almost nothing worse than the day after with sleep-deprived kids. Plus, if small children are still up past their bedtimes, they're guaranteed to fall apart. Multiply the whining and shrieking by however many children you've invited to the gathering, and it becomes apparent that it's high time for everyone to go home.

The solution to all of this is fairly simple. First, you and your spouse or cohost must agree before the invitations go out what time the affair needs to end. Second, when you extend the invitations, let the guests know what time the fun will start. Your next sentence should be a very clear statement about what time the gathering will end. Often people aren't used to a predetermined ending time, so we find it helpful to add a note of explanation up front. "We're starting a little earlier than usual so everyone can be home by nine. My kids just aren't fit to live with if they don't get to bed by then, so will ending the party at eight-thirty work for you?"

We find this usually does the trick, and many people (parents especially) actually appreciate being able to predict the schedule. Here are several other tips to ensure success.

• Plan to serve food so that the meal will be finished at least 30 to 45 minutes before the predetermined ending time. People don't feel comfortable putting their forks down and walking out the door.

• If a very close friend is on the guest list, enlist her or him to help with the plan. When one guest makes a move to leave, others usually follow.

• If the ending time is approaching and the festivities are still in full force, make a few winding down gestures. Begin some small attempts to clean up; start telling your guests how great it was to get together and how you should do it more often. Guests often expect these cues and wait for them.

• In the rare instance when guests who know the ending time just won't let the party go, you have two choices. You can suffer in silence. Or you can check your watch and gasp, "Oh, dear. My kids turn into pumpkins in precisely five minutes. Larry, Lorraine, it's been great seeing you, but you'll have to excuse me while I go put them to bed." By the time you've finished doing this, provided your fun-loving spouse refrains from serving more beer, the guests should have said their good-byes.

CONVERSION TABLES

LIQUID CONVERSIONS

U.S.	IMPERIAL	METRIC
2 tbs	1 fl oz	30 ml
3 tbs	1½ fl oz	45 ml
¼ cup	2 fl oz	60 ml
⅓ cup	2½ fl oz	75 ml
⅓ cup + 1 tbs	3 fl oz	90 ml
⅓ cup + 2 tbs	3½ fl oz	100 ml
½ cup	4 fl oz	125 ml
⅔ cup	5 fl oz	150 ml
¾ cup	6 fl oz	175 ml
¾ cup + 2 tbs	7 fl oz	200 ml
1 cup	8 fl oz	250 ml
1 cup + 2 tbs	9 fl oz	275 ml
1¼ cups	10 fl oz	300 ml
1⅓ cups	11 fl oz	325 ml
1½ cups	12 fl oz	350 ml
1⅔ cups	13 fl oz	375 ml
1¾ cups	14 fl oz	400 ml
1¾ cups + 2 tbs	15 fl oz	450 ml
2 cups (1 pint)	16 fl oz	500 ml
2½ cups	20 fl oz (1 pint)	600 ml
3¾ cups	1½ pints	900 ml
4 cups	1¾ pints	1 liter

WEIGHT CONVERSIONS

U.S.	METRIC
½ oz	15 g
1 oz	30 g
1½ oz	45 g
2 oz	60 g
2½ oz	75 g
3 oz	90 g
3½ oz	100 g
4 oz	125 g
5 oz	150 g
6 oz	175 g
7 oz	200 g
8 oz	250 g
9 oz	275 g
10 oz	300 g
11 oz	325 g
12 oz	350 g
13 oz	375 g
14 oz	400 g
15 oz	450 g
1 lb	500 g

OVEN TEMPERATURES*

FAHRENHEIT	GAS MARK	CELSIUS
250	½	120
275	1	140
300	2	150
325	3	160
350	4	180
375	5	190
400	6	200
425	7	220
450	8	230
475	9	240
500	10	260

*Reduce the temperature by 20°C (68°F) for fan-assisted ovens.

APPROXIMATE EQUIVALENTS

1 large egg = about 2 oz = about 3 tbs
1 large egg yolk = about 1 tbs
1 large egg white = about 2 tbs
1 stick butter = 8 tbs = 4 oz = ½ cup
1 cup grated cheese = 4 oz
1 cup honey or syrup = 12 oz
1 cup granulated sugar = 8 oz
1 cup (packed) brown sugar = 6 oz
1 cup confectioners' sugar = 4½ oz
1 cup dried beans = 6 oz
1 cup all-purpose flour or dried bread
crumbs = 5 oz

Note: All conversions are approximate but close enough to be useful when converting from one system to another.

INDEX